PRINCIPLES AND PRACTICE OF INSURANCE

PRINCIPLES AND PRACTICE OF INSURANCE

Dr. P. Periasamy
M.B.A., Ph.D.

Reader,
Department of Business Management (Antonomous),
Erode Arts College,
Erode – 638009.

Himalaya Publishing House
ISO 9001:2015 CERTIFIED

First Edition : 2005
Second Revised Edition : 2009
Edition : 2010, 2011, 2012, 2013
Edition : 2014, 2015, 2017, 2019, 2022
Edition : 2023

Published by : Mrs. Meena Pandey
for **HIMALAYA PUBLISHING HOUSE PVT. LTD.,**
"Ramdoot", Dr. Bhalerao Marg, Girgaon, Mumbai - 400 004.
Phone: 022-23860170, 23863863; **Fax:** 022-23877178
E-mail: himpub@bharatmail.co.in; **Website:** www.himpub.com

Branch Offices :

New Delhi : "Pooja Apartments", 4-B, Murari Lal Street, Ansari Road, Darya Ganj, New Delhi - 110 002.
Phone: 011-23270392, 23278631; Fax: 011-23256286

Nagpur : Kundanlal Chandak Industrial Estate, Ghat Road, Nagpur - 440 018.
Phone: 0712-2721215, 2721216

Bengaluru : Plot No. 91-33, 2nd Main Road, Seshadripuram, Behind Nataraja Theatre, Bengaluru - 560 020.
Phone: 080-41138821; Mobile: 09379847017, 09379847005

Hyderabad : No. 3-4-184, Lingampally, Besides Raghavendra Swamy Matham, Kachiguda, Hyderabad - 500 027. Phone: 040-27560041, 27550139

Chennai : No. 34/44, Motilal Street, T. Nagar, Chennai - 600 017.
Mobile: 09380460419

Pune : "Laksha" Apartment, First Floor, No. 527, Mehunpura, Shaniwarpeth (Near Prabhat Theatre), Pune - 411 030.
Phone: 020-24496323, 24496333; Mobile: 09370579333

Cuttack : Plot No. 5F-755/4, Sector-9, CDA Markat Nagar, Cuttack - 753 014, Odisha. Mobile: 09338746007

Kolkata : 3, S.M. Bose Road, Near Gate No. 5, Agarpara Railway Station, North 24 Parganas, West Bengal - 700 109. Mobile: 09674536325

Printed at : Geetanjali Press Pvt. Ltd., Nagpur. On behalf of HPH.

PREFACE

Principles and Practice of Insurance is a wide and diverse subject. In view of the increasing scope of Insurance, it is essential to acquire a general basic knowledge of the insurance business as a whole and this should certainly be the first step to be taken by the new entrant with an insurance career ahead of him.

Because of its increasing insurance, it has become a special subject of study in Commerce and Management courses in many universities in India. This book entitled "Principles and Practice of Insurance", provides a detailed coverage of Risk Management, General Insurance, Life Insurance, Fire Insurance and Marine Insurance in a comprehensive way, keeping mainly the interest of the undergraduate and post graduate students of Commerce and Management in view.

I hope that both the students and teachers will find this book highly useful. I would be very much obliged to receive from the readers any constructive suggestions for improving the standard of this book.

I take this opportunity to offer my sincere thanks to Shri K.N. Pandey and Shri. Niraj Pandey and Shri K. Sivadasan, Area Manager, Tamil Nadu of Himalaya Publishing House for bringing out this book in its excellent form.

Dr. P. PERIASAMY

Contents

1. NATURE AND SCOPE OF RISK MANAGEMENT 1-7
2. METHODS OF HANDLING RISKS 8-11
3. MANAGEMENT OF RISKS 12-21
4. NATURE OF INSURANCE BUSINESS 22-28
5. REINSURANCE 29-37
6. PRIVATISATION OF INSURANCE BUSINESS IN INDIA 38-47
7. CLASSIFICATION OF INSURANCE 48-51
8. PRINCIPLES OF CONTRACT OF INSURANCE 52-59
9. INSURANCE DOCUMENTS 60-63
10. LIFE INSURANCE 64-70
11. CLASSIFICATION OF LIFE INSURANCE POLICIES 71-88
12. ASSIGNMENT OF LIFE POLICIES 89-95
13. LIFE INSURANCE CORPORATION OF INDIA (LIC) 96-110
14. MARKETING OF LIFE INSURANCE 111-119
15. WORLD LIFE INSURANCE MARKET 120-130
16. LIC FINANCIAL SERVICES 131-153
17. ROLE OF THE DEVELOPMENT OFFICER 154-160
18. ROLE OF INSURANCE AGENTS 161-167
19. GENERAL INSURANCE BUSINESS AND ROLE OF GIC 168-178
20. NATURE OF MARINE INSURANCE CONTRACT 179-189
21. KINDS OF MARINE INSURANCE POLICIES 190-194
22. IMPORTANT CLAUSES IN MARINE POLICY 195-200

23. MARINE LOSSES AND ABANDONMENT 201-209
24. NATURE OF FIRE INSURANCE CONTRACT 210-215
25. TYPES OF FIRE POLICIES 216-224
26. FIRE INSURANCE CLAIMS 225-239
27. MISCELLANEOUS INSURANCE 240-243
28. NATIONAL AGRICULTURAL INSURANCE SCHEMES 244-250
29. FIDELITY GUARANTEE INSURANCE 251-253
30. PROPERTY INSURANCE 254-255
31. MOTOR VEHICLE INSURANCE 256-262
32. HEALTH INSURANCE 263-265
33. CATTLE INSURANCE AND ENGINEERING INSURANCE 266-269
34. PUBLIC LIABILITY INSURANCE 270-274
35. INSURANCE REGULATORY AND DEVELOPMENT AUTHORITY (IRDA) 275-301
ANNEXURES 302-312

PART I : RISK MANAGEMENT

Chapter 1
Nature and Scope of Risk Management

Introduction

The entire business process has to face numerous risks and uncertainties. Uncertainity comes from changes in economic, social and political trends (such as a spike in oil price or interest rates), the arrival of new technologies (like the internet), or shifts in consumer demand (preference for personal computers Day-Glo Colors versus traditional beige). Thus in business, as in private life, there are dangers and risks of every kind. The concept of risk may be explained as the possibility of unfavourable results following any occurrence. Risks arise due to uncertainties in regard to cost, loss or damage. The loss or damage may be related to financial loss or non-financial loss. In a dynamic and free economy and in life, such risks are inevitable. In business, risks include changing demand and fashions, price falls, change in desire and taste of consumers, change in the market conditions, high competitions, new inventions and their development, fire, flood, accidents etc.,

Meaning and Definitions of Risk

According to Frank Knight risk may be defined as a measurable uncertainty. A. H. Willet defined risk as an objectified uncertainty regarding the occurence of an undesirable event.

The risk may also mean that there is a possibility of loss or damage. It may or may not happen. In business, the risk may be defined as the danger of loss from unforeseen circumstances. It implies, a possibility of loss due to unpredictable or unfavourable happening in the future.

To the man in the street, "risk" means exposure to danger. But in insurance practice in term 'risk' is also used for peril or loss producing events. For example, it is said that insurance covers the risks of fire, explosion, cyclone, flood etc. Here, the risks refer to the subject matter of insurance.

According to Federation of Insurance Institutes, the risk can be thought of as the degree of variation in the possible outcome from an uncertain event, or as the variation in the possible outcomes.

According to Life Insurance Corporation of India, risk may be defined as "a condition where there is a possibility of an adverse deviation from a desired outcome that is expected or hoped for; there is no requirement that the possibility be unmeasurable, only that it must exist." When an event is stated to be possible, it has a possibility between zero and one, it is neither impossible nor definite. The degree of risk may or may not be measurable.

The concept of risk may be distinguished from peril and hazard. A peril is the cause of loss for example fire, wind, storm, hail or theft. Hazard is a condition that may create or increase the chance of a loss arising from a given peril or under a given condition. Hazards can be classified into following three categories.

(a) Physical hazard (b) Moral hazard and (c) Morale hazard.

(a) *Physical hazard* consists of those physical conditions that increase the chance of loss from any peril. For example, premises for bad repair proposed for public liability insurance.

(b) *Moral hazard* refers to the increase in probability of loss that results from dishonesty in the character of the insured person. An extreme illustration of bad moral hazard is the person who effects a policy of insurance in order to make a profit by means of false and exaggerated claims.

(c) *Morale hazard:* The term Morale refers to a mental condition or attitude of an individual or a group which determines their willingness to co-operate. Morale hazard may be reflected in a careless attitude toward the occurrence of loss or in an indifference to the cost of restoring damage. In short, Morale hazard acts to increase both the frequency and severity of losses when such losses are covered by the insurance.

Meaning of Uncertainty

The term uncertainty used to indicate situations where the possibility of occurence of a result is non-quantifiable, consequently is not possible to insure against uncertainty.

Classification of Risks

The risk is the result or effect of any unforeseen event or its happening. The business world is dynamic and full of risks of uncertainties. The future is unpredictable and full of uncertainties. Planning alone cannot solve or protect one against uncertainties. Risks are inherent in all forms of economical, political, social, environmental and business activity. Thereby risks are involved not only in life cycle of human beings but also till the movement the product reaches the consumer.

From a practical point of view, the whole process of risk can be classified into:

(a) Financial and Non-financial Risks

(b) Static and Dynamic Risks

(c) Fundamental and Particular Risks

(d) Pure and Speculative Risks

Pure Risks can also be classified further into:

(1) Personal Risks

(2) Property Risks

(3) Liability Risks

(4) Risks arising from failure of others.

Other Risks:

Risks other than above classifications can be grouped as follows:

1. Market Risks
2. Technical Risks
3. Political Risks
4. Physical Risks
5. Business Risks

The following chart show classifications of risks

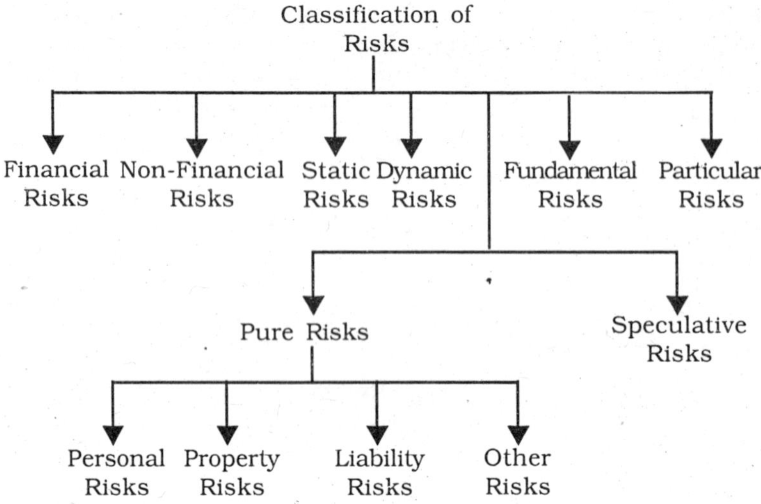

(Risk arising from failure of others)

Financial and Non-Financial Risks

If any risk is concerned with financial loss, it is termed as a financial risk. Financial risks are associated with the way in which a company finances its activities. We usually gauge financial risk by looking at the capital structure of a firm. Broadly defined, financial risks encompass risks of possible insolvency and variability in the earnings available to common share holders. For example, the presence of borrowed money or debt in the capital structure creates fixed payment in the form of interest that must be sustained by the firm. The presence of interest commitments – fixed interest payments due to debt or fixed dividend payments on preferred stock – causes the amount of residual earnings available for common-stock dividends to be more available if no interest payments were required. Financial risk is avoidable risk to the extent that managements have the freedom to decide to borrow or not to borrow funds. A firm with no debt financing has no financial risk. Other than financial consequences (only incidental) those risks are referred to as non-financial risks. As per insurance concerned with those risks that involve a financial loss.

Static and Dynamic Risks

Static Risks: Static risks involve losses resulting from the destruction of an asset or changes in its possession as a result of dishonesty or human failure. Such financial losses arise even if there were no changes in the economic environment. Normally, static risks are not a source of gain to society. Static losses arise with a degree of regularity over time and, as a result are generally predictable unlike dynamic risk; static risks are most suitable to treatment by insurance. For example, dishonesty, carelessness, incompetence etc. of the employees causes risks in the business. Death of responsible officer is disastrous to firm as a whole.

Dynamic Risk: Dynamic risk involves losses mainly concerned with financial loss. It occurs resulting from the causes relating to the changes in the price level, consumer wants and needs, income, output and development of technology. Dynamic risks also affect the public. Unlike static risks, these risks are the best indicators of progress to society over the long run since they are the result of adjustment to misallocation of resources. Foreign exchange losses, bad publicity, worker compensation claims, loss of production and assets etc. are the few examples of dynamic risk.

Distinction between Dynamic Risks and Static Risks

Dynamic Risks	*Static Risks*
1. Dynamic risks are the losses resulting from changes in the economic environment. For example, prevents repatriation of profits, labour dispute etc.	1. It involves the losses that occur even if there were no changes in the economic environment. For example, customer disfavour and defection.
2. Unlike static risks, the occurrence of dynamic loss is not easily predictable. For example, computer defects.	2. Occurrence of static loss can be easily predicted. For example, quality problem.
3. Unlike static risks, dynamic risks are not suited to treatment by Insurance. Earthquake, flood etc.	3. Static risks are more suited to treatment by Insurance than dynamic risks. Fraud security, safety etc.
4. Dynamic risks normally benefit the society. For example, foreign government appropriates assets.	4. Static risks are not a source of gain to society. For example, environmental pollution.
5. Dynamic risks also occur resulting from the causes relating to the changes in the price level, consumer wants and needs, income etc.	5. Static losses involve either the destruction of an asset or a change in its possession as a result of dishonesty or human failure.

Fundamental and Particular Risk

Fundamental Risk: Fundamental risk is also termed as a group risk. It involves those losses that occur as a result of the causes or problems relating to major factors such as changes of economic, social, cultural and political environment. The consequences of the fundamental risk severely affect the whole population. The following are examples of fundamental risks such as unemployment, war, inflation, earthquakes, floods, droughts, famine etc.

Particular Risk: As far as a particular risk is concerned, unlike fundamental risk, it involves losses that occur resulting from individual events. Burning of a house and robbery of a bank are the examples of particular risk.

Pure and Speculative Risk

The concept pure risk refers to those situations that involve the chances of loss or no loss. Speculative risk means those risks which involve a situation where there is a possibility of gain. The nature of insurable risk refers to the losses involved relating to only pure risk and not against speculative risk, because speculative risk is mainly concerned with the nature and possibility of gain.

Pure Risk can also be grouped into:

(a) Personal Risk

(b) Property Risk

(c) Liability Risk and

(d) Risks arising from failure of others

(a) Personal Risk

Some uncertainties arise out of human elements, perhaps a major source of risks. The following four are the basic elements of pure risk an individual has to face:

(1) Premature death

(2) Dependent old age

(3) Sickness or disability

(4) Unemployment

(b) Property Risk

Property risk refers to direct losses/consequential losses. Occurrence of uncertain events which cause loss to the property such as accident, fire, crash, obsolence, breakdown are called property risk. Property risk is also termed as pure risk. The following are the examples of property risk:

(1) Loss of the property

(2) Loss of use of the property and

(3) Additional overhead expenses occasioned by the loss of property.

(c) Liability Risk

Liability Risk is concerned with those losses which result from unintentional injury to other persons or damages to their property through negligence or carelessness. In other words, risk which create financial liability on any person on the occurrence of an uncertain event are called liability risk.

(d) Risks Arising from Failure of Others

Any loss that occurs resulting from failure of another person to meet an obligation is considered in this category.

Questions

1. What is meant by risk?
2. Define risk? What are the classification of risk?
3. Distinguish between dynamic risks and static risks?
4. Write explanatory notes on the types of pure risks?
5. Write short notes on:
   - (a) Fundamental risks
   - (b) Particular risks
   - (c) Property risks
6. Explain the characteristics of insurable risks.

Chapter 2

Methods of Handling Risks

Introduction

Personal or business or any type of risks is common in the day to day activities; all precautions are to be adopted in protecting ourselves against unforeseen risks. A businessman finds out means to eliminate the risks or at least minimise the effect of such risks. Burden of risk is the greatest problem in connection with risk management. This is because, it relates to risk of some financial loss. The risk occurs due to multiple causes. There are people who undertake risks because of the belief "larger the risk, greater the profit". A sensible businessman tries to minimise the risk, if losses are unavoidable.

Methods of Handling Risks

The following methods are usually adopted for handling risks:

(I) Prevention of risks (or) Avoiding of risks

(2) Reduction of risks

(3) Shifting of risks (or) Transferring of risks

(4) Acceptance of risks

(5) Spreading of risks

1. Prevention of Risks (or) Avoiding of Risks

"Prevention is better than cure". Preventive measures are designed to eliminate risks or the causes of risks. It is not possible to find a formula to avoid risks completly, but to a great extent the risk can be reduced. The following steps are generally used in preventing risks.

(a) Losses from theft, shop-lifting etc. can be minimised by giving effective training to the employees of the firm. Apart from this, Burglar alarms, watchmen, safety vaults etc. help to a great extent in preventing or avoiding the risks.

(b) Losses from bad debts can be prevented if creditworthiness of the party is known before granting credit.

(c) Loss from fire, weather change etc. can be completely avoided by constructing a fire proof building for stocking products.

(d) To avoid the non-availability of raw materials, it is advisable to adopt vertical integration, in which full control from the supply of raw materials to the distribution of final goods can be exercised.

(e) Loss from overstocking or understocking should be avoided by producing the products to meet the orders. Over stocking will block capital and understocking will result in loss of profit. This can be avoided in production to orders.

(f) Reduced demand for the products can be regulated by effective sales efforts through trademarks and brands. This will overcome the loss through bogus sales.

2. Reduction of Risks

Many risks are neither transferable nor avoidable. But business risks are reduced by concentrated efforts of risk management. Today, we know that business conditions changes day to day. Here are some suggestions to overcome loss.

(a) Loss on sale on account of fashion changes, improved products can be overcome by stock clearance sales at a discount.

(b) Loss on account of market change may be minimised by market research.

(c) Innovations invite risks and changes may lead to progress. Business cannot progress without innovations. Again, we are unable to forecast changes in the future which are beyond our control.

(d) Reorganisation of firms—amalgamations, conversion to company etc. greatly helps in improving the managerial ability, financial strength etc.

3. Shifting of Risks (or) Transferring of Risks

Some types of risks involving loss can be shifted or transferred to other's shoulders. There are professional agencies which accept the risks as their responsibility.

In the business world, there are many risks, uncertainties or losses. Generally, business people are not willing to bear such risks which bring losses to the firm and so want to transfer them. Many natural risks or losses can be avoided through insurance. The importance of insurance marketing lies in the fact that it helps in eliminating uncertainty. Insurance companies cover many risks for the payment of a sum, known as a premium, for instance, Marine Insurance, Fire Insurance, Credit Insurance, Burglary Insurance etc. A businessman can easily transfer the risk to the insurer. Insurance is a contract by which the assurer (Insurance Company) in consideration of the payment of a sum (Premium), agrees to pay a specified sum to the insured on the happening of a certain event. The insurer undertakes to indemnify the assured for the loss on the happening of the event.

4. Acceptance of Risks

Because the element of risk is incidential to life and cannot usually be avoided, it may be accepted in the following ways:

(a) Some risks are accepted in ignorance.

(b) Some risks are accepted inadvertently, for example, a family man fails to make adequate provision for his family in the event of premature death or disability through accident. He need not be callously indifferent but merely neglectful.

(c) Some risks are accepted intentionally: Where the degree of risk is slight or the possible loss is small, a man may be willing to bear it without any expectations.

Along with the acceptance of risk, provision is sometimes made against the consequences of loss by the creation or reserve fund. This is a method employed by some large concerns. Many such type of risks or loss can be accepted or covered by the professional insurance companies also.

5. Spreading of Risks

Spreading of risks is termed as 'Averaging of risks'. This involves the combination of the risks of many individuals who band together. It does not reduce the aggregate amount of potential loss, but it does achieve a reduction of uncertainty and it spreads the burden for those who are thus banded together.

For example:

(a) by writing different classes of insurance business and even within a single class, by covering various types of risks.

(b) by entering business in different geographical states within a country or different countries.

(c) by incorporating as a public company so that with the help of larger capital recourses, who is in a position to enter larger volume of business in order to achieve a larger spread of risks.

(d) by entering into reinsurance business with other companies and also accepting reinsurances from other companies.

(e) by entering into pools of certain risks particularly of difficult or more hazardous nature.

Risks cannot only be spread over a larger capital and a wider area, but also they can be spread over a period of time. The adverse effect of the risks as a result of fluctuations in economic conditions, recessions following a period of prosperity may be averaged in time. To achieve this, reserve funds are created out of profits by the insurers to be utilised in adverse trading conditions.

Questions

1. What do you understand by methods of handling risks?
2. Explain the various methods of handling risks.
3. Write short notes on:
   (a) Prevention of risks
   (b) Spreading of risks
   (c) Reduction of risks.

PART II : INSURANCE BUSINESS

Chapter 3 Management of Risks

Meaning and Definitions

Risk management is concerned with the conversion of a firm's asset and earning power against risks of accidental loss. The duties of the executive or outside professional consulting firm charged with this elimination or a avoidance, and the scientific prevention of loss that could result from non-removable or non-avoidable hazards. To the extent that the proper use of insurance to transfer non-avoidable risk to a professional risk carrier (insurance company) is one method (among several) of treating a firm's exposure to risk, insurance management also falls within the scope of risk management. Risk management may be defined as "the identification, analysis and economic control of those risks which can threaten the assets or earning capacity of an enterprise."

The definition is classified further:

(1) It brings into light that systematic methods are required to be applied for risk management.

(2) Risk can be measured before it can be identified.

(3) It can be evaluated only after their impact.

(4) Suitable cost control devices should be applied for minimising cost of handling risks.

(5) It gives importance to the assets and earning capacity of an organisation. Hence, risk management should focus on both of them. These assets can be physical or human.

(6) Finally, it suggests that the principles of risk management are applicable not only to service sectors but are also of equal importance to all sectors of the economy.

Features of Risk Management

By considering the concepts and definitions as a whole, we can conclude that risk management has the following features:

(1) Risk management is a scientific approach to the problem of dealing with only pure risks and not any other risks faced by the individual and business.

(2) Risk management gives importance to insurable and uninsurable risks and to use suitable techinques for problems dealing with all pure risks.

(3) It mainly emphasises reducing the cost of handling risk by using appropriate methods.

Importance of Risk Management

Risk management is of vital importance in the day to day business and human activities. It is essential for not only prevention of risks, but also for reduction of risks. It provides maximum social advantage. It plays a significant role in bringing about social, political and economic development of a country. The importance of risk management is laid down as follows:

(1) To create the right corporate policies and strategy.

(2) It is essential for effective managing of people and process.

(3) To evaluate the risks of the business.

(4) For effective handling of spreading the risk, monitoring and insuring against.

(5) To introduce various plans and techniques to minimise the risks.

(6) To give advice and make suggestions for handling the risks.

(7) To create awareness about risks among the people.

(8) To avoid cost, disruption and unhappiness in relating to risks.

(9) To decide which risks are worth pursuing, and which should be shunned.

(10) To fix the sum assured under the policy and to decide on whether to insure or not.

(11) To select the appropriate technique or methods to manage the risks.

Chart of Risks Insurance Management Process

The process of risk insurance management exhibit in the given below chart:

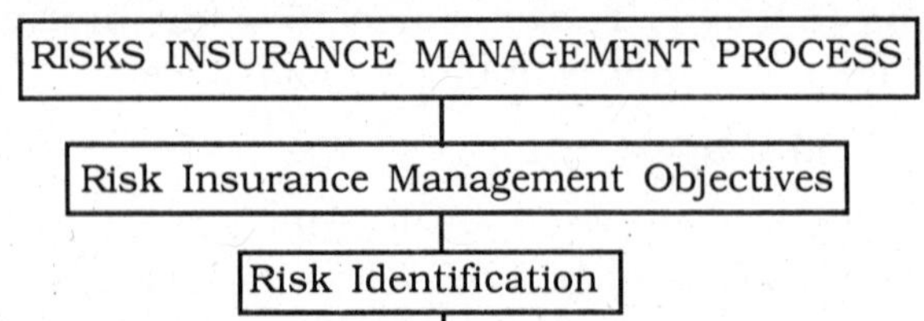

Sources of Risks	Tools Used
1. The Proposal Form	1. Insurance Policy Check List
2. Medical Examiner's Report	2. Analysis of Financial Statements
3. Agent's Report	3. Risk Analysis Questionnaire
4. Inspection Report	4. Hazards and Operability Studies
5. Private Friend's Report	5. Physical Inspection of the Operation
6. MIS	6. Flow Charts
7. Business Associates.	7. Organisational Chart
	8. Management Information System

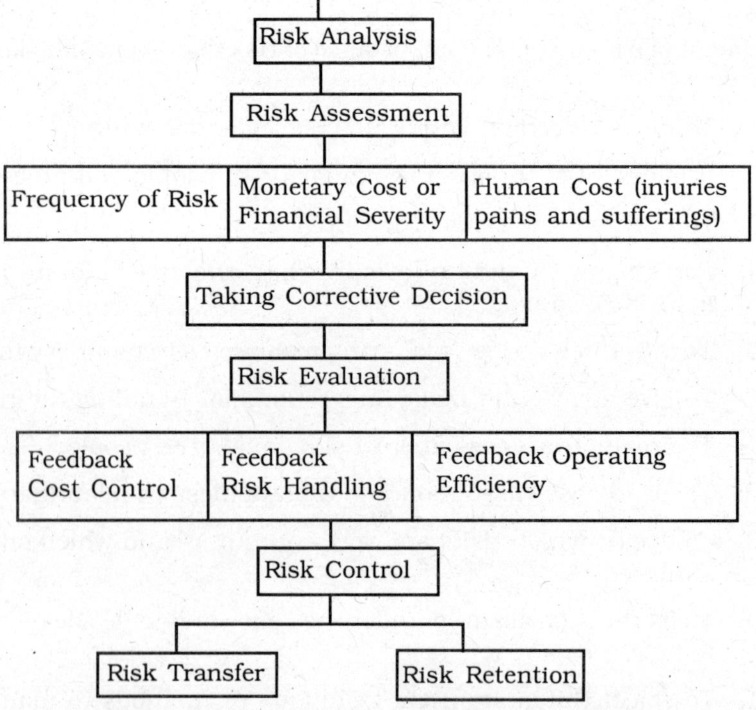

Fig: 3.1 Risks Insurance Management Process

Risk Management Objectives

Risk management is a management process with the objectives of achieving its own aims, i.e., to preserve the operating effectiveness of the organisation, to make sure that it is not prevented from attaining its other objectives by the losses arising from pure risks. In other words, risk management is one which facilitates any organisation the avoidance of any great financial losses resulting in bankruptcy. Some of the other objectives are:

(1) Protecting employees from accident is another important objectives of risk management. It is the humanitarian goal of protecting employees from accident that might result in death or injury.

(2) Another form of objective of risk management is:

 (a) due attention given on cost of handling risks,

 (b) effective utilisation of resources, and

 (c) maintaining good relations with society and public.

Purpose of Selection of Risks

The selection of risk is a process whereby less value or quality is weeded out. The function of the selection process is to determine whether the degree of risk presented by an applicant for insurance is commensurate with the premium established for persons in his category or some additional premium should be charged or the applicant's proposal should be rejected.

According to the insurance point of view, the following purposes of selection of risks are laid down:

(1) To determine whether the proposal should be accepted or not.

(2) To determine the rate of premium to be charged from the assured.

(3) To determine the risks and premium according to the classification of risks.

(4) To avoid any discrimination on the part of the lives assured.

(5) To check anti-selection or adverse selection which means selections of the persons for insurance who are not insurable and charging of lesser premium for those who are to be charged higher premium.

Sources of Risks

Before embarking on the details of analysis and evaluation of risk insurance, it seems appropriate to present a brief overview of the source of risk. Risk manager must find the source of risk and formulate for identification so that it becomes susceptible to evaluation. Like a medical doctor, a risk manager must examine all the ways and means concerning with sources of risk before he can diagnose correctly.

There are several sources of risk information available and the risk manager must decide in advance for identification. The following are the sources of information for identification of risk:

(1) Proposal Form — it may be Application form or Personal Statement

(2) Medical Examiner's Report

(3) Development Officer's, Agent's, and Broker's Report

(4) Field Officer's Report

(5) Medical Information Bureau Report

(6) Private Agency's Report

(7) Business Associate's Report

(8) Commercial Credit Investigation Bureau.

Risk Identification

Risk identification is one of the important processes of risk management. Based on the threat on the asset and earning capacity of the enterprise, the risk manager is employed to carry out the whole functions of risk management.

The task of risk identification: The risk manager should apply relevant trade techniques to discover the risks. There are various methods of risk identification. As such, the risk manager must judiciously select the method for his study to discover the risk to which the subject is exposed.

The following are the important tools generally used for identification of risk:

(1) Insurance Policy Check list

(2) Risk Analysis Questionnaires

(3) Analysis of Financial Statements

(4) Hazard and Operability Studies

(5) Physical Inspections of the Operations

(6) Flow Charts

(7) Organisational Charts

(8) Management Information System

(9) Procedure Manuals

(10) Insurance Policies

(11) Maintenance Records

(12) Plans of Specific Premises

(13) Loss Records

(14) Plus Maps, Photographs etc.

Principles of Risk Insurance Management

Risk insurance management is a science though it is one of the most inexact of the social sciences. Its principles may be defined as a systematic grouping of inter-related principles, with a view to tying together and providing a framework to significant knowledge. The principles of risk insurance management have so far been only derived from the experience of risk insurance managers. The principles of risk insurance management are brought out by the following:

(1) Principles of Risk Identification

(2) Principles of Risk Analysis

(3) Principles of Risk Assessment

(4) Principles of Taking Corrective Decision

(5) Principles of Evaluation

(6) Principles of Alternative Course of Action

(7) Principles of Risk Control

(8) Principles of Risk Retention

(9) Principles of Risk Transfer.

These principles of risk insurance management have been discussed briefly:

1. Principles of Risk Identification: Proper identification of risk is essential to achieve the several objectives of risk management such as preserving the operating effectiveness of the organisation, minimising the cost of handling risk etc. Without proper identification of risk, a firm's operations have no meaning and direction. The success of the risk insurance management depends on proper risk identification.

2. Principles of Risk Analysis: The risk manager should select various statistical tools to analyse the identified risk on the basis of principles of analysis in order to achieve the objectives of risk management. Analysis of a risk is necessary not only to know the level of severity of risk, but also to determine the accuracy and relevance of risk exposure at each stage.

3. Principles of Risk Assessment: Necessary steps are to be taken by the executives in order to make an assessment of cost of risk. This is essential to keep reducing the cost of risk within control. The following are important factors worth mentioning about risk assessment issues:

(a) frequency of risk

(b) monetary cost or financial severity

(c) human cost in terms of pain and suffering

(d) purpose of the assignment

(e) nature of the risk

(f) description of the project

(g) resources involved or affected

(h) scale of the impact

(i) benefits of the hazard

(j) mitigating factors

(k) contingency plans

(l) limitations of the assessment

(m) conclusions and recommendations

(n) action taken.

The risk manager has to evaluate the occurrence of losses or probability that it is likely to occur. Certain risks are to be easily identified and evaluated, but some other critical risks are difficult to be exposured. For example, incidents related to Bhopal and Chernobyle etc. disasters. On the basis of the possibility of losses, the assessment of risk may be described as important risk and unimportant risk. The importance of risk may vary from individual to individual and firm to firm.

4. Principles of Taking Corrective Decision: Corrective decision is an integral part of the risk manager's job. In risk management, decision-making is a process involving information, choice of alternative actions, implementation, and evaluation that is directed to the achievement of certain stated goals. The decision for dealing with the risk highlights three important aspects, they are:

(a) to retain risk — this may be achieved with or without a reserve or a fund

(b) to involve with the risk through loss prevention effective alternative solutions applied for prevention of loss

(c) to transfer the risk through insurance and this must be followed by the selection of an insurer.

5. Principles of Evaluation: There may be many alternative courses of action for handling of risk. But not all of them can be said to be equally practicable or suitable. Each alternative plan has its strong and weak points. A proper evaluation of these points is necessary for risk management to determine which of the alternatives would be the best. Such evaluation has to be from different angles. How would any plan contribute to the acomplishment of risk management's desired objectives? To what extent will it be able to face the effects of various predictable and unpredicatable factors? And so on.

6. Principles of Alternative Course of Action: The final choice from among the several alternatives will be based on how efficiently the risk manager's chosen alternative will produce results which come up to the desired level. In some cases, the decision as regards the final alternative will be objective, but in a majority of cases it is subjective, based on the value. Majority of cases are subjective based on the value judgement of the risk manager concerned.

7. Principles of Risk Control: Effective control provides the yardstick to measure the effectiveness of performance at various levels of handling risk. To achieve the risk management objectives, various financial mechanisms can be used to control risk. This is essential to keep the cost of risk within control. Risk control can be achieved through the following effective measures:

(1) Carrying out a supplier assessment

(2) Inspecting during manufacture

(3) Investigating complaints

(4) Increasing the level of supervision

(5) Improved detection

(6) Improving financial controls and management systems

(7) Better working conditions

(8) Improved staff morale and lower staff turnover

(9) Improved standing in the local community

(10) Minimising the opportunity to steal etc.

8. Principles of Risk Retention: This principle provides a valuable framework within which managers may make their decisions. When the risk has been identified, the risk manager can look to the principles of risk retention, as to how the effects are to be financed. For example, loss on account of faulty production planning can be improved by developing new technologies. High production cost may be minimised by effective control system.

9. Principles of Risk Transfer: Principles of risk transfer help to analyse the transfer of financial effect of risk to an other party. Generally, business people are unwilling to bear such risks which create losses to the firm and so want to transfer them. Many natural risks or losses can be avoided through insurance. Investment funds loosen their risk by buying the share of many companies. Companies can also push responsibility on to their suppliers by requiring them to be responsible for product quality and safety. This is a risk transfer practice which is highly valuable not only to individuals, but also to trade and industry.

Scope of Insurance Management

Generally, the insurance management function is limited to property insurance, liability insurance, workmen's compensation insurance and suretyship. However, some firms include their programs for pension, group life, hospitalisation etc., with in the duties of the insurance manager. The insurance executives must understand and negotiate an almost limitless number of forms of insurance of which the following are among the most important.

(1) **Automobile Insurance:** Numerous forms of policies are available covering automobile bodily injury and property damage, automobile collision insurance, comprehensive liability, non-ownership liability against liability from operation by others etc.

(2) **Accounts Received Insurance:** This forms of insurance provides virtually all risk coverage against the firm's inability to collect outstanding balances following the destruction of the accounts receivable records, plus reasonable expenses incurred to reconstruct accounts receivable records

(3) **Consequential Loss Insurance:** This is a form of power plant insurance and provides coverage against spoilage of property due to the lack of power, heat, light, steam, refrigeration etc. from a described accident in an insured object, both as defined by a power plant policy.

(4) **Contingent Business Interruption Insurance:** Protects the firm against interruption of its business due to fire, or other insured perils at another's premises, such as a supplier, or customer, and can be written on a scheduled peril form, or all risk form.

(5) **Credit Insurance:** Protects the firm against loss in excess of a deductible, known as a primary loss caused by the insolvency of customers or delinquent claims, filed within a prescribed period.

(6) **Electronic Data Processing Insurance:** A relatively new form of coverage that provides specially tailored property insurance coverage on virtually an 'all risk' basis. It covers the insured for the financial loss arising form damage to or destruction of EDP equipments, peripheral equipment or media.

(7) **Motor Cargo Insurance:** This coverage is intended for firms that carry their own merchandise on their own or leased vehicles.

(8) **Marine Insurance:** Probably, the oldest form of insurance. This covers merchandise being carried by ocean–going vessels on a per voyage basis, or an open form that covers all voyage and all shipments, blanket.

(9) **Power Plant Insurance:** This title applies to almost any type of power plant equipment or appliances including steam, electric,

internal combustion, and refrigeration, and insures against accident or breakdown.

(10) **Workmen's Compensation Insurance:** A form of insurance to comply with compulsory Workmen's Compensation Acts. It is statutory in form and varies by state.

(11) **Valuable Papers Insurance:** This form of insurance provides all risks coverage on valuable papers, usually on an agreed amount basis.

(12) **Manufacturer's Output Insurance:** This is a flexible designed form on a virtually all risk basis that covers virtually all personal property of larger firms whose principal activity is manufacturing as long as the property is away from the manufacturing premises; it is usually written in excess of a substantial deductible.

(13) **Export Credit Insurance:** Covers agreed percentage of loss sustained because of insolvency of firms to whom the assured has extended credit, and based on that credit, exported merchandise or services to them.

(14) **Fire Legal Liability Insurance:** Coverage against liability of the firm for damage to property of other caused by the fire, including property in the care, custody or control of the insured.

(15) **Employer's Liability Insurance:** Provides for the protection for the firm against liability arising out of injury to employees apart from that imposed by the Workmen's Compensation Laws.

Questions

1. What is meant by management of risks?
2. What are the features of risk management?
3. Explain the importance of risk management.
4. What are the importance principles of risk insurance management?
5. Explain the purposes of selection of risk.
6. Write short notes on:
   (a) Sources of risks
   (b) Risk identification
   (c) Risk management objectives
7. Write a brief note on risk insurance management process.
8. Explain the scope of Insurance management.

Chapter 4

Nature of Insurance Business

Meaning and Definitions of Insurance

According to Gosh and Agarwal, insurance may be defined as a co-operative form of distributing a certain risk over a group of persons who are expresed to it.

According to Allen Z. Mayerson define insurance as a "device for the transfer to an insurer of certain risks of economic loss that would otherwise come by the insure".

From the above definitions, it is observed that **'Insurance'** is a contract between the insurer and the insured under which the insurer undertakes to compensate the insured for the loss arising from the risk insured against. In consideration, the insured agrees to pay a premium regularly. The person whose risk is insured is called **'Insured'** or **'Assured'**. The person who agrees to compensate the loss arising from the risk is called the **'Insurer'** or **'Assurer"** or **'Underwriter'**.

Thus, the concept **'Premium'** implies that it is the consideration paid by the insured to the insurer for the risk undertaken by the latter. Premium is usually required to be paid in cash and advance payment of the premium is a condition precedent to the creation of a binding contract of insurance.

The term **'Assurance'** is applied to contracts, where the risk insured against is certain to happen but the time of its happening is uncertain.

Thus, the risk insured against death is a contract of assurance. The instrument containing the contract of insurance is called a 'policy'. The thing or property which forms the basis of insurance is called the 'subject-matter' of insurance. The interest of the assured in the subject-matter is called the insurable interest.

Characteristics of Insurance Contract

(1) Insurance is a device by which the loss likely to be caused by an uncertain event is spread over a number of persons who are exposed to it and who propose to insure themselves against such an event.

(2) The essence of insurance is the elimination of risk and substitution of certainity for uncertainty. Insurance is thus a cooperative way of spreading risk.

(3) A contract of Insurance is a Contingent Agreement.

(4) The general principles of law of contract agreement to a valid contract of insurance.

(5) Contract of insurance comes into existence where there is an offer and the underwriter or the insurer accepts it by issuing the policy.

(6) Contract of insurance must be entered into by a competent person in order to be valid.

(7) A contract of insurance other than life insurance is a contract of indemnity.

(8) The insurer undertakes to indemnify the insured for loss or damage arising as a result of the risk specified.

Difference between Insurance Contract and Wagering Agreement

It is sometimes said that a contract of insurance whether it is marine, fire or life very closely appears like a wagering agreement. In the case of the wagering agreement, Mr. 'X' promises to pay 'Y' the insured sum of money Rs. 2,00,000 on happening or non-happening of a certain event. Payment of this sum depends on the future event which, at the time of the contract, is of an uncertain nature. If the event does not happen, no payment will be made; nor will the premium paid be refunded. The following are the points of distinction between the Insurance Contract and a Wagering Agreement:

Distinction Between The Insurance Contract and Wagering Agreement

Insurance Contract	Wagering Agreement
(1) Insurable interest in the subject-matter is necessary.	(1) The insurable interest required for a valid contract is limited. Parties are interested in knowing only for the purpose of winning or losing upon the future events.
(2) Contract of insurance insurable is essential on the basis of principles of indemnity.	(2) In a Wagering agreement, there is no question of indemnity because no risk is covered.
(3) Contract of insurance is legally enforceable.	(3) Neither party has any legal remedy.
(4) Contract of insurance is based on the principles of good faith, i.e., a full disclosure of material facts is required by both parties to contract.	(4) There is no question of disclosure of material facts as it is not required by either party in a Wagering agreement.
(5) Risks and premiums are fixed on the basis of scientific methods.	(5) No such caculations are made in the Wagering agreement.

Functions of Insurance

The functions of insurance can be discussed into the following ways:

(1) Insurance is risk bearing: The main function of insurance is providing certainty of payment at the uncertainty of loss. The financial loss of the individual entity is equitably distributed over the many. In fire insurance, for example, the policy holders pay premiums into a common pool, out of which those who suffer loss are compensated.

(2) Insurance Provides Saving: The main function of the insurance is to provide to the public on terms attractive enough to encourage them to insure and yet sufficient to offer a reasonable margin of profit.

(3) Insurance Provides Protection: Insurance means protection against risk of loss. It covers the risk of loss. The insurance company agrees to give the payment of loss to the insured party against any actual loss or damage involved in business.

(4) Insurance Stimulates Business Enterprise: Insurance has made possible, and helps to maintain, the present day large scale industrial and commercial organisation. A trade or businessman wants to carry on his business free from risks whenever possible. Insurance safeguards capital and at the same time it avoids the necessity on the part of industrialist and others of freezing capital to guard against various contingencies. Thus, insurance leads to development of business enterprises.

(5) Insurance Encourages Efficiency: The insurance eliminates worries and uncertainty of risks. In personal form of insurance is relieved from hardship and anxiety. Thus, insurance improves not only his efficiency but the efficiencies of the masses are also advanced.

(6) Insurance Promotes Loss Prevention: The community would suffer much greater economic impoverishment through material losses if it were not for the loss prevention measures of Insurers. The insurance joins hands with those institutions which are engaged in preventing the loss of the society because the reduction in loss causes lesser payment to the assured and so more saving is possible which will assist in reducing the premium.

(7) Insurance Provides Capital: Insurance provides not only protection but also capital to the society. Usually, accumulated funds through savings in the form of insurance premium invested in economic development or productivity plans.

(8) Insurance Solves Social Problems: Some of the social problems which beset a modern civilised community are taken care of through insurance. At present, we have insurance against industrial injuries, road accidents, old age, disability or death etc. Thus, insurance acts as a good instrument for solving many social problems.

(9) Use of Reserve Funds: Because of the investment policy of Insurers, their reserve funds are not static, but are used productively. Thus, results in a reduction of the cost of insurance to the insuring public.

Importance of Insurance

The importance of insurance stands out in the following respects:

(1) Insurance contract protects against the possible occurrence of contingencies, i.e., perils (fire, flood, lightning, etc.)

(2) The insurer undertakes to compensate the insured for the loss arising from the risk insured against.

(3) The purpose of insurance is the elimination of risk and the loss is to be shared, i.e., substitution of certainty for uncertainty.

(4) Contract of insurance can act as a co-operative way of spreading risks.

(5) The essence of insurance is a contract by which the loss suffered by a person is spread over the whole of insured community.

(6) Payment of insurance for insurance contract is sufficient to acquire the right and remedies available to that person.

(7) The insurance provides funds to the government and public which will lead to economic development.

Uses or Benefits of Insurance

Insurance covers many risks and uncertainties in the world of business and act as a boon to the industrial or commercial concerns and general public. The following are some of the important services of insurance.

(1) Risk Transfer: Businessman can easily and conveniently transfer the risk of loss of insurance. It also safeguards the interest of individual and public.

(2) Protection: Businessman do not have to worry about losses or damage when the risk of loss to their property is duly insured. They will receive compensation against actual loss — their position becomes "as you were" even though the actual loss takes place. In life insurance, life policy gives financial protection to the dependents to the extent of the assured who may be the only bread winner in the family.

(3) Assured Profit: An insured businessman or policy holders can enjoy normal expected profits, e. g., 15% or 20% margin of profit.

(4) Benefits to Consumers: As the property of the businessman is duly insured, and he can get a normal profit margin, he can charge lower prices to consumers.

(5) Insurance Serves as a Basis of Credit: Insurance has the effect of improving credit standing of businessman, commercial banks and financial institutions insist for insurance of articles which are kept as security for loans. Life policy is a valuable asset and can raise an emergency loan against it.

(6) Investment: A life insurance contract provides not only protection but also investment, or a pension in old age. Under life policy, one can also get bonuses added to the policy amount when we have with profit life policy.

(7) Insurance encourages savings: It is particularly true of life insurance. The insured person must save out of his current income an amount equal to the premium to be paid regularly and punctually. Thus, life insurance is a compulsory form of saving for the rainy day. For persons of limited means, there is no other alternative substitute of savings.

(8) **Capital Formation:** Insurance companies as institutional investors can mobilise small national savings in the form of insurance premia. They usually invest these funds in shares and debentures of business companies and also in government securities. This leads to faster capital formation.

Insurance offers many benefits to society: Some of the more important services offered by insurance to society in general are:

(a) It creates confidence among the investing public.

(b) It ensures security and safety.

(c) It provides tax relief benefits.

(d) It encourages provision for the future.

(e) It leads to higher savings and investments.

(t) It helps as uncertainty of business losses is reduced.

(g) It attracts employees of better ability and calibre.

(h) It enables small businesses to compete with larger ones.

(i) It provides maximum economic growth of the country.

(j) It creates employment opportunities.

(k) It ensures larger industrial development.

(l) It can be used as a measuring rod during the period of inflation and deflation.

Kinds of Insurance Organisation:

The insurance organisation developed in different forms with the advancement of insurance practices abroad and India.

Some of the important forms are:

1. Self Insurance
2. Proprietary or Individual Insurer
3. Partnership Insurer
4. Joint – Stock Companies
5. Mutual Companies
6. Co-operative Insurance Organisation
7. Lloyd's Association or Underwriters
8. State Insurance
9. LIC
10. GIC

11. Employee State Insurance
12. Deposit Insurance Corporation

Questions

1. What is a contract of insurance?
2. What is the nature of insurance contract? How does it differ from an agreement by way of wager?
3. How does insurance contract differ from a wager?
4. What is the importance of insurance business?
5. Define contract of insurance? Enumerate the uses of insurance business.
6. Discuss the various kinds of Insurance organisation.
7. Discuss the role of insurance in the development of Commerce and Industry.
8. Explain the important functions of Insurance.

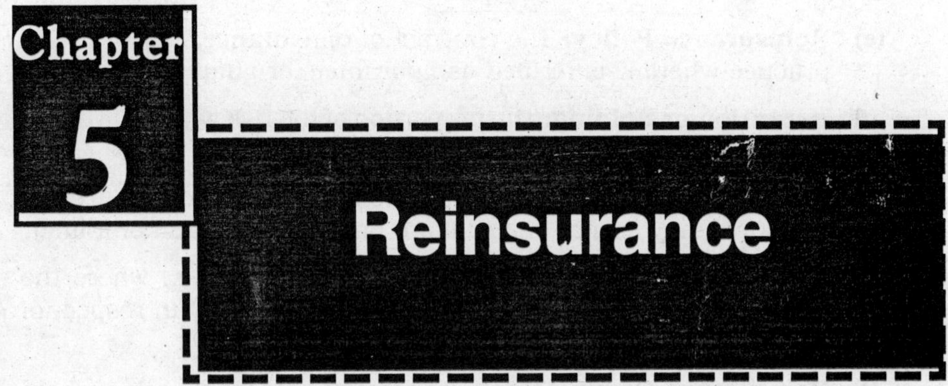

Chapter 5
Reinsurance

Meaning and Definition

The term 'Reinsurance' also termed as insurance of 'insurance' means that an insurer who has assumed a large risk may arrange with another insurer to insure a portion of the insured risk. In other words, in the event of loss, if it would be beyond the capacity of the insurer, then this reinsurance process is resorted to. In reinsurance, therefore, one insurer insures the risk which has been undertaken by another insurer. The original insurer who transfers a part of the insurance contract is called the reinsured and the second insurer is called the reinsurer. Of course, the reinsurer has to pay reinsurance premium for risk shifted. For example, a man wishing to insure his premises for Rs. 10 lakhs goes to an insurance company, which will accept the risk if it is satisfied as to the condition of the property. But if its own limit is probably Rs. 5 lakhs, it will arrange with another company to re-insure or to take up so much of the risk as exceeds its limits, i.e., Rs. 5 lakhs, so that if the house is burnt down the original insurers would pay the owner Rs. 10 lakhs, but they would be rcouped Rs. 5 lakhs by the re-insurance office.

To be effective, the reinsurance policy must be formulated after carefully considering all aspects of the situation to which it is to be applied.

Important Concepts of Reinsurance

The following are definitions of terms generally used in Reinsurance:

(a) **Direct Insurer:** The insurer who accepts the risk from the proposer and who, so far as the policyholder is concerned, is alone responsible for the obligation undertaken.

(b) **Re-insurer:** The insurer who grants a guarantee (or accepts a reinsurance) from the direct insurer.

(c) **Ceding Insurer:** The insurer who obtains a guarantee (or places reinsurance).

(d) **Cession:** The amount given off by way of reinsurance and therefore the amount accepted by the reinsurer.

(e) **Reinsurance Policy:** The contract of reinsurance, except in fire practice where it is termed as guarantee, or guarantee policy.

(f) **Retention or Holding:** The proportion of the risk which the direct insurer holds on his own account.

(g) **Line:** The amount of the retention of the direct insurer: a reinsurer may accept one or more lines (or a fraction of a line).

(h) **Retrocession:** A reinsurance of a reinsurance, i.e., where the reinsurer desires to reduce the limit of his liability in respect of business accepted.

(i) **Reinsurance Commission:** The amount paid by the reinsurer to the Ceding Company as a contribution to the acquisition and administration costs. It is calculated as a percentage of the premium received by Reinsurer.

(j) **Profit Commission:** It is a percentage of the earned profits which the Reinsurer agrees to return because the profit earned on business passing under a reinsurance treaty is deemed to be due to skill and care in the conduct of the business by the direct insurer.

(k) **Underwriter:** The person who agrees to compensate the loss arising from the risk is called the Insurer, Assurer or Underwriter.

(l) **Facultative:** Facultative reinsurance is the direct reinsurance of individual risks through the medium of a broker in precisely the same way as original insurances are placed.

Characteristics of Reinsurance

The following are the important characteristics related to reinsurance:

(1) Reinsurance is like insurance which is practised by the insurers to spread their loss.

(2) Reinsurance contract is made on the same principles which governed the original contract of insurance.

(3) An original insurer has insurable interest to the extent of the risk undertaken by him. Therefore, he can reinsure the property to that extent.

(4) Reinsurance can be terminated when the original insurance lapses for any reason.

(5) In the event of loss, the original insurer has to pay the assured sum first to the insured. Then he will recover from the reinsurer his share of the liability.

(6) In the absence of any privity of contract between the original party who has insured his subject matter and the reinsurer, the reinsurers are discharged.

(7) The reinsurer is not liable to the original insurer in the event of loss.

Types of Reinsurance

Depending on the nature and scope, the methods or forms of reinsurance are broadly classified as follows:

I. Proportional Form of Reinsurance

(1) Quota Methods of Reinsurance

(2) Share Surplus form of Reinsurance.

II. Non– proportional Form of Reinsurance

(1) Excess of Loss Method

(2) Excess of Loss Ratio Method

(3) Pools Method of Reinsurance

(4) Treaty Method of Reinsurance.

The following chart can explain this more clearly:

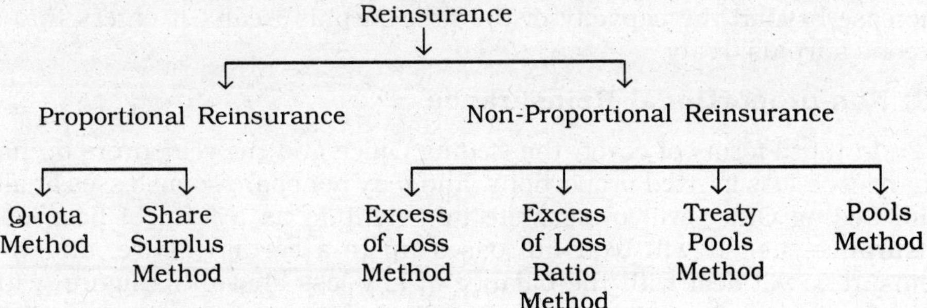

The following methods or forms of reinsurance have been discussed here briefly.

(I) Proportional Reinsurance

Under this method, the amount retained and the amount ceded will represent the fixed share of risk covered by the direct insurer, which places reinsurance with a reinsurance company (Ceding Office). Irrespective of the size of the claim, the liability of the claim will be shared by the Ceding Office and the reinsurers within the scope of treaty. The reinsurer will pay commission or brokerage to the Ceding Company or reinsurance broker at an agreed percentage of the premium ceded. The method of proportional reinsurance is further classified as:

(a) Quota Method of Reinsurance

(b) Share Surplus Method of Reinsurance

(a) Quota Method of Reinsurance: Under this method, the Ceding Office is bound to reinsurance such proportion of every risk as stated in the agreement. The Quota method of reinsurance are used where the company is new in a particular market or has no past well-known experience or has had poor experience in the past. This method is very much useful to the reinsurer. If, for example, re-insurance is arranged on a 50 per cent basis, the reinsurer accepts half of each risk obtains half the premiums, and bears half the claims while the leading company retains the balance of 50%.

(b) Share Surplus Method of Reinsurance: Under this form, surplus reinsurance treaty refers to the reinsurance, the surplus of a risk over the retention of the Ceding Office. The treaty would mention an amount as the Ceding Office's maximum retention as also the scope of geographical area and class of business. When a risk is proposed the Ceding Office has a free choice, within the liability specified in the treaty, as to how much it will retain for its own amount. If the sum insured is less than its normal retention level for that class of risk it need not take reinsurance at all. i.e., it will retain all. The number of lives of the surplus that can be reinsured is determined **by what** is specified in the treaty. Sometimes in order to increase beyond the capacity of the first surplus treaty, it enters into a second surplus treaty.

(II) Non-proportional Reinsurance

In these forms of cover, the Ceding Office and the reinsurers do not share each loss in fixed proportions, and may not share some losses at all. The Ceding Office will underwrite its retention as a form of first loss insurance, i.e., it will bear all losses up to a certain figure, and the reinsurers will deal with the balance of any loss above this figure, with usually an upper limit. Premiums under non-proportional reinsurance will be separately quoted by the reinsurer as a percentage of the total premium received by the Ceding Company for the concerned class of business. Thus, there will be a deposit premium and adjustment premium at the end of the year.

The Non-proportional forms of reinsurance can be classified into four categories.

1. Excess of Loss Method: This is another form of reinsurance which is sometimes used. This method assumes that an insurer decides the maximum amount he is prepared to bear on any one loss and seeks reinsurance under a treaty whereby the reinsurers will be responsible for the amount of any losses and above the amount retained by the direct insurer. The excess of the loss or a certain proportion of loss must be borne by the reinsurer with usually an upper limit. The net loss refers to those losses calculated after taking into account recoveries from facultative and treaty reinsurers. If the aggregate of the net loss exceeds the maximum limit mentioned in the treaty, the excess figure is paid by the reinsurer.

2. Excess of Loss Ratio Method: It does not deal with individual risks or individual events, but is designed to prevent wide fluctuations of the net claims ratio of a particular account over one financial year compared with another. The reinsurance is intended to protect the company from an abnormal experience and not just the normal year to year fluctuation. For example, if the average ratio of net claims to net premium income in a company's fire account was 40% over a period of years, it might wish to prevent the ratio going much over 50% in any year, and would arrange reinsurance accordingly. It is normal to require the ceding office to bear a share, say 10% of any layer of reinsurance.

3. Pools Method of Reinsurance: This method provides against hazardous risks or where the happening of an insured event may involve unusually heavy loss, damage etc. Under this method, the member companies accept to pool together all their business to a leading office and the payment is made by this leading office. The losses and profit shall be distributed to member companies according to their shares to the business.

4. Treaty Method of Reinsurance: Treaty is referred to an agreement between the ceding office (direct insurer) and a reinsurer or a number of reinsurers, whereby the reinsurer is bound to accept a fixed share of every risk coming within the scope of the agreement.

Double Insurance

The subject matter of the double insurance implies that it is insured with two or more insurers and the total sum insured exceeds the actual value of the subject matter. It is called as Double Insurance. In other words, the subject matter of double insurance must be insured with different insurers. If the actual value of the subject matter is more than the total sum insured, it is not treated as double insurance. In the case of life insurance, double insurance can be shown profitable because the insured can get full policy money under all policies. For example, if a premises worth of Rs. 2,00,000 is insured with 'y' for Rs. 1,40,000 and with X for Rs. 1,50,000, it is treated as double insurance because the total value of the subject-matter, i.e., total of all the policies exceeds the actual value of the premises. Suppose if it is insured with X and Y for Rs. 70,000 each, there is no double insurance.

Difference Between Reinsurance And Double Insurance

Reinsurance	Double Insurance
(1) When the risk is considered too great, get a part reinsured with another insurance company.	(1) When the same risk and subject-matter are insured with more than one insurer.
(2) The insurer has an insurable interest in the risk which he may reinsure.	(2) If insurer doubts the security of his underwriters insurers, the same risk with other underwriter no return of premium can be recovered.
(3) This reinsurance does not affect the position of the original insured. The reinsured has to pay reinsurance premium for the risk shifted.	(3) Total amount of all the policies is more than the actual value of the subject-matter.
(4) The original insurer is able to transfer a part of the risk to the reinsurer.	(4) Here, underwriters can adjust their risks and contribution among themselves.
(5) Reinsurance terminates when once the original insurance lapses for any reason.	(5) In the case of double insurance, termination is not possible.
(6) In the event of loss, the original insurer has to pay the assured sum to the insured.	(6) Assured cannot recover more than the amount of actual loss. If loss occurs, the assured may claim payment from the insurer in such order as he chooses.
(7) Original insurer will recover from the reinsurer his share of liability.	(7) The assured can recover the full value on the original policies till his total loss is made up.

Over Insurance

When the amount for which a subject-matter is insured is more than its actual value, it is called over insurance. For over insurance, the only criterion is the amount of insurance. It can even be with one insurer alone.

Lord Mansfield, while dealing with this rule of contribution in case of over insurance laid down as follows:

In the case of over insurance, the different sets of policies are considered as making but one insurance, and are good to the extent of the value of the effects put in risk; the assured can recover on the different policies, no more than their value but he may sue the underwriters on any of the policies, and recover from those, he so sued, to the full extent of his loss, supposing it to be covered by the policy on which he effects to sue, leaving the underwriters on that policy to recover a rateable sum by way of contribution from the underwriters of the other policy.

For Example:

Where a merchant, the value of whose whole interest is $ 22001, first effected a policy on his interest at Liverpool for $ 17001, and then without fraud another policy on the same interest at London for $ 22001, he is allowed to recover the whole amount on the London Policy, and the London underwriters are allowed to recover a rateable amount by way of contribution from the Liverpool underwriters.

External Insurance and Internal Insurance

Depending on their nature and scope, the risk insurance may be broadly treated as External Insurance and Internal Insurance.

External Insurance: External insurance is referred to any insurance technique that is suitable for dealing with risk related to an individual or a firm facing in the commercial market. Captive insurers, risk retention groups and risk sharing pools are the important alternative techniques that have been developed for commercial insurance. The group captive may be classified into pure captives and association or group captives. Risk retention groups are formed for the purpose of retaining or pooling risks.

Internal Insurance: Internal insurance may be described as an alternative to purchasing insurance in the commercial market. Some public organisations, enterprises, individual and institutions have established a fund to meet the insurable losses. As the risk is retained within the organisation, there is no market transaction of buying insurance cover. Internal insurance is also termed as self insurance. This mainly focuses attention and effort on the high frequency and low severity profile and implies that the losses are predictable. Own damage motor claims are the best example of self insurance.

Questions

1. What do you understand by reinsurance?
2. What are the characteristics of reinsurance?
3. Explain the various types of reinsurance
4. What do you understand by double insurance?
5. Bring out the different types of non-proportional reinsurance?
6. Write a short note on types of proportional reinsurance?
7. Write short notes on:

(a) External insurance

(b) Internal insurance

(c) Double insurance

(d) Surplus method of reinsurance

(e) Over insurance.

8. Explain the difference between reinsurance and double insurance.

Mini Cases

Case 1. A insures his house for Rs. 20,000 with A Ltd. and Rs. 40,000 with B Ltd. The house is partially damaged on account of an insured peril. The loss amounts to Rs. 24,000. State the liability of the two companies 'A' Ltd. and 'B' Ltd.

Ans : Since the same subject matter has been insured with two insurance companies, both must contribute towards the loss. Their liability will be determined on the basis of the following formula:

$$\frac{\text{Sum insured with the company}}{\text{Total Sum insured}} \times \text{Loss}$$

$$\text{Liability of A Ltd.} = \frac{20{,}000}{60{,}000} \times 24{,}000 = \text{Rs. } 8{,}000$$

$$\text{Liability of B Ltd.} = \frac{40{,}000}{60{,}000} \times 24{,}000 = \text{Rs. } 16{,}000$$

Case 2. A gets his ship insured with B for Rs. 10,000 for a certain premium. Now, if B, underwriter, wishes to reinsure half the risk, he may insure with C, for say Rs. 5,000. State the liability of the two underwriters B and C?

Ans: In case of loss, A can only put in a claim against B, but he has no rights against C, B has to pay his claim and in his turn claim half the loss from C. If, therefore, B were to fail and A's claim is not paid, A cannot claim the reinsured amount from the underwriter C with whom the reinsurance was effected. C is liable to pay in such an event only to B's trustee in bankruptcy.

Case 3. Mr. A has a building worth of Rs. 1,00,000 insured with B for Rs. 60, OOO and with C for Rs. 70,000. Is it a case of double insurance? Discuss.

Ans: The principle of double insurance is, when the same risk and subject matter is insured with more than one insurer and the sum insured far exceeds the actual value of subject matter.

In the instant case, it is insured with B and C for Rs. 60,000 and Rs. 70,000, it is a case of double insurance. If however, it is less than the actual value of subject matter, there is no double insurance.

Case 4. Mr. A is a merchant, the value of whose whole interest is $ 22001. He first effected a policy on his interest at Liverpool for $ 17001 and then without fraud another policy on the same interest at London for $ 22001. How will you decide A's claim?

Ans: In the instant case, Mr. A is allowed to recover the whole amount on the London Policy, and the London underwriters are allowed to recover a rateable amount by way of contribution from the Liverpool underwriters.

Case 5. A instructs his agent B to effect a "lost or not lost insurance on a ship at sea." During negotiation with an underwriter, B receives secret information of the sinking of the ship. Thereupon he abandons the negotiations without disclosing this information to anyone. Some days after; A instructs C to effect the insurance. Can the insurance effected by C be avoided by the underwriter on the ground of concealment of material facts?

Ans: No, the underwriter is liable to make good the loss as both A and C are ignorant to the sinking of the ship.

Chapter 6

Privatisation of Insurance Business In India

Introduction

Liberalisation, Privatisation and Globalisation have become a much talked of subject among economists, businessmen, politicians and professionals in modern days. Privatisation is expressed as the supporting pillar on which is the edifice of new economic policy of our Government has been erected and implemented since 1991.

Meaning

The term privatisation connotes a wide range of ideas. It would be therefore, appropriate to understand the meaning of the term.

In a narrow sense, privatisation implies the introduction of private ownership in publicly owned enterprises, but in a broader sense, it connotes besides private ownership (or even without change of ownership), the induction of private management and control in the public sector enterprises. Barbara Lee and John Nellis define the concept in this manner: "Privatisation is the general process of involving the private sector in the ownership or operation of the state owned enterprises. Thus, the term refers to private purchase of all or part of the company. It covers 'contracting out' and the privatisation of management through management contracts, leases or franchise arrangements."

Background of Privatisation

Privatisation, which has gathered momentum since around the 1980, has become the hallmark of the new wave of economic reforms sweeping across the world. More than 8,500 state owned enterprises have been privatised in over 80 counties during 1980-92.

Privatisation means transfer of ownership and/or management of an enterprise from the public sector to the private sector. It also means the withdrawal of the state from an industry or sector, partially or fully. Privatisation marks a change from dogmatism to pragmatism and amounts to a reversal of policy.

The trend towards privatisation has been observed in developed and developing economics; in market oriented and socialist, including communist countries; and cuts across socio cultural systems.

The fundamental reason for the reversal of policy from nationalisation to privatisation is the growing disappointment with the functioning of the public sector undertaking and state owned enterprises. In 1960, there was a trend towards nationalisation in Britain. But since 1970, this trend has been reversed and privatisation gathered ground by selling state owned enterprises. Besides UK; countries which announced the policy of privatisation included Argentina, Bangladesh, Brazil, Germany, France, Italy, Japan, Mexico, Nigeria, Spain, Turkey etc. A number of other countries including India have deregulated or liberalised the industrial sector in varying degrees. In late 1970, China also started privatisation and it spread to other communist countries like former USSR, East European countries and Cuba.

Performance of Public Sector

Contribution of the public sector in India towards economic development has been spectacular. To mention a few.

(1) Public sector has paved the way for building an industrial base in the country.

(2) It has opened up doors for tremendous employment potentiality.

(3) It facilitated the achievement of national objectives like checking concentration of economic power, poverty alleviation, redistribution of wealth.

(4) It has helped in capital formation and resource mobilisation.

(5) It facilitated technological development, research and development as well as a thrust for modernisation.

(6) It made substantial contribution towards India's exports and import substitution.

(7) Public sector's contribution towards the development of basic, heavy and large scale industries is tremendous.

(8) It facilitated to build up sound infrastructural facilities in India.

(9) It safeguards social interests of the various sections of the population.

(10) It provides essential services including transport, communication, educational and medical services etc.

(11) It helps to check monopoly and restrictive trade practices in India.

(12) It has a dominant place in critical areas like steel, coal, copper, zinc, chemical, fertilisers, and heavy machinery and so on.

(13) It helps in developing ancillary industries in India.

(14) It helps in removing regional disparities.

Defects or Criticism of Public Sectors

Thus, public sector plays a pivotal role, though it is not beyond criticism. The performance of public enterprises or state owned enterprises was far from satisfactory in several countries including India.

(1) Economic inefficiency in the production activities of the public sector, with high cost of production, inability to innovate, and cost delays in delivery of the goods produced.

(2) Capacity utilisation is very low in the public sector. In India, over 23 per cent of the public enterprises could utilise only 50-75 per cent of the installed capacity.

(3) Ineffectiveness in provision of goods and services, such as failure to meet intended objectives, diversion of benefits to elite groups etc.

(4) Labour indiscipline, idle time, inefficient management and mismanagement leads to ineffective utilisation of resources.

(5) Political interference and inappropriate controls also adversely affect the efficiency of these units though they enjoy budgetary support.

(6) Restricting the development of market mechanism which adversely affected undisturbed growth of the economy.

(7) Rapid expansion of the bureaucracy, severely straining the public budget, causing problems in labour relations within the public sector and adverse effects on the whole economy.

(8) Lack of autonomy as well as political interference affected the functions of public enterprises adversely.

(9) Uneconomic project implementation and high project cost make the public sector projects sick at its very birth.

These problems led many governments to undertake programmes of public sector reform, and pushed by a need to curb public expenditure to revaluate the possibilities for shifting publicly managed activities into the private sector.

Ways of Privatisation

There are several ways of achieving privatisation and each country adopted its own method. In Britain, the staff of the privatised company had the priority in buying shares and was entitled to a discount. For instance, 96 per cent of British telecom employees took a share in their company in defiance of the trade union opposition. Although some of them later sold them at a higher rate, they derived certain benefits financially through privatisation. One of the important methods of privatisation is divestiture, or privatisation of ownership, through the sale of equity. In countries where there are well functioning capital markets, this entails selling stock to the public. In industrial countries, privatisation had taken place mainly through divestiture of government economic activities. Bangladesh, Pakistan, Brazil, Peru and Sudan are some of the examples of this method. According to Elliot Berg, divestiture has become so common in the Western Europe that "hardly a week or month goes by without some new evidence of sale of state enterprise by such Western European countries as France, Italy, Sweden, the Federal Republic of Germany and, of course, the champion industrial company privatiser, Britain."

There is another way of privatisation. It takes the form of denationalisation or re-privatisation. Several large enterprises were denationalised in Pakistan, Bangladesh and Chile. Franchising is also one of the methods of privatisation. It this, certain services are designated in certain geographical areas which will be delivered by private companies. This is common in utility services and transport. Contracting is also common in public works. Where suppliers compete for contract and there is no less economics of scale, contracting is efficient. But there is scope for corruption in contracting. Long term contracts tend to encourage monopolistic tendencies in private companies.

Privatisation may also take the form of privatisation of management, using leases and management contracts. A public enterprise while retaining ownership may lease out to a private bidder for a specific period for use.

Contribution of Private Sector

Private sector has played a great role in the Indian economy, It may include:

(a) Promotion of economic growth

(b) Contribution to national exchequer

(c) Working to solve the problem of unemployment

(d) Contribution to global business

(e) Promoting research and development

(f) Contribution to ancillary development

(g) Concern for rural industrialisation

(h) Export development

(i) Acting as complementary and providing patronage to small scale and medium scale sectors.

(j) Stimulating the overall economic activity in India.

(k) Motivating capital formation and

(l) Stimulating resource mobilisation.

Role of Government in Promoting Private Sector

In promoting and developing an effective private sector, the Government plays a crucial role in India. Some of the important measures adopted by the Government for promoting and developing a responsible private sector include:

(1) Providing financial assistance to private entrepreneurs

(2) Developing infrastructural facilities

(3) Industrial area development

(4) Promoting raw materials, particularly scarce raw materials

(5) Developing a market, particularly export market

(6) Tax incentives are provided for new units, sick units and units in industrially backward areas

(7) Providing assistance for the revival of sick units

(8) Government's liberalisation process is envisaged to encourage private sector

(9) Appropriate industrial policy resolution and regulatory measures are adopted

(10) Providing incentives for industrial and business development, particularly to unemployed youth, women, technician

(11) Rationalisation of the tax structure

(12) Providing assistance to entrepreneurs and industrialists through District Industrial Centres and Industrial Development Centres

(13) Providing special incentives and assistance for small scale, village and tiny industries.

Liberalisation required for Privatisation

Liberalisation is an essential pre-requisite for successful privatisation. In the absence of liberalised rule and regulations, the private sector will not be willing to venture, due to several restrictions which would hinder the independent growth of the private sector institutions. The Government under former Prime Minister Narashima Rao, and former Finance Minister Dr. Manmohan Singh chose the path of liberalisation. Immediate factors which backed this policy change include (i) Global change, (ii) Position of Indian Economy and (iii) Trade deficit. As part of liberalisation, a new industrial policy was announced by Government of India in two parts on July 24, 1991 and 6th August 1991 respectively. This liberalisation has tremendously expanded the scope of the private industry in India. As a result of liberalisation, a new international economic relationship has emerged which has three aspects, viz., a multilateral business approach, regionalism and unilateralism, resulting in an international business philosophy. Even in the industries that are open to private sector, several regulations like industrial licensing, clearance from MRTP Act and Foreign Exchange restrictions liberalisation policy, these restrictions were removed. Liberalisation also facilitates unilateral trade and business relationships. Further, an outcome of liberalisation, automatic approval of foreign investment upto 51 per cent and foreign technology agreement are permitted for priority sectors.

Effect of Globalisation

The term Globalisation has been widely used in modern discussion of industrial policies and national economic policies, besides in business circles. The term Globalisation refers to the deepening relationships and broadening interdependence among people from different countries. Globalisation implies that the entire world is reckoned as one entity, one people and one market. Considering the emergence of the 'one market' norm, the business which takes place in one part of the globe can also be considered as a global business which is always highly competitive in a free market. Globalisation and liberalisation are inter-related terms. Liberation has got two dimensions (i) Domestic liberalisation, which consists of relaxing restrictions on production, investment, prices and increasing the role of market, guiding resource allocation (ii) External sector liberalisation or relaxing restrictions on international flow of goods and services, technology and capital. Globalisation is identified with external sector liberalization.

Globalisation of the market, investment, production process, technology upgradation, competitive environment and a global vision are necessary as a part of globalisation. While global companies and multinationals enter the Indian Market, Indian Companies should have the opportunity to conduct overseas business successfully. All the efforts for liberalisation and privatisation have paved the way for a global business environment in India, which is expected to progress further in the year to come.

Privatization of Life Insurance Business

As part of the wide-ranging economic reforms announced in 1991, industrial policy measures were initiated by the Government of India to liberalise the MRTP and FERA regulations. The most important aspect of the MRTP Act was amended to totally remove pre-entry restrictions on establishments of new undertaking and expansion of the existing firms. Important changes were also made in the Foreign Exchange Regulation Act (FERA) of 1973 in order to encourage foreign investment in India. FERA companies are allowed to have foreign equity holdings upto 51 per cent in high priority areas. FERA companies are granted greater freedom to operate in India, since restriction on internal operations has been removed. It means that FERA companies are now treated almost at par with the Indian companies. It is a great motivation to foreign corporate giants to freely operate in India without fear.

As part of the liberalisation process, the Government had to review the role of insurance sector and Government's investment in it. Accordingly, the Malhotra committee set up to study the insurance sector suggested in 1944 in its reports among other things the privatisation of the insurance sector. While praising the work done in achieving many of its objectives, the committee was critical about the low insurance coverage, unresponsiveness to customers needs, poor service, costly insurance cover with low returns, hierarchical management and an excessive lapse ratio policies. It stated that there was a large untapped potential for insurance in the country and this led to the first step being taken towards opening up of this sector to private player. As the results of the committee's recommendation to open up the sector to participation was implemented by the Government in 2000. The key element in the reform process was the participation of overseas insurance companies though restricted to 26 per cent of capital.

Private Life Insurers Operating in India

The Indian insurance sector was opened for private insurance sectors when the Government enacted the Insurance Regulatory and Development Authority Act 1999 leading to the establishment of IRDA. The main objective of setting up the IRDA was to protect the interest of policy holders and to regulate, promote and ensure orderly development of the insurance sectors. It is also aimed at ending the monopoly of the Life Insurance Corporation (LIC) and General Insurance Corporation (GIC) in the insurance sector of the company. The first private life insurance company was registered with IRDA in October 2000 and started operations shortly thereafter, thereby ending 44 years of public sector monopoly. Since then, many more private companies have been registered bringing the total number to a dozen as of

July 2002 all of which are joint ventures between major business houses or banks in India and renowned international insurance giants. Today after nearly fifty years, the insurance sector is a buyer's market where the consumer has the choice to select from variety of insurers. The table shows the lists of new entrants of insurers are associated with foreign shareholders to sell insurance products in India as on 2002 is given below:

List of Private Life Insurers in India

Company	Foreign shareholder	Major Local shareholder	Business of Local shareholder
(1) Allianz Bajaj Life	Allianz	Bajaj Auto	Auto Manufacturer
(2) AMP Sanmar	AMP	Sanmar	Diversified Conglomerate
(3) Birla Sun Life	Sun Life of Canada	Birla Global Finance	Diversified Conglomerate
(4) Dabur CGU	CGNU	Dabur	Medical & Consumer Products
(5) HDFC Standard Life	Standard Life	HDFC	Investment & Finance
(6) ICICI Prudential Life	Prudential (UK)	ICICI	Invesment & Finance
[7) ING Vysya Life	ING	Vysya Bank	Bank & Other Investors
(8) Max New York Life	New York Life	Max India	Diversified Conglomerate
(9) Met Life Inidia	Met Life	Jammu & Kashmir Bank : Pallonji Group	Bank and Diversified Conglomerate
(10) OM Kotak Mahindra	Old Mutual	Kotak Mahindra	Investment & Finance
(11) SBI Life	Cardiff	SBI	Bank
(12) TATA-AIG Life	AIG	TATA	Diversified Conglomerate

Performance of Private Life Insurance

The healthy development of the insurance industry in India has been boosted by the private insurers which has contributed substantially high percentage in overall performance. The private sectors brought with them international experience, cutting edge technology, new products and had the advantages technology, new products and had the advantages of starting off in the current regulated environment rather than changing over from an old environment. A report brought by Boston Consulting Group in 2003 given the performance of some of the private insurers fully operational in the year 2001-2002. The first year (2001-2002) premium income of ICICI prudential was Rs.115.9 Crores; Max New York Life was HDFC Standard Life was Rs.36.1 Crores ; Birla Sun Life was Rs.36.1 Crores ; Allianz Bajaj was Rs.18.05 Crores; SBI Life was Rs.15.20 Crores; and OM Kotak was Rs.12.83 Crores respectively. According to IRDA Life Council given the report in the year ended may 2002, more than 3,00,736 policies were issued by the private players in India. It was contributed by 1.30 per cent of the combined market share of private insurers. The same year the total policies were issued by LIC was 2,31,88,144. The total premium of LIC in 2001-2002, including renewal premium was Rs. 49,614 Crores with a growth rate of 42.25 per cent. It indicates that LIC, the premier life insurer and one of the most stable financial institutions in the country, during the forty six years of its existence has been through several trials and tribulations, but has managed to grow and metamorphose into the giant it is today.

Privatisation of General Insurance Business

The performance of the nationalised General Insurance industry was commented upon by the Malhotra committee set up the Government in the year 1994 to examine the insurance sector and suggest reforms required. It recorded in its report that objectives of nationalisation had been substantially achieved. As results of the recommendations made by the committee, a major change in the last couple of years has been the dismantling of the monopolistic status of the state run insurers. The field is no longer confined to them and has been thrown open to private insurers also. Six of them have commenced commercial operations and a few more are waiting in the wings. All of them have been promoted by major business groups and with one notable exception have tie-ups with foreign insurers. The minimum capital requirements of Rs. 100 Crores has resulted in only heavyweights of Indian commerce venturing into this area. There is now a restriction on the foreign holding, the maximum being limited to 26 per cent.

This has given a new dimension to the competitive market. While in the previous era competition was among four organisation which were similar in almost different culture, capabilities and value systems. There is one company promoted by co-operative organisation and five companies started by leading business houses.

Conditions for Success of Private Insurers

The success of private insurers primarily depends on the following conditions are:

(1) By constantly analysing the challenges and market opportunities to estimate the targets.

(2) New products should be simple and economical and also expected to give better return.

(3) Should provide more new innovative products with very competitive pricing.

(4) Should be focused on aggressive advertising. Unique advantages of promotional campaigns explain considerably success in private insurance companies.

(5) Proper training facilities should be provided to the intermediaries in order to enhance their efficiency.

(6) Large number of trained and professional agents should be appointed as intermediaries to development and expansion of insurance market.

(7) Better after sale services should be provided at the time of processing of a claim, documentation, and settlement of claims.

(8) A target of zero outstanding claims to be set.

(9) Build up a large network of office in order to take insurance close to the insuring public.

(10) Different strategies should be adopted to penetrate the market by developing multi-channel distribution models.

(11) Should be focused on direct selling or using bank network to sell insurance products.

(12) Use innovative technology to design and administering of insurance products.

(13) Emphasis on the sale of want satisfying utilities, i.e., acid-test of insurance business success is consumer's satisfaction.

(14) Making their distribution channel more productive and cost effective.

(15) Strong control over their distribution channel.

Questions

(1) What is meant by Privatisation?

(2) What are the various ways of Privatisation?

(3) Discuss about privatisation of Insurance business in India.

(4) State the conditions for success of private insurers.

(5) Explain the role of Government in privatisation of insurance business in India.

(6) Discuss the performance of public sectors and point out its deficiencies.

(7) Explain the impact on privatisation of insurance business in India.

Chapter 7

Classification of Insurance

CLASSIFICATION

Insurance can be classified two broad categories:

(a) Life Insurance

(b) Non-Life Insurance

The Non-Life Insurance can be classified further into General Insurance and Miscellaneous Insurance. The following are the four kinds of General Insurance.

(1) Marine Insurance

(2) Fire Insurance

(3) Personal Accident Insurance

(4) Vehicle Insurance

The Miscellaneous Insurance can be classified into:

(1) Fidelity Guarantee Insurance

(2) Crop Insurance

(3) Burglary Insurance

(4) Flood Insurance

(5) Cattle Insurance

(6) Cash Insurance

(7) Cash in Transit Insurance.

The following Chart explains the types of insurance:

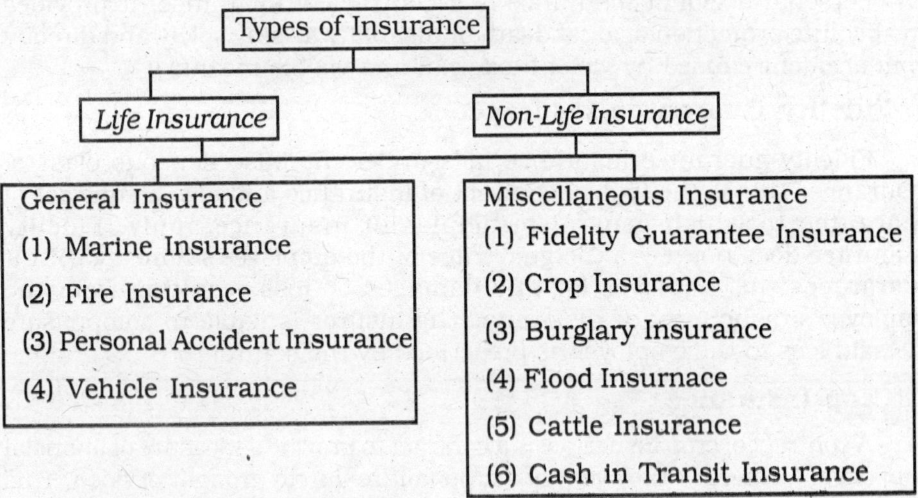

Theses are discussed briefly:

Various types of insurances are explained in the following pages.

1. Life Insurance

Life Insurance is a contract whereby the insurer in consideration of a premium paid either in a lump sum or in periodical instalments undertakes to pay an annuity or certain sum of money, either on the death of the insured or on the expiry of a certain number of years, whichever is earlier.

2. Marine Insurance

Marine Insurance is a contract of insurance under which the insurer undertakes to indemnify the insured against losses incidental to marine adventure. It may cover loss or damages to the ship, cargo, freight, vessels or any other subject of a marine adventure.

3. Fire Insurance

Fire insurance is a contract of agreement between the insurer and the insured whereby the insurer undertakes to indemnify the insured for destruction of or damage to property caused by fire or other specified perils during an agreed period of time, in return for payment of a premium in lump sum or by instalments.

4. Motor Vehicle Insurance

Motor Vehicle Insurance falls under General Insurance. Its importance increasing day by day. In Motor insurance, the owner's liability to compensate people who were killed or injured through the negligence of the motorists or drivers is passed on to the insurance company. Motor insurance business is the largest single section of accident insurance, if judged by premium income, but this relates to motor business as a whole.

5. Personal Accident Insurance

Personal accident insurance is a contract of insurance. It provides an absolute protection against death or disability arising solely and directly from accident caused by violent external and visible means.

6. Fidelity Guarantee Insurance

Fidelity guarantee insurance falls under the Miscellaneous class of insurance. This is the type of contract of insurance and also a contract of guarantee to which general principles of insurance apply. Fidelity guarantee does not mean the guarantee of the employee's honesty. But it guarantees the employer for any damages or loss resulting from the employee's dishonesty or disloyalty. The insurer is liable to compensate the said loss to the employer as prescribed by the contract.

7. Crop Insurance

A contract of crop insurance is a contract to provide a measure of financial support to farmers in the event of a crop failure due to drought or flood. This insurance covers all risks of loss or damage relating to production of rice, wheat, millets, oil seeds and pulses etc. Insurance of all crops all risks of loss or damage has not yet found a beginning in our country.

8. Burglary Insurance

Burglary insurance falls under the classification of insurance of property. In the case of a burglary policy, the loss or damages of household goods and properties and personal effects due to theft, larceny, burglary, house-breaking and acts of such nature are covered. The actual loss is compensated.

9. Cattle Insurance

A contract of Cattle Insurance is a contract whereby a sum of money is secured to the assured in the event of death of animals like bulls, buffaloes, cows and heifers. It is a contract against death resulting from accident, disease, parturitions or pregnant condition as the case may be. The insurer usually undertakes to pay the excess sum in the event of loss.

10. Cash in Transit Insurance

Cash in transit insurance is one of the contracts of insurance which falls under the category of miscellaneous insurance. This form of insurance covers to the insured against any loss in the event of money or cash being stolen from his business premises or while it is being carried from or to the bank. The scope of cash in transit insurance is important to any business as large sum of money are drawn from banks to pay wages and to meet the day to day expenses.

Questions

1. Write the different types of Insurance Business.
2. Write short notes on:
   (a) Fidelity Guarantee Insurance
   (b) Burglary Insurance
   (c) Cash in Transit Insurance
   (d) Marine Insurance
   (e) Motor Vehicle Insurance.

PART III : ESSENTIAL OF CONTRACT OF INSURANCE

Chapter

8

Principles of Contract of Insurance

Definition of Contract of Insurance

Contracts of insurance have all the essential elements of a general contract. According to Section 2(h) and Section (10) of Indian Contract Act, valid contracts must have the essential elements of offer and acceptance, consideration, legal parties, sound mind and free consent of the parties. A contract of insurance may be defined as a contract between two parties whereby a person undertakes in consideration of a fixed sum of money to pay to the other a fixed amount of money on the happening of a certain event (death or attainase in case of human life) or to pay the amount of actual loss when it takes place through a risk insured (in case of property).

Essential Elements of a Contract of Insurance

The following are the important essential elements required for a valid Contract of Insurance.

(1) Nature of Contract

(2) Utmost good faith

(3) Insurable interest

(4) Indemnity not involved

(5) Causa Proxima

(6) Contribution

(7) Risk must attach

(8) Mitigation of loss

(9) Subrogation

(10) Terms of policy

1. Nature of Contract

The nature of contract is a fundamental principle of contract of insurance required for a valid contract. A contract of insurance comes into existence when there is an offer or proposal on one side and acceptance of the same by other. It has to satisfy all the essential elements of a simple contract. The contract of insurance must be entered into by a competent person in order to be valid. The competent person must be of the age of majority according to law and of sound mind. Premium is the consideration that must be given for commencement of the insurance contract. The object of the contract should be lawful. Free consent is also one of the essential features of the contract of insurance. Every person entering into an insurance contract should enter into it by free consent.

2. Utmost Good Faith

Utmost good faith, *uberrimae fidei*, is the basis of contract of insurance. It requires that both the parties involved in an insurance contract should make disclosure of all material facts and figures relating to the subject matter of the insurance contract. If utmost good faith is not disclosed by either party, the contract may be avoided by the other. The insured's duty is to disclose all material facts known to him but unknown to the insurer. Similarly, the insurer's duty of utmost good faith is disclosing the scope of insurance at the time of contract. Any concealment, misrepresentation, fraud or mistake concerning the material facts to the risk should be disclosed. No important material facts and figures must be concealed. The duty of disclosure is absolute and positive. A few examples of disclosure of material facts may be given:

(1) Life Insurance : Age, income, education, occupation, health, family size, etc.

(2) Fire Insurance : Inflammable materials, nature and its use, fire detection etc.

(3) Motor Insurance : Type of car, value and details of driver etc.

3. Insurable Interest

Insurable interest is a fundamental principle of insurance. It is necessary for a valid contract of insurance. It means that insurable interest must be a pecuniary interest. The insured must have an insurable interest in the subject matter of insurance. Without insurable interest, the contract of insurance is void and unenforceable. A person said to have an insurable interest in the subject matter has to have benefit from its existence and prejudice by its destruction. Thus, insurable interest must be actual and real and not arising out of mere expectation.

The insured should have insurable interest in the subject matter of insurance at the following times:

(a) in life insurance at the time of taking policy

(b) in fire insurance both at the time of taking policy as well as at the time of loss and

(c) in marine insurance at the time of loss and an assured need not have an insurable interest at the time of effecting marine insurance.

There are a number of people with insurable interest. For example, a merchant may insure his cargo, while the owner of the ship or carrier may have an insurable interest in respect of his liability to damage to the cargo. A person who has advanced money on the security of a house has an insurable interest in the house. An underwriter has an insurable interest in respect of any reinsurance that he may desire to effect. Again every person has an insurable interest in his own life, since the law presumes that each one desire to remain alive.

4. Indemnity

A contract of insurance is a contract of indemnity. All contract of insurance except life, personal accident and sickness insurances are contracts of indemnity. This means that the assured, in case of loss against which the policy has been insured, shall be paid the actual amount of loss not exceeding the amount of the policy. In case of marine and fire. insurances, the insurer undertakes to indemnify the insured for loss or damage resulting from specified perils. In case of loss, the insured can recover from the insurer the actual amount of loss, not exceeding the amount of policy. A contract of life insurance is not a contract of indemnity. In the case of the life insurance, there is no question of actual loss. Whether the assured suffered any financial loss or not, thc assurer must pay the policy amount on the maturity of the policy.

Methods of Indemnity:

There are four alternative methods to indemnify an insured in the event of loss, damage or destruction of the subject matters insured. These are (a) Cash payment (b) Repairs (c) Replacement and (d) Reinstatement.

5. Causa Proxima

Causa Proxima is necessary for a valid contract of insurance. It has been defined as "The active efficient cause that sets in motion a train of events which brings about a result, without the intervention of any force started and working actively from a new and independent source."

Proximate cause means the most closely and directly connected of perils insured against with loss. Thus the insurer is liable for loss, if the risk must be insured against, is the proximate or the last cause of loss occurred. If there is one cause of loss identified, it is not required to go further into the cause of causes. If there is a series of causes of damage or loss is identified in such, the nearest peril is the one insured against the principle of causa proxima is applied. And also the insurer is bound to be responsible only if the nearest cause comes within the meaning of the risk insured. Thus, the closest peril is the one insured against risk, the loss of the subject matter would be compensated.

(1) For example, sugar was insured against danger by sea water. Rats make a hole which caused sea water to pour out and damage the goods. Though rats were originally responsible for this damage, the immediate cause of damage (the proximate cause of damage) was sea water, a peril insured against. Hence, the insured was held to be entitled to the damage.

(2) A cargo of oranges was insured against loss due to collision. The ship actually collided resulting in delay and mishandling of cargo which made oranges unfit for human consumption. The Master of the Rolls held that the damage to oranges was not the direct result of collision, but of delay and mishandling. As these causes were not insured, the insured could not recover.

(3) A policy holder sustained an accident while hunting. He was unable to walk after the accident and, as a result of lying on wet ground before being picked up, he contracted pneumonia. There was an unbroken chain of causation between the accident and the death, and the proximate cause of the death, therefore, was the accident and not pneumonia.

6. Contribution

This is another principle essential for a valid insurance contract. This doctrine of contribution applies only to contracts of indemnity, i.e., to fire and marine insurance. According to this principle, in case of double insurance, the insurers are to share the loss in proportion to the amount assured by each of them. In order to apply the right to contribution between two or more companies, the following factors must exist:

(a) The subject matter of insurance must be the same.

(b) The event insured must be the same.

(c) The insured must be the same.

"Contribution may be defined as the right of an insurer who has paid a loss under a policy to cover a proportionate amount from other insurers who are liable for the loss".

7. Risk much Attach

This principle is essential for a valid contract of insurance. A contract of insurance can be enforced only if the risk has been attached. Premium is the consideration for the risk run by the insurance companies. If there is no risk in the subject matter, there should be no premium. Thus, where the policy is avoided before the risk began to run; the assured is entitled to a repayment of the premium that may have been paid. But if once the risk has begun to run, the premium cannot be recovered. For example, if the subject-matter of insurance ceases to exist (e.g. the goods are burnt) or the insured ship has already arrived safely, at the time the policy is effected, the risk does not attach and as a consequence, the premium paid can be recovered from the insurers because the consideration for the premium has totally failed. Thus, where the risk is never run, the consideration fails and therefore the premium is returnable.

8. Mitigation of Loss

Mitigation of loss is applied in valid insurance contract. In the event of some mishap to the insured property, the insured must make necessary effort to safeguard his remaining property and minimise the loss, as much as possible. If he does make any reasonable efforts to reduce the loss, the insurer will be liable for payment of all loss resulting from the peril insured against. If he is negligent to preserve the property, the insurer may avoid payment of loss.

9. Subrogation

The term 'Subrogation' means the transfer of all the rights and remedies available to the insured in respect of the subject matter to the insurer after indemnity has been effected. It is also referred as getting into the shoes of the others. It implies substitution of the insurer in place of the insured in respect of the latter's rights and remedies. For example,

(1) when loss is caused by the wrongful act of a third party, the insurer can proceed against the third party after paying the insured his loss. This principle holds good only in the case of fire and marine Insurance.

(2) Subrogation also arises in motor insurance as, for example, where an insured motor vehicle is damaged owning to the negligence of a third party against whom the insurers will therefore claim in an endeavour to recover the cost of repairs paid by them under their policy.

(3) A private car may be damaged in a collision caused by the rash and negligent driving of a truck. The private car owner's right of recovery against the truck owner is transferred to the insurer who has indemnified the loss.

10. Term of Policy

An insurance policy specifies the terms or period of time it covers; often the nature of risk against which insurance is sought determines the period or life of the policy. A life insurance policy may cover a specified number of years or the balance of the insured life. A contract of fire insurance is normally for a period of one year.

Questions

1. What is a contract of insurance? Explain the fundamental principles of insurance.
2. Explain and illustrate the fundamental principles of insurance.
3. A contract of insurance is a contract of "uberrimae fidei". Explain.
4. Write short notes on
   (a) Causa Proxima
   (b) Mitigation of loss
   (c) Utmost good faith
   (d) Insurable interest
5. What is the doctrine of subrogation?
6. Explain the essential elements of a contract of insurance.
7. What do you mean by a proximate cause?

Mini Cases

Case1. **A** made a proposal to an insurance company for an insurance policy on his life for Rs. 80,000. He truthfully answered all questions on the proposal form and disclosed all relevant facts. A few days later but before the proposal was accepted, **A** was taken ill with pneumonia. The proposal was accepted by the company the next day. Two days after **A** died of pneumonia and the company learnt for the first time of his illness. Is the insurance company liable to make the payment?

Ans: A contract of insurance is a contract of absolute good faith. The duty of observing utmost good faith by the proposer to an insurance contract continues throughout the negotiations till the proposal is accepted by the insurance and the contract becomes operative. Thus, the insurance is entitled to get notice of any material alteration in the risk between the day of the proposal and its acceptance.

In the instant case, such notice was not given, and therefore, there was a breach of good faith. The insurer is, therefore, not liable for making payment.

Case 2. **A** took a life insurance policy from an insurance company on his life. While making the proposal of insurance, **A** in reply to a question asking whether all previous proposal on his life were accepted by insurers at ordinary rates, he replied that he was insured with two insurance companies at ordinary rates, but omitted to disclose that his proposal for insurance was declined by two other insurance companies, **A** dies and his legal representative claimed the insurance money. Is the insurance company liable to pay?

Ans: A contract of insurance is a contract of absolute good faith. It is expected form the proposer as well as the insurance company to disclose every material fact known to each other. Such liability is more on the proposer since perhaps no one knows about him more than he himself. The term material fact refers to a fact which would affect the judgement of a prudent underwriter in assessing the extent of risk or determining the amount of premium which he will like to charge.

In the instant case, the proposer was guilty of concealing material facts from the insurance company. Hence, the insurance company is not liable to pay money to the legal representative of **A**.

Case 3. The cargo on a ship was insured against loss arising on account of sea water. Some rats on the ship caused a hole in the bottom of the ship resulting in entry of sea water into the ship and resulting in loss to the cargo. The insurance company refuses to pay the money on the ground that loss was caused on account of rats, which was not an insured peril. How will you decide?

Ans: The insurer is liable to compensate the insured for any loss arising on account of a sea peril insured against. Such peril should be the proximate cause of loss.

In the instant case, the rats were a remote cause of loss and sea water a proximate one. Since loss on account of sea water is an insured peril and, therefore, the insurance is liable to pay for the loss.

Case 4. **A**'s goods in a warehouse were insured against fire with **B** insurance Company. The goods were burnt and **A** recovered the full value of Rs.10,00,000 from the insurance company. Subsequently, **A** also sued the warehouse keeper and recovered a sum of Rs.10,00,000 from him. **A** retains this money?

Ans: According to doctrine of subrogation in contracts of indemnity, an insured cannot be allowed to make any profit from an insurance claim. He cannot take benefit of an insurance policy as well as any other alternative rights or remedies.

On the basis of the above principle, in the instant case, **A** must return a sum of Rs.10,00,000 to the insurance company.

Case 5. A steamer was insured for Rs.11 lakh, though its declared value was Rs.13 lakhs. In a collision with a ship, the steamer was completely lost. The insurer paid a sum of Rs.1 lakh, the insured amount to the owner of the steamer. Later on, the insurer recovered a sum or Rs.21 lakhs from the owner of the ship responsible for collision. Can the insurer retain the sum received?

Ans: The doctrine of subrogation entitles the insurer to all alternative rights and remedies available to the insurer against a third party. However, it is to be noted that subrogation of the insurer extends to the value insured and no more than that.

Case 6. **P** effected an insurance on his goods against loss or damage by fire. **P** and his wife quarrelled and the excited wife set fire to and destroyed the goods. Can **P** recover under the policy? If yes, can the insurer sue the wife under the doctrine of subrogation?

Ans: **P** can recover under the policy as the wife had set fire to the goods without his connivance. But the insurer cannot sue the wife under the principle of subrogation because there can be no subrogation of those rights which the insured himself does not have (the husband himself cannot sue his wife for her act).

Case 7. **A** contracted to build a shop for **B** for Rs.5,00,000. All the materials were to be supplied by **B**. Can **A** get the materials insured for the period of construction?

Ans: Yes, **A** can get the materials insured because he has an insurable interest therein as he would suffer financial loss on the destruction of the materials.

Chapter 9

Insurance Documents

Introduction

There are various insurance documents used for different types of insurance, which are essential for all classes of insurance business. The object of insurance documents is to give the insurer full particulars of the risk against which insurance protection is desired. It also provides evidence of contract into which the parties have entered.

(a) Proposal Form

(b) Policy Form

(c) Cover Note

(d) Certificate of Insurance

(e) Endorsement.

(a) Proposal Forms

The company's printed proposal form is normally used for making an application for the required insurance cover. The proposal form contains questions designed to elicit all material information about the particular risk proposed for insurance. The number and nature of questions vary according to the particular class of insurance covered.

In Marine Cargo Insurance, it is not the practice to use a proposal form, although sometimes it is usual to obtain a questionnaire or a declaration form duly completed. Proposal forms are used for hull insurance.

In Fire Insurance, the practice varies among the companies. Proposal forms are not generally used for large industrial risks where inspection of the risk is arranged before acceptance of the risk. Forms are used for simple risks. Proposal forms are used in respect of risks which are normally declined but have to be accommodated to retain the goodwill of the client.

In Miscellaneous Insurance, proposal forms are invariably required and they incorporate a declaration which extends the common law duty of good faith. Fire proposal forms mayor may not have the declarations.

The following items may be considered as common to all proposal forms.

(a) Proposer's name in full

(b) Proposer's address

(c) Proposer's profession, occupation or business

(d) Previous and present insurance

(e) Loss experience

(f) Sum insured

(g) Other Section's — Signature, date, place etc.

(b) Policy Forms

Policy forms, like proposal forms, vary within wide limits as between different classes of insurance but they have certain features in common. The policy is a document which provides evidence of the contact of insurance. This document has to be stamped in accordance with provisions of the Indian Stamp Act 1899, where the insurance is governed by a Tariff or a Market agreement, the policy wording is prescribed therein itself and it is obligatory for insurers to use these wordings. In fire and miscellaneous insurance, the policy form used is on a scheduled basis, i.e., all individual details relating to a particular insurance are grouped together in a schedule.

Generally speaking, policies are divisible into certain well-defined sections and these are as follows:

(1) Recital Clause or Preamble

(2) Operative Clause

(3) Attestation Clause

(4) Conditions

(5) Schedule.

1. **Recital Clause:** The opening section of the policy is termed as Recital Clause because it recites the parties to the contract, and

if the insurance is based upon a proposal form and declaration, this is also mentioned.

2. **Operative Clause:** The operative clause sets out the circumstances in which the insurers agree to make a payment or its equivalent to the insured.

3. **Attestation Clause:** This clause governs the signature of the policy and its wording depends upon the practice of the insurers concerned for the execution of documents.

4. **Conditions:** All policies are subject to conditions which are printed on the policy. They are called Express Conditions which are necessary to regulate the contract. There are certain conditions implied namely (a) good faith (b) insurable interest etc.

5. **Schedule:** In the schedule will be found certain particulars common to most classes of polices and other peculiar to the type of insurance under consideration. The particulars common to most policies include details of the policy number, first and annual premiums, renewal date, name and address of the parties and the period of insurance, with the date of signature of the policy.

(c) Cover Note

A cover note is a document issued in advance of the policy. It is issued when the policy cannot for some reason or the other, be issued straight away. Cover notes are issued when the negotiations for insurance are in progress and it is necessary to provide cover on a provisional basis or when the premises are being inspected for determining the actual rate applicable. Pending the preparation of the policy, the cover note is issued as evidence of protection for a temporary period of time and to prove that cover is in force. Here is a brief detail of a cover.

In Marine Insurance, marine cover notes are normally issued when details required for the issue of policy such as name of the steamer, number of packages or exact value etc., are not known.

In Fire Insurance, the operative clause of a fire cover note is issued in consideration of the proposer named in the schedule having proposed the effect of an insurance against fire for the period mentioned, on the usual terms and conditions of the company's policy.

In Motor Vehicle Insurance, motor cover notes are to be issued in the form prescribed by the Motor Tariff.

(d) Certificate of Insurance

In motor insurance, in addition to the policy, a certificate of insurance is required by the Motor Vehicle Act., 1988. This certificate provides evidence of insurance to the Police and Registration authorities. It contains the essential features of the cover including the terms and conditions.

In Marine Insurance, certificate of insurance is issued to provide evidence of cover on shipments insured under cargo open cover or floating policies

(e) Endorsements

It is the practice of insurers to issue policies is a standard form, covering certain perils and excluding certain others. If it is intended, at the time of issuing the policy to modify the terms and conditions of the policy, it is done by setting out the alteration in a memorandum which is attached to the policy and forms part of it. The memorandum is called an endorsement.

Questions

1. What are the important documents used in insurance business?
2. Write short notes on:
   (a) Proposal Form
   (b) Policy Form
   (c) Cover Note
3. What do you mean by Proposal Form?
4. What do you understand by Policy Form?
5. What is Certificate of Insurance?

Chapter 10

Essentials of Life Insurance

Law relating to Life Insurance

Life insurance in its present form came to India from the United Kingdom (UK) with the establishment of a British firm. In 1818, the Oriential Life Insurance Company came into existence in Calcutta followed by Bombay. Life Insurance Company was set up in 1823. In 1829, the Madras Equitable Life Insurance Society and Oriential Government Security were established. Life Insurance Company came into force during the year 1956. Prior to 1871, Indian lives were treated as sub-standard and charged an extra premium of 15% to 20%. Bombay Mutual Life Assurance Society, an Indian insurer which came into existence in 1871, was the first to cover Indian lives at normal rates. The Indian Life Assurance Companies Act 1912 was the first statutory measure to regulate life insurance business. Later in 1928, the Indian Insurance Companies Act was enacted, *inter alia* to enable the Government to collect statistical information about both life and non-life insurance business transacted in India by Indian and foreign insurers including Provident Fund Societies.

The Insurance Act of 1938 was a well thoughtout legislation passed to perform and control the activities of the companies carrying on various businesses relating to life, marine, fire and accident. It contained various provisions of the 1938 Act relating to deposits, investments, premium, role and power of insurance companies that did not apply to life insurance business. Efforts in this direction continued progressively and the Act was amended in 1950. It was in Jan. 1956 that the management of 245 Indian and foreign insurance companies and provident societies operating in the life insurance business were taken over by the Union Government and nationalised on September 1,1956. The Life Insurance Corporation was formed with a capital contribution of Rs. 5 crores. The Life Insurance Corporation business has increased from 5 million policies at the time of nationalisation to over 56 million policies at present (2004).

Meaning and Definition of Life Insurance

Introduction

It is a common belief that one of the most difficult products to sell is, "life insurance" and one who sells life insurance can sell anything under the sun. There is no gainsaying the fact that selling life insurance is a difficult proposition primarily because what is sought to be marketed is an assurance, a belief and a faith.

Definition of Life Insurance

Life insurance may be defined as a contract in which the insurer in consideration of a certain premium either in lump sum or other periodical payments, agrees to pay to the assured or to the person for whose benefits the policy is taken, a stated sum of money on the happening of a particular event contingent on the duration of human life. Thus, under a whole-life Assurance, the policy money is payable at the death of the assured and under an endowment policy, the money is payable on the assured's surviving a stated period of years, for example, on his attaining the age of 55 or his death, should that occur earlier.

According to Sec.(2) (11) of the Insurance Act, Life Insurance business means "the business of effecting contracts upon human life. It includes:

(a) any contract whereby the payment of money is assured upon death (except death by accident only) or the happening of any contingency dependent on human life;

(b) any contract which is subject to the payment of premiums for a term dependent on human life;

(c) any contract which include the granting of disability and double or triple indemnity, accident benefits, the granting of annuities upon human life and the granting of superannuation allowances."

Difference Between Insurance and Assurance

Insurance (Non-Life Insurance)	Assurance (Life Insurance)
(1) In the case of insurance, loss due to risk is not certain to happen, loss i.e., likely to happen or not	(1) Loss due to risk is certain to happen. Risk of death is bound to happen sooner or later.
(2) Generally, goods or property of any other kind are the subject matter of non-life insurance.	(2) Human life is the subject matter of life insurance contract.
(3) Insurance contract is usually for one year.	(3) In the case of life insurance contract, the contract is a continuing contract, i.e., long term contract.
(4) Fire, marine insurance and other contracts are contracts of indemnity.	(4) It is not a contract of indemnity.
(5) In fire insurance, insurable interest must be approved both at the time policy is effected and at the time when loss occurred. In marine insurance, it must be present only at the time of loss occurring. It is not necessary at the time of effecting the policy.	(5) Insurable interest must be present only at the time of taking out the policy, but need not have insurable interestat the time of maturity of the policy.
(6) The term 'Insurance' is used to other kinds of non-life insurance contracts.	(6) The term 'Assurance' is referred only to Life Insurance business.
(7) In the case of marine and fire insurance, the policy cannot be surrendered by the assured before its maturity.	(7) In life the insurance, policy can be surrendered by the assured before its maturity.
(8) In the case of fire and marine insurance, insurance contain only the protection elements.	(8) Life Insurance contains both the elements.

Essential Features of Life Assurance

Essential Features

The following are the essential features of a valid contract of life insurance.

(1) Elements of a valid contract

(2) Insurable interest.

(3) Utmost good faith

(4) Warranties

(5) Assignment and nomination

(6) Cause is certain

(7) Premium

(8) Terms of policy

(9) Return of premium.

Now we shall consider the above features of life assurance.

1. Elements of a Valid Contract: Contract of life insurance has the essential elements of a general contract, since the life insurance contract is a contract, as defined in the Indian Contract Act. A valid contract of life insurance comes into existence where the essential elements of agreement (offer and acceptance, competency of the parties, free consent of the parties, legal consideration and legal objectives) are present.

2. Insurable Interest: A person cannot insure the life of another unless he has an insurable interest in it. The risk against this policy is the death of the insured. A person has unlimited insurable interest in his own life. A husband is presumed to have insurable interest in his wife's life and *vice versa.* A surety has insurable interest in the life of the principal debtor to the extent of his claim. In life insurance, the insurable interest must exist at the time of the contract of insurance.

3. Utmost Good Faith: Insurance contracts, however, are contracts *uberrimae fidei,* i.e., one based on utmost good faith or the contract of utmost good faith. The insured is bound to disclose all the material facts and figures known to him but unknown to the insurer. Every fact which is likely to influence the mind of the insurer in deciding whether to accept the proposal or in fixing the rate of premium is material for this purpose. Similarly, the insurer is bound to exercise the same good faith in disclosing the scope of insurance which he is prepared to grant. In life insurance, age, income, education, occupation, health, family size etc. are some examples of material facts that should be disclosed at the time of entering into the contract.

The breach of obligation of disclosing material facts with almost good faith may arise in the following cases:

1. Non-disclosure of material facts
2. International non-disclosure
3. Non-disclosure of material facts by negligence or by oversight
4. Mis-representation by material facts with fraudulent purposes.

4. Warranties: Warranties are an important feature of life insurance contract. Warranties are the basis of the contract between the proposer and insurer. If any statement, whether of material or non-material facts and figures are untrue the contract shall be null and void and the premium paid by him may be forfeited by the insurer. The policy insured will contain that proposal and the personal statement shall form part of the policy and be the basis of the contract.

5. Assignment and Nomination: Both assignment and nomination are essential features of life insurance policy. Assignment of a life policy means transferring the rights of the assured in respect of the policy holder to the assignee. In the case of the nomination, a person is merely named to collect the amount to be paid by the insurer on the death of the assured.

6. Cause is Certain: In life assurance policy, the insurer has to pay the insured amount one day or other because the death of the assured or his reaching a particular age is certain to happen.

7. Premium: The premium is the price for the risk of loss undertaken by the insurer. In the case of the insurance, premium is usually required to be paid in cash and advance payment of the premium is a condition precedent to the creation of a binding contract of insurance. The amount of premium for payment of insured is paid monthly or on annual instalments for a certain period. In life insurance, the premium is calculated on the average rate of mortality and the fixed periodical premium may continue either until death or for a specified number of years. Premium is payable till the maturity of the policy.

8. Terms of Policy: An insurance policy specifies the terms and conditions or period of time, it covers often the nature of risk against which insurance is sought, determines the period or life of the policy. A life insurance policy may cover a specified number of years or the balance of the insured life.

9. Return of Premium: Premium is the consideration for the risk run by the insurers, and if the risk insured against is not run, then the consideration fails, the policy does not attach, and as a consequence the premium paid can be recovered from the insurer. The general principle applicable to the claim for the return of the premium is that if the insurers have never been on the risk, they cannot be said to have earned the premium. But where the insurance is avoided by the insurers on the ground of breach of warranty, the premium can only be recovered if it is shown there was breach *ab initio*.

Questions

1. Define a contract of life insurance.
2. What are the features of life assurance?
3. What is the difference between Insurance and Assurance?
4. When should insurable interest be present in the case of life insurance?
5. Define Life Insurance. Discuss how far the principles of insurable interest and indemnity apply to this branch of insurance.
6. How does life insurance differ from other forms of insurance?
7. What is Insurance?

8. What is Assurance?
9. Explain the essential elements of life assurance.
10. Explain the law relating to life insurance business.
11. Under what circumstances is an insurer bound to return the premium?

Mini Cases

Case 1. P owes Q Rs. 15,000. Q insures P's life for a like amount. P pays the debt to Q, then dies. Q claims Rs. 15,000 from the insurer. Is he liable to pay?

Ans: Yes, insurable interest is necessary only at the time of taking the policy. Thus, in the instant case, the insurer is liable to pay a sum of Rs. 15,000 to Q.

Case 2. A insures his life with an insurer for Rs. 5,000. Subsequently, he becomes insane and while of unsound mind he commits suicide. Can the legal representative of A recover the money from the Insurance company?

Ans: According to the present clause inserted by the Life Insurance Corporation of India in all life insurance policies, if the life assured commits suicide at any time after expiry of one year from the date of commencement of policy, the legal representative can claim the money of the policy. Hence in the present case, the legal representative of A, subject to the terms of the policy, can recover the money from the insurance company, if one year has expired since the commencement of the policy.

Case 3. Z effected with defendants an insurance on her own life. In making the proposal for insurance, Z in reply to a question asking whether she had suffered from mental derangement replied 'no'. In fact, she had not thought of this fact, of having been confined of acute mania. In a claim on the policy the insurers declined to pay on the ground of a material concealment. How would you decide?

Ans: Insurers are not liable on account of material concealment of facts.

Case 4. On the 1st April, 1995, A takes life insurance policy for Rs. 10,000 on his life. The premium was agreed to be paid in monthly instalments of Rs. 100. A pays the first instalments due on 1st April, 1995 and subsequent instalment, but fails to pay the instalment due on the 1st April 1999. On 1st June, 1999 A dies. State the amount of the insurance, the company will pay to the legal representative or nominee of A.

Ans: The premium on a life insurance policy is payable in full in advance for the whole year. The facility to pay the premium in instalments is provided by the insurance company only for the benefit of the insured.

The insurance company will pay to A's representative or his nominee a sum after deducting the following amounts:

(i) Premium due up to the date of death, i.e., Rs. 300 with interest at a reasonable rate.

(ii) The sum due as premium up to the next anniversary (31st March 1999) Rs. 900.

Case 5. P, takes a policy on his own life on the 15th January, 2000 and later commits suicide on the 24th September, 2001. Is the LIC liable?

Ans: Yes, the LIC is liable, as the policy has already run, on the date of suicide, for more than one year.

Case 6. A, the holder of a policy of life insurance on his own life assigned it to his wife. B, on the condition that the benefits under the policy are to revert to him should B die during his life time. A year later, A revoked the assignment on the ground that it was conditional. Thereafter A died during the lifetime of B. Both B and A's legal representatives claimed the policy money. Whose claim will prevail and why?

Ans: B's claim will prevail. Section 38 of the Insurance Act permits "Conditional assignment". Hence, the assignment made in favour of B was valid. The assignor cannot revoke an assignment once validly made. As such the policy remained assigned to B and on A's death she is entitled to get the policy money.

Case 7. P, the holder of a policy of life insurance on his own life nominates Q as his nominee. Before the maturity of the policy Q dies. On the maturity of the policy Q,s heirs claim the policy money. Will they succeed?

Ans: No. Q's heirs will not succeed because as per section 39 of the Insurance Act where the nominee dies before the policy matures for payment, the policy money shall be payable to the policy holder or his heirs.

Chapter 11

Classification of Life Insurance Policies

Objectives of Life Insurance Policies

Life Insurance is a contract providing for payment of a sum of money to the person assured or failing him, to the person entitled to receive the same, on the happening of certain events. The Life Insurance Corporation came into existence with the objectives of assurance of

(a) family protection

(b) provision for old age

(c) tax concession

(d) housing loans

(e) loans advanced for educational purposes and

(f) donations to charitable institutions. To meet the above said objectives, various types of life insurance policies are being issued by the Life Insurance Corporation of India.

Classification of Policies

The Life Insurance Policies can be divided on the basis of:

I. Duration of Policy

II. Methods of Premium Payments

III. Participation in Profit

IV. Number of Lives Covered

V. Method of Payment of Sum Assured.

From the above said basis, the following are Life Insurance Policies classified futher into:

I. Policies According to Duration:

1. On the basis of Duration of Policies:

(a) Whole Life Policies

(b) Limited Payment Whole Life Policies

(c) Convertible Whole Life Policy

2. On the basis of Terms Insurance Policies:

(a) Temporary Assurance Policy

(b) Renewable Term Policies

(c) Convertible Term Policies

3. On the basis of Endowment Policies:

(a) Pure Endowment Policy

(b) Ordinary Endowment Policy

(c) Joint Endowment Policy

(d) Double Endowment Policy

(e) Fixed Term (Marriage) Endowment Policy

(f) Educational Annuity Policy

(g) Triple Benefit Policy

(h) Anticipated Endowment Policy

(i) Multi-Purpose Policy

(j) Children's Deferred Endowment Assurance

II. On the basis of Premium Payment:

(a) Single Premium Policy

(b) Level Premium Policy

III. On the basis of Participation in Profit:

(a) Without Profit Policies (or) Non-Participating Policies

(b) With Profit Policies (or) Participating Policies

IV. On the basis of the Number of Persons Assured:

(a) Single Life Policies

(b) Multiple Life Policies

Life Insurance Policies can be classified as shown in the following chart:

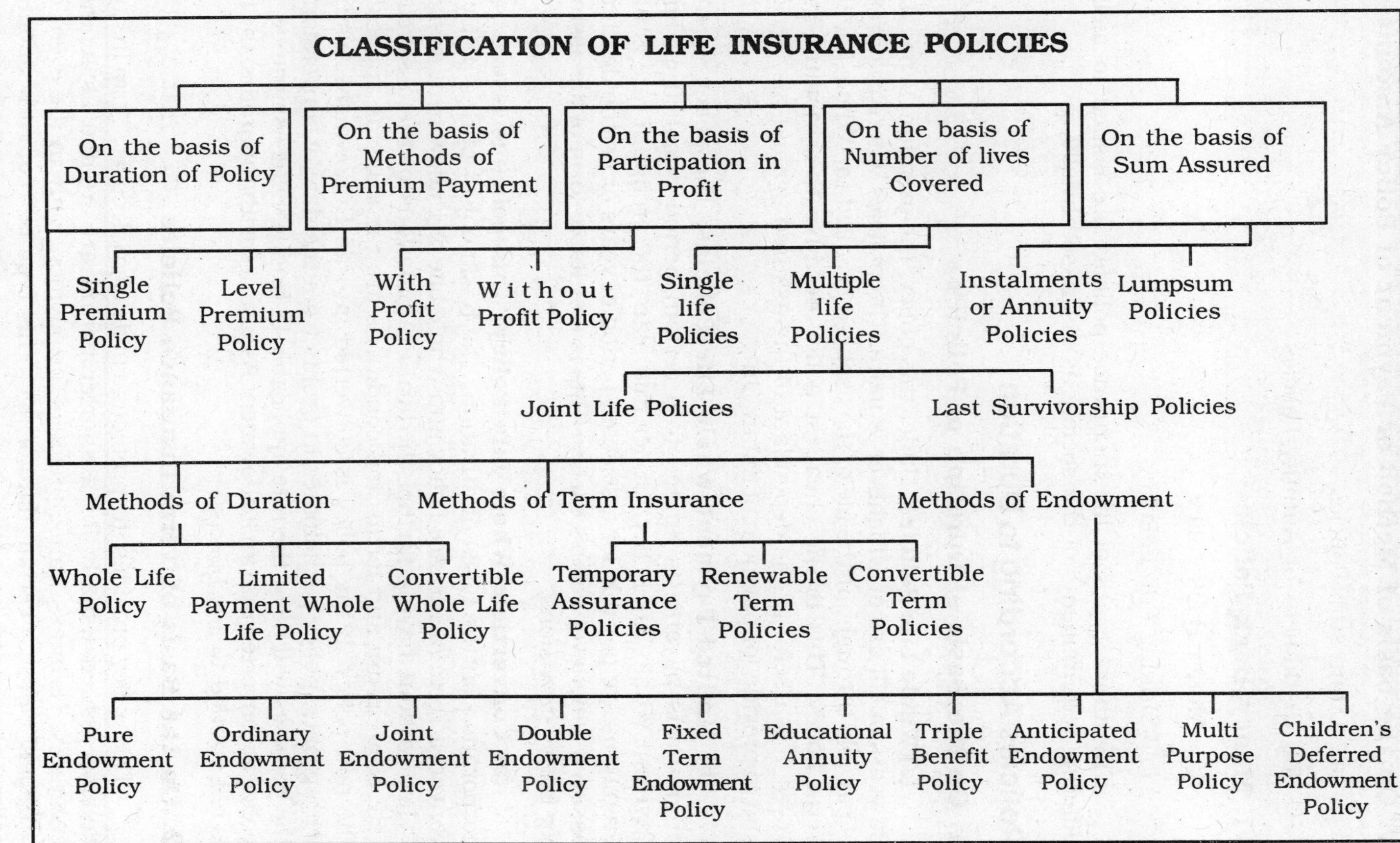

(c) Joint Life Policies

(d) Last Survivorship Policy

V. On the basis of Method or Payment of Policy Amount:

(a) Lump sum Policies

(b) Instalment or Annuity Policies

VI. Money Back Policies:

(a) Money Back Policy

(b) Sinking Funds Policy

The above types of life insurance policies are issued to meet the differing requirements of the society as discussed briefly.

Policies According to Duration

1. On the Basis of Duration of Policies

(a) Whole Life Policies: Under this policy, the premium is payable for 35 years or till age or whichever is more. The policies where the premium is payable throughout the life of the assured is called the Whole Life Whole Term Policy. This is the cheapest policy because the premium rate is lower. It is useful to the dependant of the assured against his/her death and to provide for payment of Estate Duty.

(b) Limited Payment Whole Life Policies: The policy where the premium is payable is limited to a certain period is called as Limited Payment Whole Life Policy. Under this plan, the premium rate is higher. Premiums are payable for a selected period of years or on the death of the assured whichever occurs earlier. This is a suitable form of life assurance for family provisions.

(c) Convertible Whole Life Policy: This policy is issued by the corporation on the basis of duration. The basic object of this policy is to convert a Term Assurance Policy into Whole Life or Endowment Assurance Policy without having further medical examinations of the assured. The rate of premium and terms and conditions are the same as applicable to the new policy. If the policy is converted into an Endowment Assurance with profits, policy participates in profits from the date of conversion, and the bonuses will be at the rate applicable to Endowment Assurance. If the policy is converted into an Endowment Assurance without profits, the policy is not entitled to any bonus.

2. On the Basis of Term Insurance Policies

This policy provides the protection of death risk cover. Term Insurance Policies issued usually for a shorter period are treated as temporary contracts. Term assurance provides for payment only in the event of life dropping before a certain date or age. This type is frequently adopted as collateral security for a loan.

(a) Temporary Assurance Policy: This policy is issued by the Corporation on the basis of Term Insurance Policy. This plan is designed to cover the risk against life assured for a period of less than two years. The sum assured will be payable only in the event of the life assured's death occurring within the selected period from the commencement of the policy. A single premium is required to be paid at the outset. Rates are fixed whereof per thousand sum assured are given alongside.

(b) Renewable Term Policies: Renewable Term Policies are issued on the basis of term of assurance. This plan of assurance is renewable at the end of the selected term for an additional term period without having to undergo fresh medical examination. Premiums are usually quoted according to the age attained at the time of renewal.

(c) Convertible Term Policies: This plan of assurance is designed to meet the needs of those options to convert it into Whole Life or Endowment Assurance Policy. Premiums are payable for selected terms of years or until death if it occurs within this period, but they may be limited to a shorter term of years, if so desired. The sum assured shall be payable only in the event of death of the life assured or at the end of maturity period whichever is earlier. The main object of this policy is the life assured under this plan, has an option to convert the policy, provided it is in full force, into either a Limited Payment Life Policy or an Endowment Assurance Policy without having to undergo fresh medical examination, at anytime during the specified term except the last two years. For example, the Convertible Term Insurance Plan can be converted into an endowment or whole life type contract at the end of selected term of 5,6 or *y* years. During this period, this is treated as a term assurance. The assured is expected to exercise his choice of conversion before two years of expiry of term, so as to obviate adverse selection. Selection against the insurer during last two years. If no option is exercised, the assurance comes to end at the end of the selected term.

3. On the Basis of Endowment Policies

This is a popular policy issued by the Life Insurance Corporation of India. The basic objective is that the policy for the sum assured becomes matured on the policy holder's death or on his attaining a particular age whichever is earlier. The period for which the policy is taken is called as Endowment Period. The premium under this policy is a little higher as compared with term assurance. This policy is a useful to the family in case of a sudden death of the policy holder.

Endowment policies are of many types. The important endowment policies are discussed below:

(a) Pure Endowment Policy: Under Pure Endowment Policy, the sum assured is payable on the policy holder surviving to the maturity date. The sum assured is payable in the event of death within the term of policy. In the event of death in the first and the second year of policy, the benefit will be limited to 80% and 90% of the premiums paid respectively. This is the best form of life assurance for adult and child. The basic aim of this policy is not only providing protection against risk of death but also encouraging investments.

(b) Ordinary Endowment Policy: This policy provides a fund for family provision and investment. The sum assured is payable to the policy holder for a specific term of years either on the assured's death or on his survival to the stipulated term, i.e., until the maturity date. Premiums are payable throughout the life time of the assured or for a selected period of years or until prior death of the life assured.

(c) Joint Endowment Policy: This policy is designed to cover the risk on the two or more lives under a single policy. The sum assured shall become payable on the maturity of the policy or on death of either of the two lives assured whichever is earlier. This policy is useful to partners of a firm and for husband and wife in a family. Partnership firms usually go in for such policies to provide for the return of the capital of the deceased partner.

(d) Double Endowment Policy: Under this policy, premium is payable throughout the life term of the assured or for a selected period of years or until prior death of the life assured. This is the best form of life assurance, the insurer agrees to pay the assured double the amount of the insured sum on the expiry of the term or on the death of the life assured whichever is earlier.

(e) Fixed Term (Marriage) Endowment Policy: This plan is designed to meet the needs of the provision relating to marriage of anyone of the family members of the policy holder. Under this plan, the sum assured together with profits shall be payable at the end of the maturity or on the death of the life assured whichever is earlier. Premiums are payable for the selected terms of the policy or till death of the life assured if it occurs during the selected term.

(f) Educational Annuity Policy: This plan provides for a sum assured to be kept aside to meet the educational expenses of children. Under this plan, the sum assured together with profits is payable to the insured at the end of the selected term either in a lump sum or in ten half yearly instalments at the option of the life assured/nominee/ beneficiary. Premiums are payable for the selected term of the policy or till death of the life assured if it occurs during the selected term. This policy will be issued to persons aged not less than 18 years and not more than 60 years at entry. The policies will be issued for minimum term of 5 years and maximum term of 25 years subject to maturity age of 70 years. The minimum sum assured under this plan will be Rs. 10,000.

(g) Triple Benefit Policy: This plan is most suitable for housing loan purpose. Under this plan, the benefits availing the policy holders on death of the life assured during the term of the policy is thrice the basic sum payable or on survival to the date of maturity, only the basic sum assured is payable. Premiums are payable for the selected term of the policy or till prior death of the life assured. As per the method of calculation, paid up value will be the same as a Whole Life limited payment and a Pure Endowment Policy.

(h) Anticipated Endowment Policy: Under this policy, the sum assured will be payable on the basis of half of the sum assured paid before the death of the policy holders and the balance of the sum assured is payable at the end of the maturity date. In the event of death of the assured before the attainment of the term period, full lump sum assured amount is payable to the policy holder. Premiums are payable during the selected term or till death if earlier.

(i) Multi Purpose Policy: This form of life insurance not only makes provision for the family of life assured in the event of his death, but also to meet the needs of a person in old age. It is also useful to meet the expenses relating to family and provision for education and marriage of his children. Premiums are payable during selected period of years or until prior death of the life assured. Several purposes are fulfilled under one single policy which is called Multi Purpose Policy.

(j) Children's Deferred Endowment Assurance: This policy is designed to meet the expenses relating to children's education and marriage. Policies under this plan are issued on lives of both male and female children who have not completed 18 years. This is an Endowment Assurance Policy, it provides the protection of risk from the date of commencement of policy or from the deferred date to the date on which the policy emerges as claimed by the death of child or its survival to a stipulated date. This is the cheapest form of life insurance because of low rate of premium. The main object of this policy is to cover the risk against the life of children on behalf of their parents and guardian.

(II) On the Basis of Premium Payment

The following important policies are issued by the Corporation on the basis of premium payment.

(a) Single Premium Policy: Single Premium Policy is useful to those who desire to provide the whole premium in one instalment at the time of taking the policy. Single Premium Policy becomes matured on the assured's death or on his attainment of selected term whichever occurs earlier.

(b) Level Premium Policy: Unlike single premium policy, under this policy premiums are payable on a regular basis for a selected term or till prior death. It is useful to those persons having regular earnings. Premium is lesser as compared to a single premium policy. The sum assured becomes payable if the assured reaches a particular age or on the assured's death whichever is earlier.

(III) On the Basis of Participation in Profits

Policies issued on the basis of participation in profits are discussed below:

(a) With Profit Policies (or) Participating Policies: With Profit Policies are also termed as Participating Policies. Unlike Non-participating Policies Participating policy holders are entitled to get the share of profits or bonus or benefits or paid up facilities as per the terms and conditions of the Corporation. The sum assured with profits shall become payable to the insured at the end of the maturity or in the event of death if earlier.

(b) Without Profit Policies (or) Non-Participating Policies: Under this policy, sum assured will become payable without any paid up facilities to the insured at the end of the selected term or on the death of life assured if earlier.

(IV) On the Basis of the Number of Persons Assured

Important policies on the basis of Number of Persons assured are discussed below:

(a) Single Life Policies: This policy is designed on the basis of number persons assured. Single Life Policy covers the risk on one individual, it may be issued on one's own life or on another's life. The policy amount is payable to the insured on attaining a selected term or on the death of the life assured whichever is earlier.

(b) Multiple Life Policies: Multiple Life Policies is a policy issued on the basis of the number of persons assured. The Multiple Life Policies may be Joint Life Policies and Last Survivorship Policies. Unlike Single Life Policy, Joint Life Policy covers the risks of more than two individuals. The sum assured is payable at the time of maturity or on the event of the death of the first assured whichever is earlier. This policy is useful to partners of a firm or on the lives of husband and wife of a family. Under Last Survivorship Policy, the sum assured shall be payable at the last death of assured or on the attaining a selected term if earlier.

(V) On the Basis of Methods of Payment of Policy Amount

On the basis of Methods of Payment of Policy amount, the policy may be:

(1) Lump sum Policies

(2) Instalments (or) Annuity Policies.

(1) Lumpsum Policies: Lump sum Policies are designed by the corporation on the basis of methods of payment of policy amount. Under this policy the sum assured shall be payable in a lump sum to the policyholders at the end of the maturity date or on the assured's death whichever is earlier.

(2) Instalments (or) Annuity Policies: This is a plan of assurance designed to provide a large amount of risk cover on payment of a premium which is comparatively a small amount. Under this policy, the full amount is not payable in lump sum but the insured amount is payable to the assured by periodical instalments for a selected period of terms or till the death of the assured.

(VI) Money Back Policies

(a) Money Back Policy: This type of policy provides money back at regular intervals before the policy expires. For example, on a 15 years policy, one gets 20 per cent of the sum assured after five years, another 20 per cent on the expiry of another five years and the balance at the end of 15 years. In case death of the assured occurs during the 2 years, the full sum assured is paid irrespective of instalments already paid. Thus, the policy gives money in hand plus insurance cover. Premiums are payable for the selected term of years or till death if it occurs within that period. The bonus additions to the policy will be reckoned on the full sum assured and are payable at the end of the selected term of years or at the life assured's death, if earlier. No loan will be granted under this policy.

(b) Sinking Funds Policy: Such a policy is taken with a view of providing for the payment of liability or replacement of an asset.

(VII) Special Plans

(1) Jeevan Shree: This plan also refers to "an exclusive policy for exclusive people". Under this plan, the minimum sum assured is 5 lakhs. Hence, it is specifically suited to high-income groups. Basically, an endowment plan with flexibility in premium paying term including single premium. The investment will be so managed as to ensure of guaranteed and loyalty additions — higher liquidity (relaxed conditions for availing loan)

(2) Capital Redemption Assurance: This plan provides for payment of a sum of money (sum assured) on a specified date in exchange for periodical premiums. There is no life assurance element and they are independent of the duration of human life, the main factor being accumulation of interest. In other words, to secure a capital sum to replace a wasting asset such as machinery or leasehold property.

(3) Jeevan Aadhar: Specially designed for the benefit of specific type of handicapped dependents. This is limited payment whole life policy with guaranteed additions at the rate of Rs.100/- per 1000 sum assured per annum, where the claimant is paid partly in lump sum and partly in the form of an annuity. Full Income Tax benefit under section 80 DD up to a premium of Rs. 40,000 per annum. Minimum age entry is 22 years and maximum per annum. Minimum age entry at 60 years. Minimum sum assured is Rs.50,000 premium payment term is 10, 15, 20, 25, 30 and 35.

(4) Jeevan Vishwas: Specially designed for the benefit of board categories of handicapped dependents. This is an endownment type with guaranteed additions where the claimant is paid in lumpsum and in the form of annuity.

(5) New Jeevan Akshay: A policy that provides for the maximum possible income on the invested capital, consistent with absolute safety. The income is assured throughout life but ceases on death of the annuitant. Options to have definite annuity payments for 5, 10, 15, 20 years and thereafter for life are available. Minimum age at entry 40 years and maximum age at entry 79 years. Minimum purchase price Rs.25,000. All modes annuity payments, i.e., monthly, quarterly, half yearly and yearly etc.

(6) Jeevan Suraksha: Jeevan Suraksha plan was introduced on 15th August 1996. This is a pension plan with life cover and various options. The policy holder taking policy with life cover provides minimum of 50% of the target pension to spouse on death during the deferment period.

(7) Komal Jeevan: Komal Jeevan plan was introduced as a children's Money Back Policy on 14th November 2002. The plan is available to children from 0 to 10 years of age. The premium are payable upto age 18 of life assured. The policy vests in life assured on attaining age 18 years. The very purpose of this plan is to provide for expenses for higher education-cum-start in life. The minimum sum assured under this plan is fixed at Rs.1 lakh and the maximum sum assured is Rs.25 lakhs. Guaranteed additions @ Rs.75 per thousand sum assured per annum is payable at the end of 26 years as a maturity benefit and the policy contract comes to an end.

(8) BIMA Nivesh: A single premium savings/investment oriented plan of assurance with compounding guaranteed addition to the sum assured at the rate of 6 per cent available in 5 years and 10 years terms. The scheme accepts premium for minimum sum assured of Rs.25,000 and the upper limit, touches the sum of Rs.50 lakhs.

(9) BIMA Plus: Bima plus is a unique insurance plan with investment facility besides getting tax benefits. It offers unmatched package of benefits. They are (a) Life Insurance Cover, (b) Accident Benefit Cover, (c) Maturity Bonus, (d) Returns and (e) Tax rebate @ 20% u/s 88. The sum assured is 10 times the annual premiums (i.e., if annual premium is Rs. 5,000 then the sum assured will be Rs.50.000) or 20 times the half yearly premiums or equal to the single premium.

(10) Jeevan Anand: Jeevan Anand plan is a combination of Whole Life and Endowment Assurance Plan. The premium can be paid yearly or half yearly. Even after the premium paying term is over, risk cover continues till the death of the policyholder. Under this policy, accident benefit is available during the premium paying term and thereafter upto age 70. The sum assured along with vested bonus and final additional bonus, if any, will be payable on maturity or on death if earlier, provided the death occurs on or after the date of commencement of risk.

(11) Key-Man Insurance: It is an insurance taken by a company on the life of important employee-key–man of the company— against financial loss that may occur from the employee's premature death. Under this plan, key-man (KM) can be an expert, a Technocrat, a Director, a Shareholder and an Executive. The key-man may be defined as an employee whose death would result in a financial loss to the company (including replacement). There can be any number of key-man in a company.

Eligibility: Key-man insurance is allowed if

(1) The key-man is holding less than 51 % shares in the company.

(2) Key-man and his family is holding less than 70 per cent shares in the company.

(3) Key-man is a matriculate.

(4) Age at entry is less than 50 years.

Salient Features

(1) Company will be the proposer for key-man insurance.

(2) Term allowed is 10 to 15 years subject to retirement age or service contract.

(3) Key-Man Insurance is restricted to 10 times of Key-Man's Annual compensation package. Annual package include: Salary + perquisites. National value of perquisites will be taken at 30% of Gross Annual Salary.

(4) Maximum Sum Assured: For Public Ltd. Companies; 5 times of average 3 years net benefit or 3 times of average 3 years gross profit whichever is lower. Private Ltd, or closely held Public Ltd, Companies:

   (a) No. of shareholders or employees 10 or more

   (b) No. of shareholders or employees — less than 10; maximum allowable cover will be 3 times of average net profits of at least 3 years.

(5) Double Accident benefit, extended permanent disability benefit and Term riders benefits are not allowed under key-man insurance policy.

Advantages of Taking Key-man Insurance

(1) The company is protected against the financial loss in the event of key-man's death.

(2) It gives substantial income tax savings to the company (while paying the premiums and while receiving the proceeds).

(3) The company is able to create an asset for itself in the form of premiums paid and added bonus.

(4) It protects the interests of other employees, salesmen, shareholders, and customers, and keep the company's position stabilised in the market.

(5) It generates confidence, sense of security and loyalty in the minds of key-men.

(6) It can be given as security to bankers, it is a guarantee to the creditors.

(12) Jeevan Mitra Policy: This plan is designed to meet needs of the people who are insurance oriented and also want to provide a big sum insurance protection to their family, in the case of their unfortunate death. This plan is most preferred by travelling persons like, sales representatives, marketing executives, medical representatives etc. This plan is not allowed to non-earning majors including students, pilots and crew members. Under this policy, maturity benefit and death benefit will be calculated on the basis of double risk cover endownment policy and triple risk cover endownment policy. Under double risk cover endownment policy, the maturity benefit will be basic sum assured plus accrued bonus is given. On death, 2 times of sum assured plus bonus is given. In case of accident death, 3 times of sum assured plus bonus is given provided policy was covered for accident benefit. On the other hand, under triple risk cover endownment policy, the maturity benefit will be basic sum assured plus accrued bonus is given. On death, 3 times of sum assured plus bonus is given. In the case of accidental death, the benefit will be 4 times of sum assured plus bonus is given, provided policy was covered for accident benefit. However, accidental benefit is subject to a maximum of Rs.25 lakhs basic sum assured including existing policies.

(13) New Janaraksha Policy: This plan is best suited for people with irregular income and whose job is not secured. For example, farmers, milk vendors, petty businessmen etc. Under this plan, the maximum entry age at entry is restricted to 40 years in case of non-medical subject to the maximum sum assured of Rs. 50,000. Under this plan, the sum assured with accured bonus is payable on the maturity date or in the event of the unfortunate premature death of the life assured. The maximum accident benefit increased from 5 lakhs to 7.5 lakhs effect from 23.11.2002.

(14) Jeevan Sukanya: A generation to generation policy for girl child. It is a plan exclusively designed for female children aged between 1 and 12 years. This a limited premium payment plan, which provides risk cover (after a certain deferment period) on the life of the female child and, when she gets married extends the risk cover to the life of her husband also. Premiums will cease on the policy anniversary falling after completion of age 20 years by the life assured on which data on sum assured is payable. Similarly, the policy matures at the age 50 of the life assured when the bonus additions are paid to the life assured.

(15) Bhavishya Jeevan with Profit: This plan is designed to meet the needs of persons having a very short span of high earnings, where after the income decreases or stops. The premium paying capacity for such persons (Film Artistes, Professionals on foreign assignment etc) is quite high during the period of high income. The plan accordingly envisages a high premium during the first 5 years. Thereafter, the premium comes down significantly.

(16) Jeevan Kishore: This plan is designed for both boys and girls. The risk cover after waiting period, i.e., 2 years from the commencement of the policy or from the policy anniversary falling immediately after the attainment of 7 years of age whichever is later. The policy will vest in the life assured — child on attaining maturity. The maximum sum assured allowed is Rs.15 lakhs, if the age at entry is less than 10 years and Rs.40 lakhs, if age at entry is 10 years or more. Under this policy, the maximum term allowed is 15 years. This policy is useful for child's marriage or start in life. Bonus for the policy including the waiting period will vest on the policy anniversary from which the risk is covered or 5 years from the commencement whichever is later.

(17) Jeevan Saathi: This policy suitable for husband and wife who wants to take joint life risk cover under a single policy.

Salient features

(a) Issued only to working couple, the wife should be an income tax assessee. For sum assured Rs. 1,00,000 and less, wife need not be a earning person.

(b) Plan is not allowed for female lives who have undergone 3 or more caesarean operations. For female with one/two caesarean is allowed to take plan with 3% extra premium.

(c) Maximum sum assured allowed under the plan to housewife and self employed female lives category 111 is Rs.1 lakhs with standard age proof.

(d) Maturity benefit — if both husband and wife are alive upto maturity, sum assured plus bonus is given. On death of either husband/wife, survivor gets sum assured immediately and further premiums are waived.

(18) Jeevan Surabhi: This plan is designed for businessmen and professionals as money is available periodically. Under this policy, for a policy of 15 years, one has to pay premium only for 12 years. Similarly, for a policy of 20 years, one has to pay premium only for 15 years and for a policy of 25 years, one is required to premium only for 18 years. The Jeevan Surabhi plan is an improved vision of Money Back Plan with an added element of increasing Term Insurance Cover. The premium paying terms are lesser than the policy term to cater to the needs of people who want to pay for shorter period, but want to enjoy benefits for a longer period. The proposal under the plan would be entertained under non-medical special scheme upto Rs.1,00,000 sum assured if eligible is to come under scheme. The policy will participate in profits till the end of policy term provided it is in force for full sum assured on the date of valuation. The bonus will be calculated on the basic sum assured. The vested bonus will be payable on the date of maturity or on death, if earlier. In case of death during the term of the policy, the basic sum assured along with the additional cover and vested bonuses will become payable.

Group Insurance Schemes

LIC offers life insurance protection under group policies to various groups such as employer-employees, professionals, co–operatives, weaker sections of society etc. It also provides insurance coverage to people under certain approved occupation at subsidised rates under social security groups schemes. Besides providing insurance coverage which provide funding of gratuity and pension liabilities of the employers.

The main features of the schemes are low premium, simple insurability conditions such as employee not being absent from duty on grounds of ill health on the date of entry, and easy administration by way of issue of a single master policy covering all the employee/members, premiums are based upon age, combination of members, occupations and working conditions of the group. However, there are certain conditions as to minimum group size and the maximum participation to make the scheme viable. The standard schemes offered by LIC are as follows:

(1) Group Term Insurance Schemes: Employer-employee groups may be offered group insurance schemes providing uniform or graded cover. These groups may also be offered schemes covering outstanding housing loans and outstanding vehicle advances granted by an employer to its employees. Group insurance schemes providing uniform cover can be granted to associations of professionals (such as doctors, lawyers, chartered accountants etc), members of co-operative banks, welfare funds, credit societies and weaker sections of society.

(2) Group Insurance Scheme in lieu of EDLI: The Employees Deposit Linked Insurance scheme is applicable to all establishments and undertakings contributing employees provident fund under EPF and MP Act 1952, with effect from 1.8.1976; the scheme provides for an insurance cover to an employee, which is linked to his balance in the PF Account, subject to a maximum of Rs.35,000.

(3) Group Gratuity Scheme: Gratuity is a statutory liability of most of the employers which accrues to an employee for every year, of service put in by him. As the liability accrues every year, from the point of view of sound accounting practice year, it is desirable to provide for this liability before the profits are determined. The Group Gratuity Scheme provides a scientific method for funding gratuity as the premiums are based on actuarial principles. The attractive features of the scheme is the life insurance cover to every employee due to which, in the event of the premature death of an employee, his dependents become entitled to substantially higher benefits.

(4) Group Superannuation Scheme: This plan is designed to provide pension to employees on their retirement from service. The scheme may be financed by the employer alone or jointly with the employees. A decreasing group insurance cover in conjunction with superannuation benefits may also be provided under the scheme. The scheme is of two types :

(a) Money purchase scheme: The contribution are fixed generally as a percentage of the salary. The accumulated value of such contributions is utilised to purchase the pension.

(b) Benefit purchase scheme: The amount of pension is fixed by the employer in advance generally in relation to the salary drawn by the employee at the time of exit. LIC determines the contributions payable for funding of pension benefits.

(5) Group Savings Linked Insurance Scheme: This plan offers insurance cover together with a savings element. The contribution under this scheme is deducted from the monthly salary of the member. The scheme is allowed to selected employer-employee groups such as quasi-Govt. bodies, public sector corporations and reputable companies in public and private sectors who keep accurate records of their employees. Under this scheme, out of the contribution received in respect of each employee, a portion is utilised for the insurance cover and the balance, known as contribution for savings, is accumulated till exit at an attractive rate of interest, which at present is 10% p.a. The savings contribution is returned with interest at the time of retirement, or exit by any other mode.

(6) Voluntary Retirement Scheme (LIC's Plan): The VRS benefits to employees generally provide for payment of an annuity (depending upon the salary and length of service) which ceases at the national retirement age. The LIC has evolved plans by which the VRS requirements of employees can be taken care of.

(7) Group Leave Encashment Scheme: This plan is designed to provide for employers to meet the liability of leave encashment facility available to employees in annual books of accounts. Under this plan, cover of a flat sum assured has also been provided to employees. The scheme shall be administered by the employer.

(8) Social Security Schemes: As per the direction of the Central Government, a social security fund was created in 1988-89. The object of the fund is to extend insurance benefits to economically weaker sections of society in the unorganised sector. Half of the premium will be drawn from the social security fund maintained by the LIC. The remaining 50% of the premium is collected from a designed Nodal Agency which may be contributed by the State Government and/or the beneficiaries. Insurance cover up to Rs.5,000 can be granted under these schemes.

(9) LALGI Scheme: All Landless Agricultural Labourers of India have been covered for a uniform sum assured of Rs.2000 (payable to the family of the deceased labourer). The entire premium is met from the social security fund maintained by LIC.

(10) Rural Group Life Insurance Schemes (RGLIS): The Govt. of India has announced the introduction of Rural Group Life Insurance Schemes which are administered by designated branch offices of LIC through intermediate level panchayats. The effective date of the scheme is 15th August 1995. The following are some of the salient features of the scheme.

Entry Age : 20 years (minimum and 50 years maximum)

Premium : Rs.60 p.a. for those who enroll up to the age of 40 years and Rs.70 p.a. for those who enroll beyond 40 years.

Two types of schemes are offered. Under the General Scheme and person within the jurisdiction of the concerned Intermediate Level Panchayats can be covered by charging full premium. Under the subsidised scheme, only one person from each of the households below the stipulated poverty line will be covered. The premium will be subsidised to the extent of 50% to be shared equally by the State/Union Territories and the Central Government.

(11) Integrated Rural Development Programme (IRDP Scheme): To offer greater security to the families and mitigate the hardship in the event of sudden death of the head of the family, a group insurance scheme was launched for the beneficiaries under the Integrated Rural Development Programme (IRDP), which provides cover of Rs.5,0001. In case of death by accident, the amount payable is Rs.10,000/-. The claims are paid out of the fund set up by the Government for the purpose and no premium is charged from the beneficiaries. So far, about 2.30 crore people have availed the benefit of this scheme. During the last 10 years, 74276 claims for Rs.30.66 crore have been paid to the beneficiaries.

(12) Group Insurance Scheme for Students: It has been decided to offer a Group Insurance Cover to the students pursuing professional courses through a recognized University. This has been allowed to fulfil the needs of insurance cover to professional students on whose studies the parents spend a substantial sum of money. If such a child dies, the loss to the parents/family is quite significant.

Some of the features:

(1) The institution which is a recognised body for imparting education in professional courses will act as a Nodal Agency for its students.

(2) The premium paid to the corporations and collected by the institutions along with the fee from students at the time of admission of the students.

(3) Full time benefited students of the institution aged less than 30 years shall be covered under this scheme.

(4) An insurance cover, ranging between Rs.50,000 and Rs.1 ,50,000 may be allowed.

(5) No Double Accident Benefit will be allowed under the scheme.

(6) A Flat premium of Rs.2.30 per thousand sum assured per annum will be charge.

Partnership Insurance

Introduction: In our country, nearly 50% of the business is done by partnership forms and proprietorship concerns. Proprietorship concern is a one man show and that an individual may take a policy or two to cover his life. However, it is not the same case with partnership firms.

Need of Partnership Insurance

The partnership firm will be in trouble when a partner dies unfortunately. The death results in dissolution of the firm and the firm has to pay lumpsum amount to the deceased partner's family. But still, many a partnership firms have not realised the importance of partnership insurance in our country. One must utilise this opportunity and bring about a partnership insurance awareness.

(1) In the event of the early death of a partner, it may not be possible to pay such a heavy sum out of the partnership fund.

(2) The remaining partners may have to sell some of the assets of the firm.

(3) In some cases, the remaining partners may have to close down the firm.

To fight against such a high risk, the LIC field force may advise the firm to take an insurance policy individually in the name of the partners.

Eligibility

(a) All partners should be first class male lives.

(b) Number of partners maximum is 5 and minimum is 2.

(c) The sum assured should be for a minimum of Rs.25000 and should not exceed the minimum amount of capital brought in by any single partner.

(d) In the case of individual partner's Insurance, the maturity age should not exceed 70 years of age of partner.

(e) The term offered should be such that the policy would mature before the eldest partner reaches the age of 70.

(f) A deed informing that in case of death of a partner the partnership will be dissolved and capital will be withdrawn.

(g) Nomination is not allowed.

(h) Assignment is not allowed.

Requirements

(1) Duly signed proposal Form No. 340

(2) Copies of original partnership deed and supplementary deed

(3) Copies of Income Tax Returns or Assessment orders of last 3 years

(4) Copies of Audited Profit and Loss A/c and Balance sheet of last 3 years

(5) Endorsement letter to meet with the requirement of point no. (f) above

(6) Special reports depending upon age, sum proposed etc.

Advantages

(1) The insurance premium paid under partnership insurance on the lives of partners is allowed as 100% business expenditure U/S 37 (1) of IT Act. However, the policy proceeds on the death claim will be treated as income of the firm and is subjected to tax.

(2) The remaining partners can pay the amount out of the policy maturity proceeds without touching the assets of the partnership firm.

(3) The risk of closing down the business is avoided.

(4) Partnership insurance cover provides business stability as it provides protection to remaining partners, in case one partner is unable to continue working.

(5) It also guarantees cash settlement readily available to other partners. This payement can be used in many ways.

(6) In the event of death of a partner, the surviving partners retain full control over the business by buying out their deceased partner's share of the partnership.

Questions

1. Endowment life policy ¾ Explain.
2. Explain the various kinds of life policies.
3. Explain the terms:
   (a) Endowment Policy
   (b) Money Back Policy
   (c) Joint Life Policy
   (d) Annuity Policy
4. What is Whole Life Policy?
5. What is Level Premium Policy?
6. Explain with profit and without profit policies.
7. Explain the various group insurance policies.
8. Key-man Insurance — Explain.
9. Explain the advantages of Key-man Insurance.
10. Briefly discuss about partnership insurance.

Chapter 12

Assignment of Life Policies

Meaning and Procedure

In life insurance policies, the term assignment indicates that it is a method of transferring rights of the assured in respect of the life policy to another party or assignee or a third party. According to the Insurance Act 1938 under Section (38) provides the following procedures as laid down:

1. **Procedure:** A transfer or assignment of life insurance can be made either by endorsement on the policy itself or by executing a separate instrument. It must be signed by the assignor or by his duly authorised agent and attested by at least one witness. The endorsement or transfer must specify the facts of assignment.
2. **Notice:** On valid assignment, a written notice must be given to the insurer together with a certified copy of the endorsement or instrument. Only then the assignment or transfer becomes complete and effective on the insurer.
3. **Priority:** The date on which the notice of assignment or transfer is delivered to the insurer regulates the priority of all claims between an assignee and a third person. If the policy has been assigned to more than one assignees, the priority of the claims of the assignee shall be governed by the order in which the notice to the insurer is delivered.
4. **Acknowledgement:** On the receipt of the notice referred to above, the insurer shall record the fact of such transfer or assignment

together with date thereof, and the name of the transferee or assignee. The insurer shall on the request of the person, who gave the notice, grant a written acknowledgment of the receipt of such notice of payment of a fee not exceeding one rupee.

5. **Recognition:** From the date of the receipt of the notice, the insurer shall recognise the transferee or the assignee named in the notice as the only person entitled to the benefits named under the policy and such a person shall be subject to the liabilities and equities to which the transfer was subject at the time of the transfer or assignment.
6. **Conditional Assignment:** Conditional assignment has been held to be valid. Thus, an assignment in favour of a person made with the condition that it shall be operative or that the interest shall pass, to some other person on the happening of specified event during the life time of the person whose life is insured is valid.

Nomination of Life Policy

The holder of a life policy has the right to nominate any person to whom the insured money shall be payable in the event of death before the maturity of the policy, it is called as Nomination. The person to be nominated is called Nominee. Nomination can be made at the time when policy is taken. In the case of nomination, a person can nominate only on the insurance of his own life. Thus, a policy holder of insurance is entitled to make a nomination. The assignee or transferee of a policy cannot do this. Nomination can be changed or cancelled any number of times by the insured before the policy matures for payment under notice to the insurers.

According to Sec. 39 of the Insurance Act, the following provisions are made regarding nomination by a policy holder.

(1) The nomination in order to be effectual, by incorporating in the text of the policy or by an endorsement on the policy itself and communicated to the insurer who shall register it.

(2) The policy holder is entitled to receive from the insurer an acknowledgement of having registered a nomination or a cancellation or change thereof.

(3) When a policy is transferred or assigned, any nomination made in that policy automatically stands cancelled.

(4) Where the policy matures for payment during the life time of the person whose life is insured, or where the nominee dies before the policy matures for payment, the amount is payable to the policy holder or his heirs or legal representatives.

(5) Where the nominee survives the person whose life is insured, the amount shall be payable to the nominee.

Difference Between Assignment and Nomination

Assignment	Nomination
(1) In an assignment of life policy, all the rights pass to the assignee.	(1) Nomination does not deprive the insured of his disposing power over the policy.
(2) Consideration is essential for a valid contract.	(2) Consideration is required for nomination.
(3) Assignment can be completed and effected either on the policy itself or by a separate deed.	(3) Nomination can be made by endorsement on the policy itself not by a spearate deed or separate instruments.
(4) In the case of assignment, it is irrevocable.	(4) Nomination can be changed or cancelled if the party holder is alive on the date of maturity or in the event of death of nominee if death occurs earlier.
(5) In the case of assignment, the assignee is entitled to collect the amount under the policy.	(5) Nomination gives the nominee a bare right to collect the policy money in the event of his death.
(6) On valid assignment, the property in the policy passes to the assignee.	(6) In nomination, the nominee gets a right to receive the insured money but it does not provide for the title or the ownership of the money.

Surrender Value

The term surrender value refers to the amount of money which the insurer agrees to pay, in case the assured decides to surrender his policy before its maturity. It is said that the policy holder wishes to surrender his policy to the insurer and gives up his claim on it. Surrender of policy indicates termination of the contract of insurance. The amount of surrender value is calculated on the basis of actual premium paid and number of years the policy has been alive. Surrender value increases with each payment of premium.

According to Life Insurance Corporation of India, a policy acquires surrender value only after payment of two or three years premium. Thus, the policy is required to have run for three years before it acquires surrender value. In this regard, some insurance companies guarantee a minimum surrender value of 40 per cent of the total premium paid.

Paid Up Value

If a policy holder discontinues the payment of premium after at least two years premiums have been paid and subsequent premium is not paid, the policy does not become void but continues as a paid up policy. According to Insurance Act, it is defined as the policy paid up for an amount bearing the same proportion to the amount of original sum assured which the number of premiums paid bears to the total number of premiums payable under the policy as a whole, the policy with this reduced amount is called "Paid Up Policy".

In the case of With Profit or Participating Policy, it is assured that bonus or profits will be added to the paid up value but future gains or profits are not entitled to such policy.

Difference between Surrender Value and Paid Up Value

Surrender Value	Paid Up Value
(1) Surrender Value is the amount which the insurer is prepared to pay before the date of the maturity.	(1) In paid up value, the policy holder is entitled to the paid up value of the policy at the maturity.
(2) If a policy holder wishes to surrender his policy, it means the assured does not want to continue the policy.	(2) If a policy holder discontinues the payment of premium, the policy does not become void but continues to be paid up policy.
(3) Surrender value represents the present cash value of a policy.	(3) Paid up value represent the value payable on assured's death or at the maturity of the policy.
(4) Surrender Value is calculated on the class of policy and number of years it has been in force.	(4) Paid up value is calculated on the basis of number of years premium paid, number of years premium payable and sum assured with accrued profits.
(5) Surrender value increases with each payment of premium.	(5) Paid up value is always higher than the surrender value since it is not required to be paid immediately.

Days of Grace

Insurance company allows certain days after the stipulated period of insurance during which the insured can pay the premium to renew or continue the policy. Life Insurance Corporation allows fifteen days of grace from the due date to pay monthly premiums and thirty days of grace for the payment of quarterly, half yearly and yearly premiums.

A life insurance policy creates a continuing risk and it merely lapses if the premium is not paid. Death of the insured during the days of grace makes the insurance company liable to pay the money due under the policy.

Revival (or) Discontinued (or) Lapsed Policies

When the premium is not paid within the days of grace, the policy lapses. It may be revived during the life time of the life assured. It can be revived within a period of five years from the due date of the first unpaid premium and before the date of maturity.

Loans on Policies

Where a policy has a surrender value, it also has a loan value, and assurance companies usually lend 95 per cent of the surrender value, keeping the balance of 5 per cent as margin for a year's arrears of interest. The loan may be repaid at the convenience of the borrower. In case it is not repaid it keeps alive with interest accumulation, to be deducted from the policy money. It can be payable by the insurers either on its final surrender or on its maturity. This is the best investment that an insurance company can make, as there is never any danger of the money being lost.

Proof of Age

In life assurance, the age of the life to the assured is important because premium and annuity rates are based upon age attained at inception of the contract. It is particularly important in endowment policies wherein the money is payable to the assured on attaining a certain age. The insurer may require proof of age to be furnished at the time of proposal itself or at any time after the issue of the policy. The evidence may be a horoscope or the birth certificate or any family record of document.

Proof of Death

In case of policies payable at death, the death of the insured has to be proved. The usual proof is a death certificate and a declaration as to the identity of the person described in such certificate. Death may be proved by direct evidence or by death certificate or by evidence of prolonged absence or other facts from which the fact of death may be properly inferred. In case of death in a foreign country, the death certificate and the declaration of the medical practitioner who attended with the attestation of the Indian Council is required. Death is presumed where it is shown that a person who went abroad, or disappeared, has not been heard of for seven years nor has he communicated with those he would have communicated when alive.

Suicide by the Insured

Suicide means a willful and intentional act on the part of the self destroyer. It includes every act of self-destruction. Policies of life insurance contain conditions by which the liability of the insurer is modified and limited in case of suicide by the assured. Where there is such a clause in a policy, the insurer can avoid payment on the policy on death by suicide.

The position in England and in India is different on this issue.

In England, suicide is a crime and hence no money is payable if a person commits suicide in a sane state of mind. On the other hand, if the assured was insane at the time of committing suicide, the sum due can be recovered by his legal representatives.

Under the Indian Law, suicide in itself is not an offence, and as such a policy cannot be avoided on the ground of suicide, unless the policy otherwise provides. Suicide will, however, not affect the rights of assignee, if the policy holder had assigned policy for valuable consideration.

The burden of proving suicide is upon the insurers and where the cause of death is not known, the presumption is against suicide and the policy cannot be avoided.

Payment of Claims

A person claiming money on the maturity of the policy must satisfy the insurer that he is entitled to receive the money either.

(a) as the owner of the policy or

(b) because the actual claim is vested in him as legal representative or as nominee or as assignee.

On the maturity of the life policy, the insurer requires a satisfactory and reasonable proof of age and death of the assured. Death may be proved by direct or indirect evidence.

In the absence of any conditions to the contrary, suicide does not avoid the policy in India.

Questions

1. What do you understand by surrender value?
2. Distinguish between assignment and nomination in life insurance.
3. What do you understand by paid up value?
4. What do you understand by assignment of an insurance policy? How does an assignment differ from nomination?
5. Discuss the liability of insurers on a life insurance policy in case of suicide of the assured.
6. What do you understand by nomination of life policy?
7. Write short notes on:

   (a) Days of Grace

   (b) Proof of death

   (c) Proof of Age

Mini Cases

Case 1. A insures his life with an insurer for Rs. 5,000. Subsequently, he became insane and while of unsound mind, he commits suicide. Can the legal representatives of 'A', subject to the terms of the policy, recover money from the insurer?

Ans: Yes, provided one year has expired since the commencement of the policy.

Case 2. 'A' assigned his life insurance policy to 'B' on 15th January 1988 for valuable consideration by a separate deed of assignment. On

15th February 1988, 'A' transferred the same policy by endorsement thereon to 'C' as a gift and gave a notice of transfer in favour of 'C' to the Life Insurance Corporation of India in the prescribed manner and enclosing therewith the original deed of assignment. Both B and C claim the policy money on maturity. Decide.

Ans: In the instant case, notice of assignment in favour of C has been given to the Life Insurance Corporation. Hence, C would be entitled to get the policy money.

Case 3. M is the holder of a life insurance policy on his life. Mrs. M is mentioned in the policy as his nominee. Afterwards, M nominates by will his brother R in place of his wife and sends a notice of change by post to Life Insurance Corporation. The letter is lost in transit. The Corporation pays the policy money to Mrs. M upon the death of Mr. M. R disputes the payments. Is the contention of R correct?

Ans: The holder of a life insurance policy has the right to nominate any person to whom the insurance money shall be payable in the event of his death. Notice of such nomination must be delivered to the insurer.

In the instant case, the notice of nomination in favour of R has not been delivered to the insurer and the insurer has made payment bonafide. Hence, R's contention is not correct and the insurer has no liability towards him.

Case 4. A had taken a life insurance policy for Rs. 10.000. He became indebted to a Bank which instituted a suit against him, got his policy attached and obtained a decree. A died. His wife who had been nominated as the person entitled to receive money due under the policy in the event of his death also died. His son filed a claim petition that the policy amount be paid to him. Is he entitled to the money? Discuss.

Ans: The nominee of life insurance policy gets the right in the property subject to all the liabilities of the policy holder. In view of this position of law, 'A's son will not get any prior claim in the policy over the claim of the Bank particularly when the life insurance policy had been attached during life time of the assured.

Case 5. A effects a policy on his own life with LIC and deposits with a bank for securing payment of an existing debt. A dies and the bank claims the amount from the LIC against A's heirs. Is the transfer to the bank valid?

Ans: In the instant case, A has simply deposited his policy with the bank as security for the debt due to the bank. There has been no valid assignment and therefore the bank cannot have any claim against A's heirs.

Chapter 13

Life Insurance Corporation of India (LIC)

Introduction

The Corporation has been established by the Insurance Act 1956 passed by parliament. According to the provisions of the Act, the Corporation began to function as an autonomous body and has necessarily run on sound business principles. The Government of India nationalised life insurance business in the year 1956. The initial paid up capital of Rs. 5 crores is wholly contributed by the Central Government to the Life Insurance Corporation of India.

Aims of LIC

Life Insurance Corporation of India has come into force with the following aims:

(a) To assure full protection to the policy holders

(b) To encourage and mobilise public savings

(c) Effective utilisation of those savings in different forms of investment for national and economic development

(d) To create liquidity position in public

(e) To motivate saving habits among the public

(f) Provisions for old age and tax concession.

Organisational Structure

To perform the functions of the Life Insurance Corporation of India, a Board of Directors consisting of 15 members is appointed by the Central Government. One of the members is also appointed as the chairman. The organisational structure of Life Insurance Corporation of India has a four tier structure. They are (1) Central Office (2) Zonal Offices (Seven) (3) Divisional Offices (100) (4) Branch Offices (2048 Branches). The Central Office is to perform the activities relating to investments, framing and administering the rules and regulations of corporation. In Branch office, almost 90% of the functions relate to policyholders. There are seven Zonal Offices and 100 Divisional Offices, which are established on the basis of geographical areas. They discharge their coordinating functions relating to the Central Offices and Zonal Offices. The Central Office of Life Insurance Corporation of India is located at Mumbai. There are several executive committees appointed by the Government of India from time to time to review the activities of the Life Insurance Corporation of India.

The chart can explain this more clearly:

LIFE INSURANCE ADMINISTRATION

(Organisational Structure)

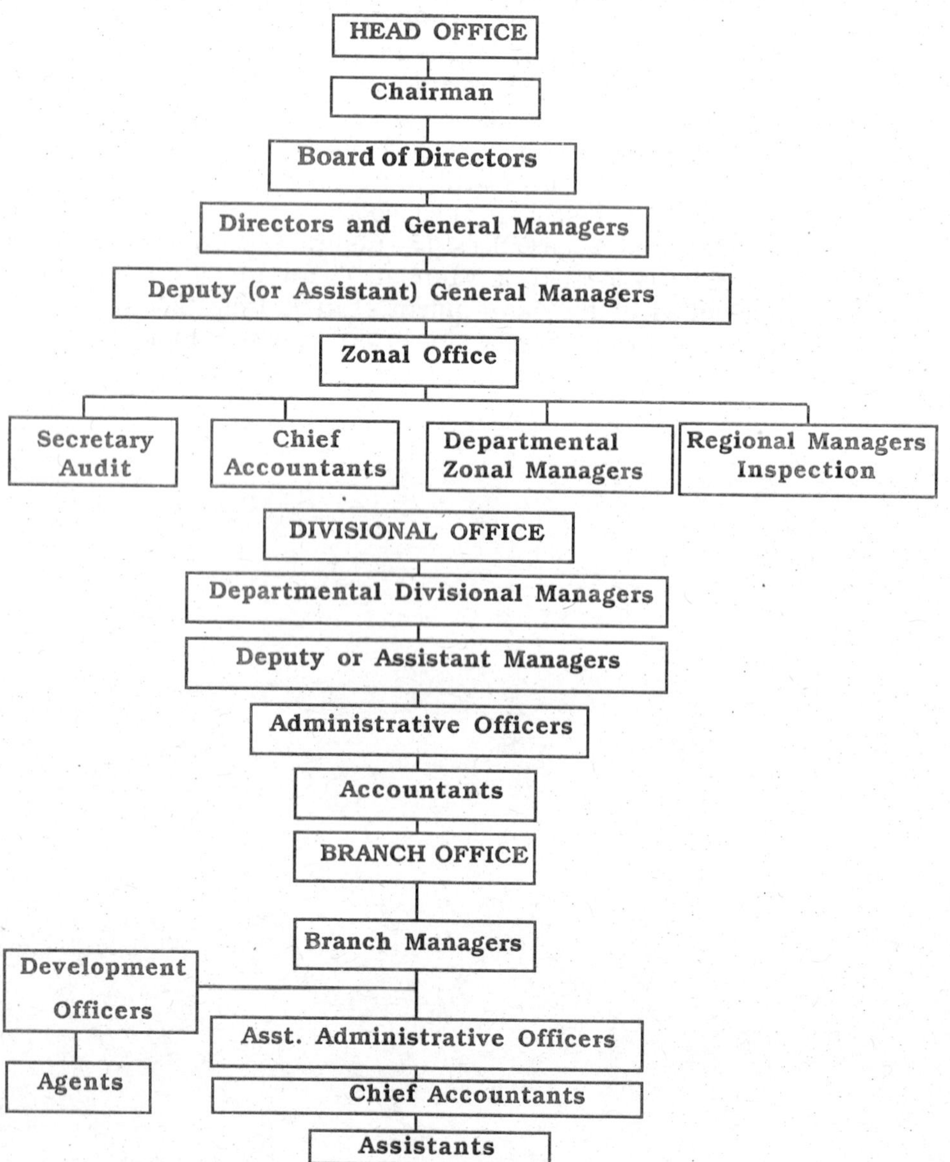

Advantages of Life Insurance

(1) It ensures absolute protection against the risk of death.

(2) Insurance encourages compulsory savings.

(3) Life Insurance facilitates easy settlement and the beneficiaries are fully protected from creditors.

(4) Policy holders of life insurance are eligible to get tax exemptions from Income Tax liability.

(5) It facilitates easy marketability and suitability for quick borrowing through commercial loan (or) housing loan or surrender the policy for a cash sum.

(6) It involves all the people working in the Corporation to the best of their capacity in furthering the interest of the insured public by providing efficient service.

Important Functions

The following are the important activities of Life Insurance Corporation:

(1) To ensure absolute security is the first and foremost function to the prospective policy holders of life insurance.

(2) Underwriting is the important activity of Life Insurance Corporation, i.e., scrutinising and making decisions on the proposals for the insurance.

(3) Issuing policy documents to the policy holders for evidence of the insurance contract.

(4) Life Insurance vitally protects the common man by providing cover through individual policies, group schemes and social security schemes.

(5) Development and prosperity of insurance companies will create employment opportunities in rural and urban areas.

(6) To make intensive and extensive publicity drives in public for mobilising insurance business.

(7) To encourage resource mobilisation for development through mopping up of savings and also to have better utilisation of those savings.

(8) To contribute social oriented investment to improve the quality of the society, especially with respect to electricity, water supply, housing and agro based industries.

(9) Life Insurance Corporation has been giving high priority for rendering various services to the policy holders. The focus of LIC is on service related to registration of nomination, assignment,

change in address, revival of a lapsed policy, payment of loan and surrender or settlement of claims.

(10) Other important functions are maintaining accounts, management of personnel, processing of data, formulating policies, procedures, setting up of objectives and goals, compliance with regulations and law of the country.

Role of LIC in National Economy

The role of Life Insurance Corporation involves all the activities relate to national economy, individual and society. The following are the important areas identified:

1. Investment
2. Underwriting
3. Disbursing Loans
4. Subscribing to Debentures and Bonds
5. Socially Oriented
6. Shareholding
7. Control
8. Mutual Fund
9. Boosting Industrial Growth
10. Claims and Settlement.

(1) Investment: Life Insurance Corporation is acting as capital market intermediaries. It provide long-term investments in Government Securities, Public Sector, Co-operative Sector, Private Sector and Joint-Sector. On the Stock Exchange, it is considered a very powerful security holder.

(2) Underwriting: LIC has been the largest underwriter of capital issues in the Indian Capital Market till the year 1978 after which it has reduced its activities in favour of socially oriented projects. During the year 1983 onwards, LIC underwrites firms and prefers large and established companies. It also prefers 'further' issues. As an underwriter, it influences the capital market considerably and is also able to stabilise the market during the downswings or depression periods.

(3) Disbursing Loans: Since 1970, LIC has been disbursing 'loans' for industrial development. One of the major avenues of investment in every year constituted financing through loans. It has given loans for generation and transmission of electricity for agriculture and industrial use, housing schemes, piped water supply schemes and development of road and transport. Out of the total disbursement of all financial institutions to the industry, LIC's contribution comes to around 8%.

(4) Subscribing to Debentures and Bonds: Financial Institutions and corporate enterprises requiring burgeoning funds to meet their expanding needs find it easier and cheaper to raise funds from the market by issuing commercial papers. LIC also subscribes to debentures and bonds of various financial institutions and development banks like IDBI and IFCI. In 1983, LIC subscribed to the Debenture of ICICI of the value of Rs.8 crores.

(5) Socially Oriented: A basic feature of financial liberalisation and many innovations are the trend towards social orientation. LIC has resorted to socially oriented schemes in a big way since 1978. This has brought down its activities in the capital market. The rationale behind this change has been to go in for developmental work. Own Your House (OYH) Schemes have been given priority. Apart from these schemes, loans for sewerage, road and transport and electricity generation have also been given priority in the recent years.

(6) Shareholding: By virtue of its shareholding, LIC has been recognized amongst the top ten shareholders in one of every three companies listed in the stock exchange on which it has a sharehold in companies. While LIC has invested in large blocks of equities and in later years in debenture holdings, it had kept away and did not interfere in the decisions of the management in the past.

(7) Control: In the recent years, LIC has influenced the management to take proper decisions and to tone up the quality of working in the companies financed by it. This is intended to promote confidence in the minds of the public and to exercise control in the corporate sector which often has a very small shareholding. In 1984, LIC dominated Indian industries scene. These changes in the direction of the LIC are bound to exert some pressure on the industry and change the complexion of the Indian industrial scenario.

(8) Mutual Fund: It has set up in 1989, a Mutual Fund for operating various schemes for mobilisation of savings from the public particularly from the rural and urban areas and channel these funds to the capital market. The LIC has considerable expertise in investment management by virtue of its earlier operations of funds.

(9) Boosting Industrial Growth: The corporation helps boost the industrial growth in the country. It helps small scale and medium scale industries by granting loans for setting up co-operative industrial estates and an amount of Rs. 45 crores has so far been advanced to industrial estates and industrial development corporations. The corporation also makes investment in the corporate sector in the form of long, medium and short term loans to companies/corporations. The total investment made by way of loans upto year 2001 was Rs.2812 crores and by way of subscription to shares/debentures was Rs.35048 crores. All this makes a distinct contribution towards growth in industralisation and generation of skilled and unskilled employment opportunities in the country.

Progress of Life Business of LIC							
Year	Total New Business		Business in Force			Total No. of lives covered	
	Individual Schemes (Rs. in Crores)	Group Insurance Schemes (Rs. in Crores)	Individual Schemes (Rs. in Crores)	Group Insurance Schemes (Rs. in lakhs)	No. of Policies (in force (in lakhs)	Group Insurance Schemes (in lakhs)	Life Fund (Rs. in Crores)
1957	336.37	–	1476.52	5.29	56.86	–	410.40
1969-70	990.03	46.05	6348.09	77.17	140.40	–	1611.03
1974-75	1772.61	1339.82	11852.25	1457.00	188.20	23.34	3033.79
1979-80	2744.33	5262.06	19242.55	6137.46	220.94	58.41	5818.09
1998-99	25606.26	69558.14	459201.04	77918.45	912.26	242.29	127389.06
1999-2000	91214.26	66619.43	536450.82	76384.53	1013.89	243.02	154043.73
2000-2001	124757.14	78134.66	645041.69	89326.19	1131.11	245.52	186024.75
2001-2002	192572.31	99446.11	81011.00	100597.64	1258.76	256.99	227008.98

(10) Claims and Settlement: The settlement of claims constitutes one of the important functions of the corporation. Indeed, the payment of claims may be regarded as the primary services of insurance to the public. Proper settlement of claims will be provided on the basis of sound knowledge of law, principles and practices governing, insurance contracts, terms and conditions of standard policies etc.

Progress of Life Business of LIC

The progress of life business of LIC can be evaluated by various indicators such as growth of new business, performance of business in force, progress of number of lives covered, investments, claims settlement and so on the Table given below shows the progress of life insurance business of LIC from 1957 to 2001-2002.

From the above table, we have observed the new individual business has increased from Rs.338.3 crores in 1957 to Rs.1,92,572.31 crores in 2001.02. On.the other hand, the group insurance schemes has increased from Rs.46.05 crores in 1969-70 to Rs.99,446.11 crores in 2001-02. It indicates that the LIC is trying hard to increase its new business at a very rapid speed from 1957 to 2002. The above table also highlights that the individual life insurance in force has been continuously increased from Rs.1,476.52 crores in 1957 to Rs.811011.00 crores in 2002. The business in force of group insurance schemes has rapidly been increasing from RS.5.291akhs in 1957 to 1,00,597.64 lakhs in 2001-02. The number of policies in force has increased from 56.86 lakhs in 1957 to 1131.11 lakhs in 2001-02. This reveals that the total business in force has been constantly and rapidly rising in India. It is a very good indicator of the popular form of life insurance which can be adopted to benefit the masses, individually as well as a group. The total number of lives covered under group insurance scheme has also increased from RS.23.341akhs in 1974-75 to 256.99 in 2001-02. It indicates a significant increase in life insurance business. The life insurance fund has been increasing at a faster rate during the period of 33 years. It is a very encouraging sign that the life insurance fund has increased from Rs.410.42 crores in 1995 to 2,27,008.98 crores in 2001- 02.

Highlights the Performance of LIC (1999-2000)

A survey was conducted by LIC in 2000 indicates that the following financial record of LIC's performance during 1999-2000 highlights the growth of life insurance.

(1) The total income amounted to Rs.45,174.15 crore registering a growth of 23.59%.

(2) The total premium income amounted to Rs.27,849.46 crore, registering a growth of 21.21 %.

(3) The income from investments and rent was Rs.16,113.11 crore reflecting a growth of 21.95%. The corporation has also generated a profit of Rs.845.47 crore on the sale of equities.

(4) The total payment to policy holders amounted to 11,170.50 crore as against Rs.9,106.02 crore paid in the previous year.

(5) The total life fund as at the close of the year increased to Rs.1,54,043.73 crore, the percentage increase over previous year being 20.92% Rs.26,654.67 crore was added to the life fund during 1999-2000.

(6) The value of the total asset of the corporations stood at Rs.1,60,935.76 crore, the growth rate being 21.28%.

Performance of LIC (2001-2002)

The following points highlight the performance of the corporation during the year (2001-2002).

(1) New policies under individual assurance at 169.77lakhs grew by 14.37% over the previous year.

(2) The new business premium income at Rs.4,393.90 crore including single premium, group business and individual pensions represents a growth rate of 35.41 %.

(3) Sum assured under individual assurance also registered a healthy growth of 21.11% at Rs.91,213.42 crore

(4) Individual pension business grew tremendously with the sale of 2,23,343 policies generating a first premium income of Rs.31.80 crore showing phenomenal growth rate of 111% and 18% respectively.

(5) Under group insurance businesses excluding social security schemes, 13.93lakhs lives were covered generating a new business premium income of Rs.598.42 crores, registering a growth of Rs.10% and 35% respectively.

(6) Under social security schemes, the Corporation registered growth rates of 155% and 179% in lives and new business premium income respectively.

IRDA Guidelines for Investment of LIC's Funds

Life insurance is a long term business and for determining the premium, the expected interest rate over the term of the policy is one of the key inputs. Bonus rates are decided on the basis of surplus determined by actuarial valuation which is done every year. Investment income, which depend also upon the return on fixed interest investments is a significant contributor for surplus. Decline in rates of return obtainable on investments necessitate from time to time revision of rates of returns offered by the Insurers.

As per IRDA Regulations, life insurer shall invest and at all times keep invested his controlled fund in.

(1) Central Government Securities – Not less than 25%

(2) State Government Securities or other approved securities – (including (1) Above) – Not less than 50%

(3) Infrastructure and social sector – Not less than 15%

(4) Balance Investments can be made as per Prudential and Exposure Norms, subject to other than approved investments not exceeding 15% of the fund.

It may be seen that at least 50% of the funds are to be invested in Government and other approved securities which may provide highest safety and consequently lower expected returns.

Insurer lays down certain norms internally within stipulated IRDA guidelines, which are expected to be followed in respect of all proposals that come up for investment. These proposals could be in respect of debenture, convertible debentures, equity, semi-equity, term loans, working capital loans etc.

Identification of Various Types of Investments

The following are the various types of investments areas identified by LIC on the basis of their merits and demerits.

(1) Government Securities
   (a) General Government Securities
   (b) State Government Securities

(2) Industrial Securities (Public Sectors and Private Sectors)
   (a) Investments in Shares
   (b) Investments in Debentures

(3) Mortgages or Investments in real estates
   (a) Mortgage of Buildings
   (b) Mortgage of Land

(4) Investments in the form of granting loan to policyholders

(5) Investments in housing sectors

(6) Investments in other assets
   (a) Investment in plant and machinery
   (b) Investment in machinery
   (c) Investment in properties

Performance of LIC's Socially Oriented Investments

Year	Total Investments (Rs. in Crores)	Socially Oriented Investments	Percentage (%) to total Investment
1957	381.90	–	–
1969-70	1514.26	513.21	2.95%
1974-75	2798.43	1218.52	2.29%
1979-80	5747.51	2472.29	2.32%
1992-99	120445.00	88831.00	1.35%
1999-00	146364.00	117888.00	1.24%
2000-01	175491.00	139926.00	1.25%
2001-02	216883.00	173370.00	1.25%

The above table reveals that the total amount of investment has been constantly increasing form Rs.381.90 crores in 2001–02. It indicates that LIC's investment has contributed significantly in the development of the nation. The share of LIC's investment also highlights that LIC has favoured socially oriented securities has increased from Rs.531.21 crores in 1969–70 to Rs.1,73,370.00 crores in 2001–02 by more than 337.81 times. On the other hand, it has been observed that the percentage of socially oriented investments to total investments has declined from 2.95% in 1970 to 1.25% in 2002. Thus, the overall performance of LIC's investments towards socially oriented sectors considerably satisfied.

Progress of LIC's Investment in Various Sectors

The Life Insurance Corporation (LIC) helps boost the industrial growth in the country. It helps small scale and medium scale industries by granting loans for setting up co–operative industrial estates. The corporation also makes investments in the corporate sector in the form of long, medium and short term loans to companies/corporations. LIC's investments has been directed towards socially oriented securities. It is a great achievement that LIC has tried to develop power generation, roadways, port, railways, water supply and sewerage schemes, housing and other infrastructures. The given below table shows the some highlights the allocation of LIC's investments in various sectors:

Allocation of LIC's Investment in Various Sectors From 1997 to 2002
(Rs.in crores)

Type of Investment	Investment Up to							
	31.3.77	31.3.87	31.3.97	31.3.98	31.9.99	31.3.00	31.3.01	31.3.02
1.Central Govt. Securities	981	4675	37330	45876	56185	70533	85181	109938
2. State Govt. & Other Govt. Guaranteed Marketable Securities	715	1683	8906	10471	12928	14156	17877	21463
3. Electricity (SEBs)	733	2603	8241	9153	10591	11931	12402	13447
4. Housing	618	1872	10967	12242	14207	15885	17998	19054
5. Water supply & Sewerage (Mun+Z.P.)	203	718	2028	2264	2508	2997	3657	4000
6. State Road Transport Corporation	–	180	540	551	671	736	784	893
7. Loans to Industrial Estates	9	37	45	45	45	45	45	45
8. Loans to Sugar Cooperatives	22	37	37	37	37	37	37	37
9. Development Authority	–	1	1	1	1	1	1	1
10. Roadways, Port, Railways	–	–	–	25	25	85	325	681
11. Power Generation (Private Sector)	–	–	–	25	801	1478	1615	3797
12. Municipalities	–	–	–	4	4	4	4	4
Total	**3281**	**11806**	**68068**	**80945**	**98003**	**117888**	**139926**	**173370**

From the above table, we can observe that the amount of investments in Central Government Securities has rapidly been increasing from Rs.981 crores in 1977 to Rs.1,09,938 crores. It indicates that the allocation of LIC's investment in Central Government Securities is more than 112 times. The distribution of LIC's investment to State Government and other Government Guaranteed Marketable Securities has been significantly gone up from Rs. 715 crores in 1977 to Rs.21,463 crores in 2002 by more than 30 times during this period. Investments in electricity sector has been considerably high from Rs.733 crores in 1977 to Rs.13,447 crores in 2002 by more than 18 times. The allocation of investments to housing sector has also increased from Rs.618 crores in 1977 to Rs. 19,054 crores in 2002 by more than 30 times. Similarly, the share of investments in water supply and sewerage sectors has gone up from Rs.203 crores in 1977 to Rs.4,000 crores in 2002. The amount of investment in state road transport corporation has constantly raised from Rs.180 crores in 1987 to Rs.893 crores in 2002. On the other hand, the allocation of investments to industrial estates, loans to cooperatives and development authority has slightly increased from 1977 to 2002. Distribution of investments in power generation sectors (private) has also been rising from Rs.276 crores in 1999 to Rs.3,797 crores in 2002 by more than 13 times. Thus, all these make a distinct contribution towards growth in industrialization and generation of skilled and unskilled employment opportunities in the country.

Performance of Claims Settlement

The life insurance is essentially an instrument for providing financial compensation in case of unexpected death of the person taking the insurance cover. On the basis of the policies in force at the end of a year, the insurer will generally estimate the expected number and the amount of claims during the year. The corporation strives to settle maturing claims on or before the due date itself. The branch office which serves the policy send out an intimation regarding the payment along with the necessary discharge voucher for execution by the assured approximately two months before the due date of such payment. In the event of the death of the policy holder, the claimant (the nominee assignee or next of skin) should immediately intimate the fact of such death to the branch office, where the policy is served along with the following particulars (a) Policy Number (b) Name of the policy assured (c) Date of death and (d) Claimants relationship with the assured. Soon after the receipt of the intimation of death, the branch office concerned will send the necessary claim forms for completion along with instructions regarding the procedure to be followed by the claimant. The claims is usually payable to the nominee assignee or the legal successor as the case may be. However, if the deceased policy holder has not nominated/assigned the policy or he/she has not made a suitable provision regarding the policy moneys by way of a will certificate or some such evidence of title from a court of Law. The given below table shows the performance of claim & settlement operations.

Claims Settlement Operations (1989-90 to 2001-02)

Year	Claims Intimated (Rs.in Crores)	Claims Settled (Rs.in Crores)	Claims Outstanding (Rs.in Crores)	Percentage (%) of Claims Outstanding to Intimated
1989-90	1,211.08	1,126.37	84.71	6.61%
1990-91	1,425.14	1,334.58	90.56	5.96%
1993-94	3,845.45	3,673.95	171.50	4.86%
1994-95	4,130.80	3,904.57	226.23	5.26%
1995-96	4,595.69	4,305.99	288.70	6.28%
1996-97	5,722.38	5,691.49	319.59	5.28%
1997-98	6,673.07	6,677.04	315.62	4.73%
1998-99	7,615.78	7,583.18	348.22	4.57%
1999-00	9,266.25	9,211.30	403.17	4.35%
2000-01	11,666.82	11,637.98	432.01	3.70%
2001-02	14,358.55	14,519.25	273.34	1.85%

The above table highlights that the performance of LIC's claims settlement operations from 1989- 90 to 2001-2002. It is seen that the number of claims intimated has increased from Rs.1211.08 crores in 1989-90 to Rs. 14,358.55 crores in 2001-02. The amount of claims settled during the same period were significantly higher than Rs. 1,126.37 crores to 14,519.25 crores. It has also been observed that the amount of claims outstanding. Compare to claims intimated has considerably declined from Rs. 84.71 crores in 1989-90 to Rs. 273.35 crores in 2001-02. It indicates that the efficiency of the LIC in meeting claims-obligations were significantly achieved. Expressed as percentage, the claim outstanding to claims intimated has gradually decreased from 6.61 % in 1989 - 90 to 1.85% in 2001-02.

This indicates that the special efforts were made to improve claim settlement and the outstanding has been brought down to 1.85% in 2001-02. Thus, if all reflection on the quality of the life insurance business.

Wide Network Progress

Since 1956, LIC has worked resolutely towards spreading life insurance and in the process has built a wide network across the length and breadth of the country, consisting of 2048 branches 100 divisional offices, 7 Zonal offices and Corporate office. The number of new policies sold each year grew from 14.62 lakhs in 1961 to 1.79 crores in 2001, of which 55.10 per cent in rural. The rural share of 1961 was 36.53 per cent. Similarly, the annual premium income rose from Rs. 88.65 crores in 1957 to 27,859 crores in 2000. The life fund and asset of the corporation also grew from 410 crores to Rs. 1,54,044 crores and 456.04 crores to 160936 crores, respectively since 1957. Investment which were Rs. 329.74 crores in 1957 rose to Rs. 1,44,954 crores in 2000, all of which is deployed in nation building activities.

In its endeavour to be economical, LIC has strived to reduce its expenses. The renewal expense ratio is an indicator of the expense incurred for collecting renewal premiums and keep policies from lapsing, dropped to 5.01% in 2000 from 28.40% in 1957. The overall expense ratio, which indicates the total cost of operations also fall from 27.3% in 1957 to 21% in 2000.

Training Facilities

LIC has a well established training infrastructure to cater to the training needs of employees consisting of a management development centre for senior officials, seven Zonal training centres for supervisors, line managers and for top salesman and for computer based training for all the employees.

There are also 25 sales training centres to provide training to other sales force. These centres are located in various zones. Training needs are analysed and a training profile to employees is kept at the offices; training modules have been standardised. In addition to imparting training to the work force consisting of over 1.24 lakhs employees and officers, LIC has concrete programme of training its sales force of over six lakhs agents.

Questions

1. Write a brief note on the Life Insurance Corporation of India.
2. Explain the important functions of Life Insurance Corporation of India.
3. Discuss briefly the administration of Life Insurance Corporation of India.
4. Explain the features of Life Insurance Corporation of India.
5. Explain the role of LIC in national economy.
6. Explain the progress of Life Business of LIC.

Chapter 14

Marketing of Life Insurance

Introduction

The economic activities can be divided into three main categories — Primary, Secondary and Tertiary. The primary activities include agriculture, fishing, forests and mining. The secondary activities cover manufacturing, construction, and industry. The tertiary activities include services like insurance, banking, finance, transport, communication etc. The list of services includes utilities, civil, insurance banking, defense services, transport etc.

In LIC, life insurance services are rendered with a view to protect the people against the risk of loss due to accident, fire, death, sickness, unemployment and so on.

Some people might argue that there is service marketing, but only marketing in which the service element is greater than the product element. We do agree that, in the sale of majority of the goods, there are both product parts as well as a service part. However, there are so many service organisations like insurance companies, banks, transport companies who do not think of themselves as marketers of goods. They see themselves as providers of services.

Definition of Services

The term service has been differently defined by different authors. According to Ivanovic, "Service is the work of dealing with customers, or payments for the work, services are benefits which are sold to customers or clients such as insurance, transport and education."

According to Philip Kotler, "A service is an activity or benefit that one party can offer to another that is essentially intangible and does not result in the ownership of anything. Its production may or may not be tied to a physical product."

Characteristics of Life Insurance Services:

Life insurance services, as described above, have a number unique characteristics that place them in separate category compared to physical goods. These characteristics create special marketing challenges. They are given below:

(1) Intangibility

(2) Heterogeneity

(3) Inseparability

(4) Changing Demand

(1) Intangibility: Life insurance services are intangible in nature. It is quite different from other commercial products. The consumer has to have faith in the services of life insurance provider. Services are intangible and therefore, cannot be seen, felt or tasted. The customer has to be encouraged, enthused and helped to visualise the unforeseen tomorrow and usefulness of a life insurance products. Unlike tangible products, there are no factories and production lines for life insurance.

(2) Heterogeneity: Life insurance services are heterogeneous in their nature. That is, they are highly variable. Each life insurance product of the service is some what different from other products of the same services. Different kinds of insurance products are developed from time to time to cater to the specific needs of customers.

(3) Inseparability: Very often, services cannot be separated from their provider. It is very important to understand the heart and soul relationship between product and service, cost and quality. Life insurance products continues to exist over a long period of time, and for making its service available, the insured person has to go on paying the purchase price (premium) throughout the term of the policy. This ensures that the benefits already accrued under sale are not lost. Hence due to inseparability, direct sale of services, is the only channel of distribution. In LIC, insurance agents represent and help in promoting inseparable services.

(4) Changing Demand: The success of life insurance service marketing in turn depends on the ability of the firm to find a customer and to satisfy his wants. For this purpose, instead of trying to sell what can be produced the business firm should produce what is really needed by the customer and what would satisfy his wants. It is a buyer's market, by and large, the seller, i.e., the LIC has to take decision whether to sell a particular policy to a particular person or not on the basis of information disclosed by the buyer himself in the proposed form.

Objectives of Life Insurance Marketing

The first and foremost objective of all marketing activities is the satisfying of human wants. Besides life insurance has other objective too. Some of the objectives are:

(1) Spread of life insurance message

(2) Mobilisation of savings in the form of pension

(3) Profit maximisation

(4) Successful distribution of life insurance products

(5) Improving customer services

(6) Increasing customer base and its spread

(7) Developing corporate image

(8) Developing guiding policies and their implementation for a good result

(9) Suggest solution by studying the problems relating to life insurance business.

Life Insurance Marketing Mix

Marketing mix is the policy adopted by any concern to get success in the field of marketing. The life insurance marketing emphasises the importance of the consumers preference. Therefore, a life insurer first analyses the nature of the consumer's needs. All the life insurance marketing efforts focus attention around the consumers needs. Then the management plan his product in such a way that he can give satisfaction to the consumers and face the competitors. All these programmes involve a number of functions which are to be planned carefully. Planning needs analysis of the insurance market to take a decision, prediction and forecasting as to the future needs of the consumers. Thus, identification of demand and supply involves various functions of life insurance marketing to attain success in the insurance market and the combination of this function is known as Life Insurance Marketing Mix.

According to Prof. Neil H. Borden, "The marketing mix refers to the apportionment of efforts, the combination, the designing and the integration of the elements of marketing into programme or mix which, in the basis of an appraisal of the market forces will best achieve the objectives of an enterprise at a given time. Thus, the marketing mix is an integration of marketing elements."

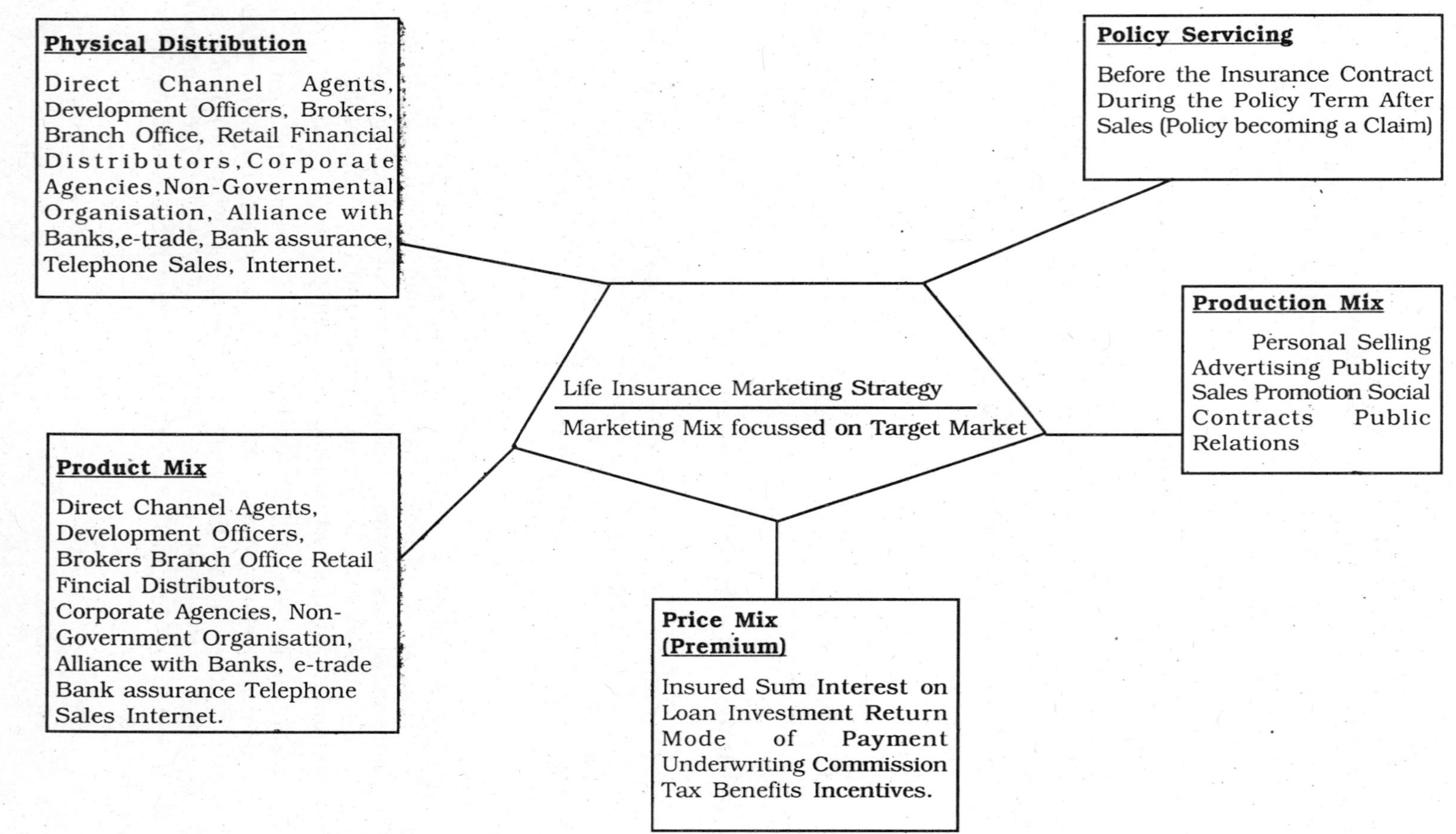
Life Insuramce Marketing Mix
Physical Distribution
Direct Channel Agents, Development Officers, Brokers, Branch Office, Retail Financial Distributors, Corporate Agencies, Non-Governmental Organisation, Alliance with Banks, e-trade, Bank assurance, Telephone Sales, Internet.
Policy Servicing
Before the Insurance Contract During the Policy Term After Sales (Policy becoming a Claim)
Life Insurance Marketing Strategy
Marketing Mix focussed on Target Market
Production Mix
Personal Selling Advertising Publicity Sales Promotion Social Contracts Public Relations
Product Mix
Direct Channel Agents, Development Officers, Brokers Branch Office Retail Fincial Distributors, Corporate Agencies, Non-Government Organisation, Alliance with Banks, e-trade Bank assurance Telephone Sales Internet.
Price Mix (Premium)
Insured Sum Interest on Loan Investment Return Mode of Payment Underwriting Commission Tax Benefits Incentives.

Elements of Life Insurance Marketing Mix

The definition cited above clearly indicate the four components of marketing mix. In the case of life insurance, marketing of services requires an expanded marketing mix comprising (1) the product, (2) price (premium), (3) physical distribution/place, (4) promotion, and (5) policy servicing. These elements should be taken as intruments by the life insurance management when formulating life insurance marketing plans.

The marketing mix is a dynamic concept, it keeps on changing with changing marketing conditions and environmental factors. The following chart depicts the life insurance marketing mix of a business enterprise. The four ingredients of the marketing mix are discussed briefly as under:

(1) Product (Scheme): It is the first element, product is the sum total of physical, social and psychological benefits. Managing the product component involves product planning and development. The life insurance marketers must define their market in terms of product function. What the customer expects from the product. It may offer a single product or several products. Life insurance as product has also to be designed, keeping in view these basic requisites, in case of life insurance the needs are in the form of two broad economic contingencies, viz., death of the breadwinner and the subsequent financial insecurity of his dependents, and secondly, longer life insurance is sold as plan of LIC of India developed term assurance and whole life policies and for the second category various pension plans and annuities. Apart from whole life insurance, endowment insurance and money back plans, LIC has several products specially suited for children, exclusively for women, the handicapped, senior citizens, to cover occurrence of terminal diseases, term assurance and pension plans. There are also group insurance schemes that can be taken by employer for their employees. The LIC also administers schemes for people who are below or just above the poverty line.

(2) Price (Premium): The price is another powerful element in the life insurance marketing mix and vitally affect the volume of sales. Price is the valuation placed upon the product by the offerer. In the case of life insurance, premium is the price which the person seeking Insurance pays to LIC for purchase in the life insurance policy. The management must take decisions regarding pricing (premium), investment return, level of premium, mode of premium, commission, insured sum, life to be covered, interest on loan, price strategy, underwriting and price related situations. It deals with price competition.

(3) Physical Distribution/Place: Marketing channel policy is another integral part of the life insurance marketing mix. Physical distribution is the delivery of insurance products at the right time and at the right place. In the case of life insurance, it is the combination of decisions regarding channels of distribution, Agents, Development Officers, Brokers, Branch Office, Retail financial service distributors, alliances with banks, tie-ups with non-governmental organisation, corporate agencies, Bank assurance, e-trade, proper infrastructure and training facilities, technical and material know-how on part of instructor etc. At present, the strength of LIC's distribution channel comprising over 6.10 lakhs active agents and over 19,000 Development officers appears to be phenomenal. This is indeed a great advantage to cover the vast Indian population, diverse in nature and spread, for which a strong marketing network is imperative. The network duly supported by 2100 servicing branches.

(4) Promotion: The business enterprise should inform the customers about its products and persuade them to buy. It covers methods of communicating with consumers through personal selling, advertising, publicity, sales promotion, social contracts, public relations, exhibition and demonstration used in promotion. For promoting life insurance, business sales promotion activities are carried out by the agent, development officers and branch offices. Calendars, diaries, bags etc. are also given to policy holders as a token of gifts. All these activities increase the volume of sales by expanding as well as retaining the market share for the insurance products.

(5) Policy Servicing: Customer satisfaction predominates the success of an enterprise. In the service industry where intangibles are marketed, the importance of customer satisfaction is all the more significant. Service is said to be the sharpest edge of any marketing strategy. Sales and services are the two powerful wings of life insurance industry. Prompt and effective service boosts the morale of the sales force to present a bold form and hold their prospects. Service encompasses the service rendered to clients before the insurance contract, during the policy term and after sales (policy becoming a claim).

Importance of Life Insurance Marketing

Life insurance marketing is the design, implementation and control of programmes seeking to increase the acceptability of a social idea or practice in a target group. It utilises concepts of market segmentation, consumer research idea configuration, and communication, facilitation, incentives and exchange theory to maximise target group response.

Absence of insurance market acts as a deterrent factor to capital formation and economic growth. The insurance market serves as an important source for the productive use of the economy's savings.

The importance of life insurance market can be briefly summarised as follows:

1. It mobilies the savings of the people for further investment in unproductive uses and thus avoids their wastage.
2. It provides incentives to saving and facilitates capital formation by offering stable rate of interest and bonus as the price of their investment.

3. It facilitates increase in production and productivity in the economy and thus enhances the economic welfare of the society.
4. Insurance market consisting of expert intermediaries promotes stability in value of different insurance schemes.
5. Insurance marketing generates employment.
6. It makes available new variety of useful and quality life insurance products to consumers.
7. Insurance marketing is the sole sources of business income.
8. Insurance marketing converts latent demand into effective demand and thus enables people to raise their standard of living.
9. It is a connecting link between the consumer and producer.

Scope of Life Insurance Marketing

In the present day insurance marketing scenario, the LIC and GIC play the role of an encouraging and supporting force to the entrepreneurs, corporate sector, investors, Government, Co-operatives, individuals and general public. There is vast scope for LIC to enlarge its operations both in domestic and international market.

The following areas are identified for the scope of insurance marketing:

1. Changing policy of LIC
2. Evolving consumer needs
3. Distribution gains importance
4. Innovations in insurance marketing
5. Development of rural markets
6. Entry of public sector banks
7. Pension plans.

(1) Changing Policy of LIC: With the opening up of the insurance sector at the dawn of the 21st century. LIC has revised its objectives and has focused its vision, mission, values and culture by constantly analysing the challenges and opportunities, and also considering its strength and weakness. LIC is designed to plan, price, promote and distribute want satisfying products and services to present and potential consumers.

(2) Evolving Consumer Needs: Insurance today has emerged as an attractive and stable investment alternative that offers total protection in life, health and wealth. In terms of returns, insurance products today offer competitive returns ranging between 7% and 9%. Besides returns, what really increases the appeal of insurance is the benefit of life protection from insurance products along with health cover benefits. Consumers today also seek a variety of insurance products that offer flexible options, prefer insurance schemes with benefits unbundled and customisable to suit their diverse needs. This offers good opportunity to insurance marketers to extend the area of operations.

(3) Distribution Gains Importance: The intermediaries in the insurance business and the distribution channels used by carriers will perhaps be the strongest drivers of growth in the sector. Multi-channel distribution and marketing of insurance products will be the smart strategy for the Indian market. While tied agents will continue to play an important role in distribution of insurance products, alternative channels like Development Officers, Inspectors, Executives will assume a greater role in distribution of insurance schemes. The trend is expected to continue in future.

(4) Innovations in Insurance Marketing: The Indian insurance market has witnessed innovations in the constantly explored avenues to increase the number of distribution channels through a variety of distribution patterns, given the rapidly changing customer profile. Internet and telemarketing is also expected to play an increasingly critical role in customer relationship. Rational intermediaries have played an important role as a distribution outlet for insurance services and products. This is likely to provide good business to insurance marketers in future.

(5) Development of Rural Markets: India is a predominantly rural country of more than one million people, mass marketing is always a profitable and cost effective option for gaining market share. The rural sector is a perfect case for mass marketing. The predominant insurance market leader, the LIC of India, feels that the lion's share of its new business comes from the rural and semi-rural markets. The development of rural insurance market offers tremendous opportunity to insurance market.

(6) Entry of Public Sector Banks: The Insurance Regulatory and Development Authority Act 1999 seeks to open up the insurance sector for private companies with a foreign equity of 26 per cent. It is also aimed at ending the monopoly of the Life Insurance Corporation (LIC) and General Insurance Corporation (GIC) in the insurance sector of the country. LIC entered into strategic alliance with corporative banks at the corporate level to improve its reach and also take advantages of mutually beneficial competencies. It also tied up with several other banks and organisations for marketing its insurance products and rendering services like collection of premium.

(7) Pension Plans: As a result of liberalisation and globalisation, the competition in the insurance sectors is becoming intense. To survive in the competition, the Insurance Regulatory Authority is permitting insurance companies into the pension business without forming separate companies for the purpose. As the Hindu/Indian joint family concept intended to disintegrate the social security cover, it had thus far provided was no longer available to a population increasingly adding numbers to the old generation. This is likely to provide good business to Insurance companies in future.

The above discussion highlights, that the scope of insurance business is vast and there lies immense opportunities ahead of insurance companies.

Questions

1. Discuss briefly Life Insurance marketing.
2. Explain the characteristics of Life Insurance Services.
3. What is Life Insurance Marketing Mix?
4. Discuss the importance and scope of Life Insurance Marketing.
5. Explain the objective of Life Insurance Marketing.

Chapter 15

World Life Insurance Market

Introduction

The life insurance markets are quite developed in many countries. Insurance markets are an important sources of financing trade, industry and government. The life insurance markets are an integral part of a country's economy. Various types of life insurance products available on the developed international insurance markets from the USA, UK and Japan etc. are given below:

1. Term or temporary insurance
2. Convertible term insurance
3. Income benefit
4. Whole life insurance
5. Endowment insurance
6. Unit linked plans
7. Income bonds
8. Building society linked savings plans
9. Universal plans
10. Variable life

11. Annuities
12. Pensions
13. Group life insurance.

The major insurance markets in the world have shown growth in life insurance business. It would be worthwhile here to have a look at a few performance indicators of the developed life insurance market in the world.

Share of World Insurance Market

The insurance market of the world in 1995 in terms of premium income was US $ 1140926 million. The share of Japan, the world leader, was 41.28% and followed by the U.S.A being 21.39%, France 6.73%, the U.K 5.88%, West Germany 5.04%, South Korea 3.78%, Switzerland 1.65%, Netherlands 1.52%, South Africa 1.34%, Canada 1.32%, Australia 1.19% and Italy 1.15%, of world market share during the year 1995. The other countries had a world share in the range of 0.02% to 1.76%. It can be observed that Japan, the USA, the UK and France are obviously the top four countries in the world insurance market and together they hold 75.28% share in the world life insurance market.

Insurance Operations in the U.S.A

Number of Insurance Companies in the U.S.A in 1960 was 1441, and it has increased to 2350 in 1989. The majority of small new companies formed in recent years remain in business by specializing in meeting the needs of families in specific regions. Others are national and global companies whose number is less. The population of the U.S.A is around 30 crore. But the number of policies in force was 39.4 crore in 1989. It included ordinary, group, industrial and credit policies. Life insurance was owned by 81% of American households, the average amount of life insurance owned by the insured household was $ 1,15,500.

The average length of a person's life in United States has increased from 47.3 years in 1900 to 75.2 years in 1989. Hence, 40% of insurance policies sold in America relate to pension schemes. In 1989, about six crore Americans were covered under the pension plan. The insurance business in the United States employed 21,27,800 persons in all in 1989. It included 14,68,000 employees in the offices and 6,59,800 insurance agents. The life insurance premium of US $ 2,64,509 millions in 1995 represented about 21.39% of the total world insurance market.

As the insurance market of the USA is considerably saturated, the American companies are pressing for opening of the insurance sector elsewhere particularly in Asia.

U.K. Scenario

Insurance market of the United Kingdom (UK) is free, but is subject to strong regulations. There are over 200 insurance companies transacting insurance business. The concept of welfare state has undergone a change with the collapse of socialism. State pension, unemployment and other social security benefits, medical benefit facilities are under increasing attack in the Western world. The emphasis has shifted on private provision of such benefits through insurance companies.

The break up of the traditional nuclear family, aging population, taxation policy, massive decline in the power of trade unions and excellent infrastructure have contributed to the change in the insurance scenario of the U.K. There are 700 life insurance and pension products available in the U.K. The design of the product is influenced by legislation, demand of sales force pressure from competitor's product and investment opportunities of the life fund.

Historically, banks and insurance companies were separate by regulations. As a result of deregulation of 1980s, this barrier between these sectors has disappeared. Hence, emergence of bank assurance is a new phenomenon in the U.K. The U.K is the fourth in the world insurance market with a total premium of US $ 72674 millions in 1995 represented about 5.88% of the world market share.

Life Insurance in Japan

Japan's share in the world insurance market in terms of premium income in 1990 was 28.74% next only to the U.S.A. 93.7% households in Japan have some kind of life insurance. Japan's population was 12.45 crore in 1992. The number of policies in force in this year was around 18 crore. The total premium increased to US $ 510448 million by the end of 1995, which represented about 41.8% of the world insurance market share.

Japan has unique sale force of 4,50,000 insurance sales agents consisting almost exclusively of housewives. Japan's high growth during the decades of the 70s and 80s caused labour shortages. Hence, housewives were recruited as insurance sales agents.

At present, there are 30 insurance companies in Japan, eight out of which are subsidiaries of the life insurance companies. Foreign insurance companies are selling their traditional insurance like Term insurance in Japan, which is most popular. Increasing population of Japan has shifted to the focus of insurance companies on pension and health care schemes. About 17% of Japan's population was covered in the age group of over 65 years during the year 2000.

Other Asian Countries

The opening up and economic restructuring of China in 1979 osculated the insurance industry. There are 18 insurance companies in China but the state owned insurer, the People's Insurance Company of China still dominates the domestic market. According to estimation, more than 90% to 95% of the business in the market is held by People's Insurance Company of China.

Recent growth in the South Korean market has left many participants perplexed. Following the opening of the market to foreign companies in 1987, the number of life insurance operations has grown from six to thirty-three. South Korean's life insurance sector, with its US $ 46738 million premium volume during 1995 results in the 6th ranking country in the worlds insurance business.

Australia's life insurance industry ranks 11th in the world. Japan takes the top spot, while South Korea the sixth position. Australia's life insurance market, therefore, is the third largest in the region. In the last 15 years, Australian Insurance companies have unbundled the traditional products and have introduced investment-linked products. Obviously, insurers marketing maturity-refund type contracts command unprecedented loyalty from their clients.

Performance of Global Life Insurance (1995 –2001)

Today, insurance has moved to the centre stage of the world economy. The growth of insurance worldwide and its manifestly increasing relevance to major aspects of Government action (social polices, savings, environment and industrial risks, health schemes, liability issues, catastrophic and systematic risks) provides a clear indication of where some key issue of the Global economy are to be found. With the opening up of the insurance sector, policy holders/investors will be exposed to a wide range of products. In a liberalised market, the country can gather enormous investment for infrastructure growth, competition can bring in a dynamic and health insurance industry. The given below table shows the performance of Global life insurance measured in terms of insurance penetration, i.e., premium in % of Gross Domestic Product and insurance density, i.e., premium per capita from 1995 to 2001.

Global Life Insurance (1995-2001)

Insurance penetration: Premium In % of Gross Domestic Product

(The Continents and India)

Year	North America			Latin America			Europe			Asia		
	Life	Non-Life	Total	Life	Non-Life	Total	Life	Non-Life	Total	Life	Non-Life	Total
1995	3.59	4.86	8.45	0.43	1.44	1.87	3.40	3.12	6.52.	7.92	2.20	10.12
1996	3.66	4.71	8.37	0.45	1.33	1.78	3.55	2.97	6.52	6.38	2.03	8.41
1997	3.80	4.61	8.41	0.49	1.37	1.86	3.85	2.93	6.78	6.27	1.90	8.18
1998	4.04	4.52	8.97	0.54	1.40	1.95	4.07	2.86	6.93	5.99	1.80	7.80
1999	4.17	4.25	8.42	0.63	1.36	1.99	4.69	2.88	7.57	5.66	1.71	7.38
2000	4.40	4.22	8.62	0.69	1.36	2.05	5.34	2.84	8.19	5.96	1.76	7.72
2001	4.30	4.50	8.80	0.72	1.46	2.17	4.89	2.95	7.84	5.84	1.76	7.60

Year	Africa			Oceania			World			India		
	Life	Non-Life	Total	Life	Non-Life	Total	Life	Non-Life	Total	Life	Non-Life	Total
1995	5.19	2.11	7.30	4.03	3.70	7.73	4.55	3.27	7.82	1.41	0.60	2.01
1996	3.90	1.82	5.72	4.30	3.82	8.12	4.17	3.12	7.28	1.29	0.55	1.84
1997	4.13	1.59	5.72	4.99	3.72	8.71	4.26	3.06	7.32	1.39	0.56	1.95
1998	3.63	1.20	4.84	5.74	3.66	9.40	4.32	2.99	7.44	1.90	0.71	2.61
1999	3.42	1.18	4.60	5.75	3.46	9.20	4.57	2.95	7.52	1.39	0.53	1.93
2000	3.03	1.06	4.09	5.43	3.44	8.87	4.88	2.96	7.84	1.77	0.55	2.32
2001	3.38	1.16	4.54	5.09	3.47	8.56	4.68	3.15	7.83	2.15	0.56	2.71

The above table gives the Global view of insurance penetration, Life and Non-life insurance business separately. Insurance penetration is measured in terms of premium (in USD) as a percentage of Gross Domestic Product of the country. North America's Penetration for Life and Non-life insurance business in 1995 was 3.59% and 4.86% and it has increased to 4.30% and 4.50% in 2001 respectively. In Latin America, it was 0.43% and 1.44% in 2001. In Europe, the Penetration for Life in 1995 was 3.40% and went up to 4.89% in 2001. On the other hand, the Non-life was 3.12% in 1995, but it was declined to 2.95% in 2001. In Asia, it was decreased from 7.93% and 2.20% in 1995 to 5.84% and 1.76% in 2001. Similarly, in Africa, the penetration for Life and Non-life in 1995 was 5.19% and 2. 11% and it was gone down to 3.38% and 1.16% in 2001. The world penetration for Life in 1995 was 3,27% and it was went up to 4.68% in 2001. But for Non-life, it was slight improvement from 3.27% in 1995 to 3.15% in 2001. India's penetration for Life and Non-life in 1995 was 1.41% and 0.60% and it has increased to 2.15% and 0.56% in 2001 respectively. It reveals the India's growth rate of 52.48% from 1995 to 2001.

From the below table highlights the Insurance Density measured in terms of Prima Capita (in USD). The premiums per capita was given from the year 1995 to 2001 for all continents for Life and Non-life insurance business. In North America, the premium per capita for Life and Non-life in 1995 was 959.7 USD and 1299.5 USD and it was continuously increased to 1508 - 6 USD and 1575 - 4 USD in 2001 respectively. Similarly, Latin America's premium per capita for Life and Non-Life in 1995 was 16.5 USD and 42.4 USD and it has gone up to 26.3 USD and 53.5 USD in 2001. The premiums per capita for life business in Europe has also gone up significantly from 464.9 USD in 1995 to 573.2 USD in 2001. But in case of Non-life business, it declined from 426.2 USD in 1995 to 345.6 USD in 2001. The premium per capita of Asia did not rise satisfactory. The Life and Non-life premiums per capita continuously declined from 208.1 USD and 59.2 USD in 1995 to 124 USD and 37.6 USD in 2001 respectively. Likewise, in Africa, it was decreased from 51.6 USD and 21.0 USD in 1995 to 22.4 USD and 7.7 USD in 2001. In Oceania, it went down from 761 USD and 697.2 USD in 1995 to 698 USD and 475 USD in 2001. Similarly, premium per capita of World was 277.2 USD and 197.9USD in 1995, but it was declined to 235 USD and 158.2 USD in 2001. On the other hand, India's premiums per capita was 4.5 USD and 1.9 USD in 1995 and it has increased to 9.1 USD and 2.4 USD in 2001 at a growth of 102.22% from 1995 to 2001.

Global Life Insurance (1995-2001)

Insurance Density: Premium Per Capita (in USD)

(The Continents and India)

Year	North America			Latin America			Europe			Asia		
	Life	Non-Life	Total	Life	Non-Life	Total	Life	Non-Life	Total	Life	Non-Life	Total
1995	959.71	299.5	2259.2	16.5	42.4	58.9	464.9	426.2	891.1	208.1	59.2	267.3
1996	1021	1212.6	2333.1	17.9	53.6	71.5	477.3	399.3	876.6	164.3	52.3	216.7
1997	1114	1353.1	2467.4	21.7	60.9	82.6	482.5	367.8	850.3	153.0	46.4	199.4
1998	1224	1368.4	2592.1	21.4	55.1	76.5	360.6	252.9	613.5	23.8	12.0	35.8
1999	1369.0	1396.6	2765.5	22.5	48.8	71.3	576.3	354.0	930.3	133.3	40.4	173.7
2000	1526	1462.1	2987.6	26.6	52.9	79.5	445.2	237.0	682.2	138.8	40.4	179.6
2001	1508.6	1575.4	3084.0	26.3	53.5	79.8	573.2	345.6	918.8	125.0	37.6	162.6

(Contd.)

Global Life Insurance (1995-2001) (*Contd.*)

Year	Africa			Oceania			World			India		
	Life	Non-Life	Total	Life	Non-Life	Total	Life	Non-Life	Total	Life	Non-Life	Total
1995	51.6	21.0	72.6	761	697.2	1458	277.2	197.9	475.1	4.5	1.9	6.4
1996	46.4	21.7	68.0	894	792.7	1686	246.7	184.5	431.1	5.0	2.0	7.0
1997	52.7	20.3	72.9	1023	761.6	1784	246.4	176.8	423.3	5.4	2.2	7.6
1998	27.1	9.1	36.2	842	536.5	1378	145.3	125.7	271.0	6.2	2.3	8.6
1999	24.1	8.3	32.4	901	542.2	1443	235.4	151.9	378.3	6.2	2.4	8.5
2000	23.5	8.2	31.7	806	510.0	1316	239.9	145.5	385.4	7.6	2.3	9.9
2001	22.4	7.7	30.1	698	475.0	1173	235.0	158.2	393.3	9.1	2.4	11.5

Insurance Density (per Capita Premium) — Selected Countries

Insurance Density is measured in terms of per capita (in USD) for selected countries including India during the year 2001 is highlighted in the given below table:

Insurance Density (per capita premium) — Selected Countries (2001)

Selected Countries	Non Life (In USD)	Life (In USD)
U.S	1381	1079
Canada	709	501
U.K	677	1433
France	790	1559
Japan	896	3236
Malaysia	121	98
Pakistan	2	2
India	2	5
South Africa	99	367
Australia	794	1011
New Zealand	787	305
Brazil	77	18
Mexico	28	14

It is observed from the table that the insurance density in terms of premium per capita for non-life and life insurance business in USA was 1381 USD and 1079 USD in 2001. It is seen that USA is a leading highest insurance density country for Non-life business among the selected countries. On the other hand, premium per capita for life business Japan secured a top rank of 3236 USD during the same period. But for non-life business Japan leading a second position of 896 USD. It is important to note here that next to Japan, the non-life business of Australia was 794 USD, next to France was 790 USD; New Zealand was 787 USD: Canada was 677 USD respectively. It shows that the significant impact of insurance density among the above said countries. It also seen that the premium per capita for life business of France was 1559 USD; U.K was 1433 USD; U.S was 1079 USD and Australia was 1011 USD respectively. Thus, it had shown a satisfactory progress of life insurance business during the same period. While per capita premium for life and non-life insurance business of South Africa was 99 USD; Brazil was 77 USD and 18 USD; Mexico was 28 USD and 14 USD; India was 2 USD and 5 USD; and Pakistan was 2 USD and 2 USD respectively. This is poor reflection on insurance density of Malaysia, Brazil, Mexico, India and Pakistan. Particularly, India and Pakistan shows very low per capita premium during the year 2001. This is most discouraging sign which needs more attention.

Perception of Asian Insurers on Liberalisation

The Asian insurance markets, identified as the fastest growing in the world, are slowly gearing up to face the current trends and pressures towards global liberalisation of trade in insurance services.

Japan, Korea and Taiwan by their sheer size and potential are considered the three most sought after markets by the foreign insurers, They also have been eyeing opportunities in Southeast Asia while casting their long-term plans on the potential opening of the giant nationalised market of China and India.

Challenges faced by Life Insurance Industry

Life insurance industry all over the world is in a state of turbulence and turmoil due to rapid changes in the financial global market place and challenges from the competitors. The challenges being faced by the life insurance industry at present are the result of:

(a) Reforms in industrial policy and industrial licensing investment promotions expenditure control etc.

(b) Reforms in trade policy and changing regulations, price stability and taxation etc.

(c) Industry image problems and methods of conducting business;

(d) Low productivity and high cost of agency organisation;

(e) Reducing controls on imports of investment norms;

(f) Changes in the external environment for life insurance market;

(g) Impacts on inflationary pressures;

(h) Changes in the population structure;

(i) Changes in the structure of personal financial assets;

(j) Aggressive inroads made by banking and other financial institutions;

(k) Aggressive competitors whose publicity is targeted to ridicule traditional life insurance companies;

(l) High expense margins specially for companies who solely rely on captive insurance agents for selling;

(m) Change in product design with shifting of priorities from product to distribution channel to product designed to suit the customers;

(n) Customers expectations – return on investment;

Factors Consider to meet the Challenges

To meet the emerging challenges the life insurance industry has to gear itself up with:

(1) Innovative work technology;

(2) Proper information system;

(3) Creating product designs capable of meeting the challenge of consumerism;

(4) Merger and working arrangements with other financial services with a view to developing composite financial services aimed at providing total consumer satisfaction;

(5) Enlisting total employee support for its strategic plans and programmes for marketing various kinds of policies;

(6) Product diversity to penetrate into rural and semi urban market segment more extensively which was hitherto been some what given inadequate attention

(7) Adequate training for agents and development officers who from the core marketing personnel, making them more professional in their attitude and approach very much necessary in marketing activity, and above all;

(8) Educating customers and creating a saving habit and investment culture, especially in semi urban and rural areas.

It must be observed here that meeting the emerging challenges must be a collective responsibility and must be shared by the officials and staff in policy servicing/claims and accounts departments in addition to the field force.

Questions

1. Briefly explain the World Insurance Market.
2. Explain a brief note on Insurance Operations in the U.S.A.
3. What is Life Insurance Marketing Mix?
4. Explain the progress of global life insurance business.

Chapter 16

LIC Financial Services

Advances Against Life Insurance Policies

Introduction

In the present day liberalised policy of advances to borrowers in the neglected sectors, where sometimes a small margin is required, insurance policy as security has come into great prominence. The insured generally approaches LIC or the bank for money to tide over an urgent but unexpected difficulty of a personal nature. Nobody would normally offer his life policy as security, which he has taken as a provision for his old age or for the benefit of his dependants in the event of his death. It is not intended to convey that advances against life policies are undertaken for business purposes. Many businessmen take such advance for their trade requirement.

Insurance is taken on the life of the borrower for the amount of the advance and the policy is assigned in the LIC's or bank's favour. The policy may or may not have any surrender value. In the event of the death of the borrower, the advance amount would be adjusted from it. Life policy with or without any surrender value is also taken as a supplementary security where the prosperity of a borrowing concern depends mainly or entirely on the life of the borrower himself and the concern may collapse in the event of his death.

Points in Favour

1. Life policies in India are issued by LIC, which is a nationalised institution known for its stability and integrity.
2. There is no change, therefore, of the LIC denying its liability or not paying the amount, if the policy and claim are in order.
3. The value of the life policy-surrender value-does not-decrease. On the other hand, it steadily increases if the premiums are regularly paid.
4. The amount of the advance is automatically repaid in the event of the death of the borrower. There is hardly any difficulty in the recovery of the amount from the LIC.
5. Little supervision is required because the life policy remains in the custody of the bank or LIC.
6. If the policy is 'with profits', the surrender value of the policy increases over and above the normal expectation.

Drawbacks

1. A life policy depends for its continued validity of the amount insured, on regular payment of premium.
2. A contract of insurance is a contract of utmost good faith and any fraudulent statement on a material fact, made by the insured in the proposal may render the policy invalid.
3. The life policy usually contains a number of conditions and special restrictions. For example, life policies state in the suicide clause that if the assured commits suicide during the particular period the policy will become invalid.
4. A policy under which the entire policy amount does not become payable on the death of the insured should also not be accepted.
5. Complication may arise if a duplicate policy is issued and the lending bank has no knowledge of it.

LIC Housing Finance Ltd

LIC Housing Finance Ltd. and its Role

Introduction:

Housing is one of the basic necessities of human beings. Yet, in India, the number of persons in need of this basic necessity far exceeds the number having a roof of their own over their head. Accordingly, the demand for housing has been growing at a rapid place. Housing has become far more affordable in recent times. A decade ago, a house cost nearly 15-20 times an individual's annual salary. Today, the cost has declined to a smaller

multiple. Further, interest rates on housing loans have come down and are much lower — between 7% and 9% as compared to 14-15 per cent five years ago. The government has been offering attractive tax incentives for purchasing houses. Stable property prices, lower interest rates, tax concessions and rising income levels have contributed to the increased demand for housing. Thus, housing finance acts as an impetus to the housing sector and is essential for a substantial growth of the economy and for housing the country's homeless.

Organisation and Capital Resources

The LIC Housing Finance Ltd. was set up as a shareholders' organisation. It was incorporated on 19th June, 1989 under the Companies Act 1956. From the 15th September 1994, it became a widely held public limited company. With the setting up of the LIC Housing Finance Ltd. as a subsidiary of LIC with equity participation from UTI, IFCI, GIC and others, and ICICI. Among the shareholders, as on 31st March 2000 the major share of the company which was held by LIC of India is 38.43%.The shareholdings of others are: UTI 12.17%, IFCI 12.07%, GIC and its Associates 3.03% and other individual 34.30%, respectively. The company has 6 Regional Offices and 67 Operating Offices along with 23 Extension Counters and over 100 Camp Offices making it the housing finance institution with widest marketing network in the country and it is a premier Housing Finance Company in our country.

Objectives of LIC Housing Finance Ltd

1) To undertake as a socio-purposive investment
2) To provide long-term finance for construction
3) To provide finance for purchase of individual houses and flats
4) To serve better the needs of the economy by providing value-added services
5) To ensure that lower probability of losses arising out of non-performing loans
6) To ensure effective utilisation of strong potentials for further growth
7) To ensure effective management of all types of risks — maturity risk, interest rate risk, foreign exchange risk, and credit risk
8) To provide home loan on life insurance policies as collateral security
9) To provide financial assistance to State Governments for social housing schemes for the economically weaker sectors.

Housing Scheme Loans

Consequent on the declaration of the National Housing Policy, the LIC Housing Finance Ltd. gave special importance to housing loans, which was till then a subdued activity and coined a new slogan "housing loan as a marketing tool". Finance is provided for housing to individuals, co-operative housing societies and private undertakings. The housing scheme loans of LIC Housing Finance Ltd. may be grouped into:

I. Individual Housing Schemes

II. Non-Individual Housing Schemes.

I. Individual Housing Schemes

The following are the various individual housing schemes are available to meet the needs of the individual.

Individual Loan Schemes

The company has several housing finance schemes tailor-made for individuals. The schemes are briefed as under:

(a) Griha Prakash:

1. Loan up to 85% of property cost
2. Minimum and Maximum loan — Rs. 25,000 and Rs.50 lakhs
3. Maximum Term - 20 years
4. Any LIC policy equal to loan amount.

(b) Griha Tara:

1. Loan up to 85% of property cost
2. Minimum and Maximum loan — Rs. 25,000 and 25 lakhs
3. Maximum Term — 20 years
4. Only Bima Sandesh Policy as collateral security.

(c) Griha Jyoti:

1. Loan up to 85% of property cost
2. Minimum and Maximum loan — Rs. 50,000 and 1 lakh
3. Maximum Term — 20 years
4. Group Insurance Cover. No individual policy.

(d) Griha Lakshmi:

1. Exclusive loan for non-insurable lives
2. Loan up to 85% of property cost
3. Minimum and Maximum loan — Rs.1 lakh and 50 lakhs
4. Maximum Term - 15 years
5. No LIC Policy as collateral.

(e) Griha Shobha:

1. Exclusive scheme for NRI's
2. Loan up to 85% of property cost
3. Minimum and Maximum loan — Rs. 25,000 and 50 lakhs
4. Term 7 to 10 years
5. Subject to RBI regulations
6. Any LIC policy equal to loan amount.

(f) Griha Sudhar:

1. Loan for repairs/renovation
2. Loan up to 85% of cost of repairs or 25% of market value of property as per our assessment
3. Minimum and Maximum loan — Rs. 50,000 and 10 lakhs
4. Term — 5 to 10 years
5. Insurance not compulsory
6. Age of the flat/house not > 40 years.

(g) Loans for plots:

1. For purchase of plots site from Govt./statutory bodies
2. Loan up to 75% of property cost
3. Minimum and Maximum loan — Rs. 50,000 and 10 lakhs
4. Term — 6 years.

(h) Sampurna Griha (A & B):

1. Loans for purchase of consumer durables like T. V., Music system, computer. Furniture etc to existing/New loans at select centres.
2. Minimum and Maximum loan—Rs. 25,000 and 2 lakhs
3. Term— Existing loans — 3 years; New loans — up to 20 years.

(i) Clean Channel facility for prossionals:

1. Practicing Doctors, Computer Engineers, Chartered Accountants, Senior Executives etc.
2. Only latest year's IT returns
3. Policy equal to 50% of the loan amount
4. 15 years Term.

(j) Scheme for Pensionable Employees:

1. For Government employees eligible for pension (aged 50 and above)
2. Extended loan term beyond retirement (up to 15 years or 70 years whichever is less)
3. 1/3 of outstanding loan to be repaid out of retirement benefits
4. Reduced EMI on balance loan term.

II. Non-Individual Schemes

With a view to solving the housing shortages in the country institutions like LIC join in a big way in a massive effort by granting loans for purchase/construction of houses/flats to the following agencies:

1. State Governments Social Housing Schemes
2. State Level Apex Co-operative Housing Finance Societies
3. Loans to Other Housing Agencies
4. Other Non-Individual Schemes.

1. State Government Social Housing Schemes: Since 1959 LIC has been advancing loan to State Governments for financing social housing schemes for the commercially weaker sections, low income groups, middle income groups, state government employees and for rural population.

2. State Level Apex Co-operative Housing Finance Societies: Since 1959 LIC has been advancing loan to State/Union territory and Apex Co-operative Housing Finance Societies who, in turn, advance loans to their affiliated primary co-operative societies for construction/purchase of houses.

3. Loans to Other Housing Agencies: Loans are advanced to other housing agencies like Housing Development Finance Corporation, Housing and Urban Development Corporation, National Housing Bank and State Police Housing Corporations in a few states.

Examples of Corporate Loan Schemes

Apart from individual loan schemes, the company also lends to reputed public limited companies/public sector undertakings for the following are examples:

Staff Quarters

1. Loan up to 70% of property cost or 10% of the net worth of the company, whichever is less
2. Minimum and Maximum loan — Rs. 20 lakhs and Rs. 7.5 crores
3. Term — 5 to 7 years.

Office Premises

1. Loan up to 50% of the project cost or 5% of the net worth
2. Minimum loan — Rs. 25 lakhs; Maximum loan — as per limitation above
3. Term — upto 7 years.

Line of credit to the company

1. To the company for their house building scheme
2. Minimum and Maximum loan — Rs. 25 lakhs and 10% of the net worth of the company
3. Term — upto 5 years.

Apna Chikitsalaya

1. Loan for purchase/Constructions of clinic/Nursing home/ Diagnostic centre
2. Loan up to 50% of the property cost
3. Minimum and Maximum loan - Rs. 5 lakhs and Rs. 50 lakhs
4. Term - 5 to 7 years.

Document required (common for all):

(a) Duly filled in application form

(b) Copy of sanctioned plan and letter

(c) Copy of N.A. Permission/ULC Clearance, whichever applicable

(d) One guarantor and his/her salary certificate in LIC Housing Finance Ltd. format. If guarantor is in business, profession, a copy of his/her latest IT returns/Assessment order

(e) Bank passbook or statement for the last two years

(f) Power of attorney whichever applicable.

Additional requirements (for salaried person)

(a) Employer's salary certificate in LICHFL format/latest salary slip

(b) Identity card of the applicants

(c) TDS certificate of applicant

(d) PE/ESI slip of applicants.

For Businessmen/ Self-employed

Three years IT returns/assessment orders along with computed income and statement of accounts certified by Chartered Accountant.

Income Tax Reliefs

For principal loan repayment, a rebate @ 20% for amount up to Rs. 20000 is allowed u/s 88. Deduction u/s 24(2) is allowed upto Rs. 1,50,000 towards interest payable on housing loan borrowed for housing purpose provided the construction/acquisition is completed within 3 years from the end of the financial year in which the loan was allowed. The deduction is applicable only for self occupied house property and unoccupied self-occupied house property.

Performance of LIC Housing Finance Ltd. (1999 – 2000)

A survey conducted by LIC Housing Finance Ltd. in 2001, highlights the following performance of its financial operations during the year (1999 - 2000):

(1) The company's income from operations was Rs.644.92 crore registering a growth of over 15%.

(2) The company sanctioned Rs.1433.58 crore of individual housing loans rising the cumulative sanctions to Rs.7416.55 crore.

(3) It distributed Rs.1312.59 crore for the year the total disbursements being Rs.6363.53 crore which is a growth of 35.9% and 24.9% respectively.

(4) The gross profit of the company came to be Rs.138.58 crore and the net profit Rs.109.08 crore.

(5) The company's reserve rose to Rs.493.95 crores over last year's Rs.410.72 crores.

The company put equal emphasis on recovery of its loan and the individual default has came down to 1.49% of the total portfolio. The gross non–performance assets on individual loans has come down to 3.20% as compared to 3.46% of the earlier year.

4. Other Non-Individual Schemes: (a) Direct loans to Corporate Bodies (Public limited company) for construction/ purchase of staff quarters. (b) Construction finance to Builders and Developers. (c) Loans to members of Co-operative Housing Society of employees of public sector undertaking/ Public Limited Companies. (d) Line of credit for financing House Building Advance Scheme of a company for its employees. (e) Financing Housing Projects of public agencies like housing board, Development Authorities etc. (f) Loans to corporate bodies for purchase or construction or repairs/ renovation of office premises.

LIC Mutual Funds Schemes

Introduction:

Mutual Funds are the backbone of an economic system and aid allocation of scarce capital across the productive sectors of the economy.

While Indian economic growth is inevitable, stability and dynamism of the mutual fund system is necessary for proper allocation of resources, which in turn, helps sustain a healthy climate for savings and investment.

People prefer mutual funds to bank deposits, life insurance and even bonds because with a little money, they can get into the investment game. Thus, mutual funds help bring together savers and users of capital.

Meaning and Definition

The term "Mutual Funds" refers to collecting the savings from small investors, invest them in Government and other corporate securities and earn income through interest and dividends, besides capital gains.

The Securities and Exchange Board of India (Mutual Funds) Regulation 1993,defines a mutual funds as "a fund established in the form of a trust by a sponsor, to raise monies by the trustee through the sale of units to the public, under one or more schemes, for investing in securities in accordance with these regulations."

Classification of Mutual Funds

The mutual fund industry in India launching of various innovative schemes in terms of year wise is grouped into (1) Open-ended schemes and (2) Closed-ended schemes. Open-ended schemes refer to under which units are purchased and sold throughout the year and a member can enter the scheme anytime or walk out of it also any time. On the other hand, closed-ended with contributions from members collected during a definite time-frame of a few days to a few months.

Further, the funds can be classified into various types based on the pattern of their investment objectives such as income schemes, income and growth schemes, growth schemes, tax saving schemes, industry specific schemes and special purpose schemes.

Mutual Funds in India

The first mutual fund, in a strict sense, started in 1868 by Foreign and Colonial Government Trust of London. Thereafter, a large number of closed-ended mutual funds were formed in USA in 1930's followed by many countries in Europe, the Far East and Latin America. In India, the mutual fund industry has been monopolised by the Unit Trust of India (UTI) ever since 1963. Thereafter over ten years period, number of other mutual funds, both in private and public sectors, came up. All of them are active in the market, though not popular. It was only with the advent of the Securities and Exchange Board of India (SEBI), that comprehensive guidelines for the mutual industry were put up in place.

The growth of mutual funds Industry in India was very slow till the end of the 1980's primarily due to Government controls and over regulations. Leaving aside UTI, which has been existing since 1964, two financial institutions namely Life Insurance Corporation of India (LIC) and General

Insurance Corporation (GIC) has set up their mutual funds in 1989 and 1990 respectively. Since 1987 starting with State Bank of India (SBI), a number of public sector banks have set up mutual funds, which have been regulated by the Reserve Bank of India (RBI). The mutual funds of LIC and GIC were regulated by the Investment Division of Ministry of Finance.

Indian Mutual Fund Report 1996 indicated that the total number of mutual fund schemes in India went up from 47 in 1970 to 197 in 1996. According to a survey conducted by Securities and Exchange Board of India (SEBI) Mumbai, 2002, highlights some of the important dimensions of the mutual fund industry.

(1) About 60 - 70 per cent of the investments come from the cooperative institutional sectors.

(2) Mumbai, Chennai, Bangalore and Calcutta account for a majority of the inflows.

(3) Less than one per cent of the adult working population are aware of mutual funds.

(4) Private sector funds are rapidly growing and gaining in market share.

The Indian mutual fund industry, in a rather short period has grown from infancy to adolescence. Among the 36 Securities and Exchange Board of India (SEBI)registered funds, are the Unit Trust of India (assets under management Rs.49,000 Crores) public sector funds (Rs.8,000 crores) and the private sectors funds (Rs.44,000 Crores). The industry assets under management has been growing at 6 per cent compound annual growth rate.

LIC Mutual Funds (LICMF)

LIC Mutual Fund was setup in June 1989 as a separate trust by the Life Insurance Corporation of India. LIC made an initial contribution of Rs. 2 crores towards the Trust Funds and appointed a Board of Trustees to supervise the activities of the Funds. The Board of Trustees have entrusted the work of management of the fund to Jeevan Sahayog Asset Management Company Ltd., which is a company promoted by the Life Insurance Corporation of India with an authorised capital of Rs.25 crores. The day-to-day operations of Jeevan Bima Sahayog Asset Management Company Ltd., the investment manager to LICMF are looked after by senior officials on deputation from LIC of India, which has the experience of handling and investing large funds for more than 40 years. It is one of the largest insurance companies in the world serving over 9 crores policy holders and managing of funds over Rs. 5000 crores.

Importance of LIC Mutual Funds

The mutual funds industry has grown at a phenomenal rate in the recent past. It helps bring together savers and users of capital. One can witness a revolution in the mutual funds industry in view of its importance to the investors in general and the country's economy at large. The following are the important advantages of mutual funds:

1. LIC Mutual funds help to channelising savings for investment.
2. It facilitates the investors to enjoy a wide portfolio investment.
3. It proves better yields due to higher market rates and lower rates of brokerage.
4. LIC Mutual funds render expert investment and research services at lower cost.
5. It ensures tax benefits to its customers.
6. LIC Mutual funds provide greater affordability, liquidity and a flexible investment schedule.
7. It plays a vital role in supporting the development of the capital market.
8. It enables simplified record keeping.
9. It promotes industrial development.
10. LIC Mutual funds help reduce the marketing cost of new issues.

Types of LIC Mutual Funds Schemes

In order to meet the needs of investors, objectives and risk taking capacities, LIC Mutual Funds Schemes have the following types:

I. Open-Ended Funds Scheme

1. DHANARAKSHA1989
2. LICMF Children's Funds
3. LICMF Bond Funds
4. LICMF Liquid Funds
5. LICMF Tax Plan 1997

II. Close-Ended Funds Scheme

1. Dhanvikas 1998
2. Dhanasamriddhi

III. Income and Growth Funds Scheme

1. LICMF Securities Funds
2. Dhanasahayog

I. Open-Ended Funds Scheme

Under this scheme, the size of the funds and or the periods of the funds are not pre-determined. The investors are free to buy and sell any number of units at any point of time. The main features of the open-ended Funds are:

1. There is complete flexibility with regard to one's investment or disinvestments.
2. These units are not publicly treated, but the fund is ready to repurchase them and resell them at any time.
3. The investor is offered instant liquidity in the sense that the units can be sold on any working day to the fund.
4. The main objective of this fund is income generation.
5. Since the units are not listed on the stock market, their prices are linked to the Net Asset Value of the units.

Under LIC Mutual fund, many products have been offered for investment. The following are on-going open ended schemes and investors can buy units anytime throughout the year:

1. Dhanaraksha 1989: "Dhanaraksha" open-ended scheme opened in 1989. With the basic objective of providing long term capital appreciation along with benefits of a tax rebate and insurance. It is an insurance linked recurring investment scheme with a 10/15 years term with the option of yearly or half yearly payment of subscription. The maximum target amount of savings under the scheme is Rs.75,000 with accident cover upto Rs.30,000.

2. LICMF Children Funds: It is an open-ended scheme, which seek to generate long-term capital appreciation through a judicious mix of investment in quality debt and equity instrument at relatively moderate risk levels, through research based investments. Under this scheme, there is an entry load of 1%. No exit load for redemption after completion of 18 years of the child. It is an accident insurance benefits scheme; accordingly it provides free personal accident cover to domestic resident beneficiaries up to 10 times the invested amount subject to a maximum of Rs.3 lakh.

3. LICMF Bond Funds: LICMF Bond Fund is an open–ended scheme launched in 1999, with the chief aim to generate returns for investors through investment in quality debt instruments. Under this scheme, the minimum amount of investment is Rs 5000. The scheme has three options such as (1) Dividend, (2) Dividend Reinvestment and (3)Growth. The investors can enter into the scheme within 6 months from the date of allotment for amounts upto Rs.50 lakh. If the amount is more than Rs.50 lakhs, the investors can enter within 3 months.

4. LICMF Liquid Funds: It is an open-ended Gilt Fund scheme launched in 2002 with the basic objective to generate returns for investors by timing the Government Securities market. It has three options such as (1).Dividend, (2). Dividend Re–investment and (3).Growth. Under this scheme, the minimum amount of investment is Rs. 10,000.

5. LICMF Tax Plan 1997: LICMF Tax Plan 1997 was launched as a open-ended scheme in 2000. The, main objective is to provide capital growth along with Tax rebate and Tax relief through prudent investments in the stock markets. Growth is the only option. The investors can enter into the scheme at any time, subject to the minimum investment of Rs.500.

II Close-Ended Funds Scheme

It is just the opposite of open-ended funds scheme. Under this scheme, the corpus of the funds and its duration are prefixed. In other words, the corpus of the fund and the number of units are determined in advance. Once the subscription reaches the predetermined level, the entry of investors is closed. After expiry of the fixed period, the entire corpus is disinvested and the proceeds are distributed to the various unit holders in proportion to their holding. Thus, the fund ceases to a fund, after the final distribution.

Salient Features

The following are the salient features of close-ended funds are:

1. The period and or the target amount of the fund is definite and fixed beforehand.
2. Once the period is over and or the target is reached, the door is closed for the investors. They cannot purchase any more units.
3. The main objective of this fund is capital appreciation.
4. The whole fund is available for the entire duration of the scheme and there will not be any redemption demands before its maturity.
5. At the time of redemption, the entire investment pertaining to a close-end scheme is liquidated and the proceeds are distributed among the unit holders.

1. Dhanvikas 1998: It was launched as a close-ended pure growth scheme in 1993. This scheme was made open-ended with effect from 1998. The main objective of this scheme is to obtain maximum possible capital growth consistent with reasonable levels of risk by investing mainly in equities. Under this scheme, the Net Asset Value and sale or repurchase prices are declared on a daily basis. The investor can enter or exit at any time, subject to a minimum investment of Rs.2000.

2. Dhanasamriddhi: This is five-year close-ended growth scheme. It came up during the year 1999. Owing to adverse market conditions during the entire tenure of the scheme, it was decided to continue the scheme as an open-ended scheme and the investors were given the option either to redeem their units at Net Asset Value of Rs.4.77 on the original redemption date or continue in the open-ended scheme. The majority of the investors have continued in the scheme

III. Income and Growth Funds Scheme:

It concentrates more on the distribution of regular income and it also sees that the average return is higher than that of the income from bank deposits. Growth funds concentrate mainly on long run schemes, i.e., capital appreciation. It is also described as "Nest Eggs" investment.

Main Features

1. The investor is assured of a regular income at periodic intervals.
2. The pattern of investment is oriented towards high and fixed income yield securities like debentures, bonds etc.
3. The growth oriented fund aims at meeting the investors' need for capital appreciation.
4. This is best suited to salaried and business people who have high risk bearing capacity and ability to defer liquidity.

1. LICMF Securities Funds: The LICMF Securities Fund Scheme was launched in 1999. The main objective of this scheme is to generate returns for investors by timing the Government Securities market. It has three options such as: (1)Dividend, (2)Dividend Reinvestment and (3)Growth. The entire corpus of the scheme is invested in central and state Government Securities and is thus insulated from credit risk to meet the needs of specific investors seeking this category of investment. The minimum amount of investment under which is Rs.10,000.

2. Dhanasahayog: Dhanasahayog was launched as an income and growth scheme. There are three plans under this scheme such as: Plan A— the dividend will be remitted to the investors, plan B—dividend will be reinvested under the scheme, and plan C— growth with capital gains. There is no lock-in period for encashment of the units purchased under this scheme.

Benefits of LIC's Mutual Funds Schemes

The major benefits of the LIC's mutual funds are

(1) Availability of mutual funds at low cost

(2) Mutual fund reduce the risk of shareholding for the holder

(3) Wider range of low cost information services

(4) Highly professional management services

(5) Record keeping is simplified in mutual funds

(6) Low cost and high value diversification

(7) Investors to switch over from one funds another

(8) Adequate protection from state agencies

(9) It facilitates low initial investment

(10) Mutual funds investment offers enough liquidity to investors

(11) Investors are exempted from certain taxes which in turn increases the net yield of investments.

(12) Mutual funds increase the mobilisation of investible funds of the community by pooling the resources of a large number of small savers for corporate investment.

(13) Mutual funds can promote the investment habit of the rural and semi-urban areas.

Progress in LIC Mutual Funds

In the developing countries like India, mutual funds have a very important role to play in channelising savings into the capital market. By building up expertise to assess financial viability of projects and prospects for individual scripts, these institutions help cushion the risks for individual investor.

LIC Mutual Funds has mobilised more than Rs.4000 crore (cumulative as on 30.3.2002) from over 17 lakhs investors during 13 years of operations by successfully launching 35 schemes of various types. In the wake of liberalisation, it has the distinction of being the only mutual fund to launch the largest number and greatest variety of schemes. It has the highest investor base of over 4 lakh investors since inception, one of the largest amongst mutual funds, which emphasises the trust it commands from the common investors.

The BS-JMRB Survey of Dec.2001 rated LIC Mutual Fund in the top 5 Fund based on investor satisfaction in key parameters like service, performance and brand strength and though it comes as a recognition for more than a decade of hard work and investor satisfaction it has not brought in complacency. Far from it, LICMF team seems driven to better its performance. LIC Mutual Funds has valued the trust of its investors and applied it to a conservative approach to investment to ensure a consistent performance. It has withstood the test of time by remaining active in all good and bad phases of the market and the economy.

Factors which determine the Mutual Funds:

There are many factors which have influenced during selection of a mutual fund. Hence, the investors should consider the following factors before determining the mutual funds:

I. Company or Industry related factors:

(1) Competence of the management

(2) Historical background of the company

(3) Sound financial background

(4) Distribution and network forces

(5) Product and market specialisation

(6) Effective corporate planning and control

(7) Objectives of the company

(8) Company's growth, equity and price stability

(9) Assurance about the benefits to investors in terms of return on their investments

(10) Investment yield and risk associated returns.

II. Product related factors:

(1) Cost of the present product

(2) Nature of the proposed new product

(3) Comparison with competitive product

(4) Types and uses of the product

(5) Risk and rate of return of the product

(6) Nature of distribution of the product

(7) Availability of alternatives.

III Operations related factors

(1) Cost of operations

(2) Efficient operations

(3) Account of flexibility

(4) Steady and consistency performance

(5) Cost and benefits of the various distribution systems.

IV Market related factors

(1) Market potential for existing product

(2) Market share based on market trend

(3) Significant segment of the market

(4) Stock Market Index

(5) Interest rate and inflation rate

(6) Competitive strength and weakness

(7) Estimated sales potential

(8) Market facilities and proposed sales market

(9) Effectiveness of promotional mix

(10) Market size and future expansion of market.

V Consumers or Investors related factors

(1) Optimum consumer satisfaction

(2) Consumer's expectation or preference

(3) Prompt and efficient servicing

(4) Rate of savings of the investors

(5) Growth of disposable income

(6) Immediate encashment of products

(7) Quality of after sale service

(8) Consumer's product knowledge.

VI Other factors

(1) Socio political trends

(2) Changes in economic behaviour

(3) Size of spending and savings

(4) Level of inflation and currency fluctuations

(5) Governments economic policy.

Information Technology in LIC

Introduction:

The positive role the IT industry is playing in our lives is no longer a debatable issue. Most countries today are beginning to understand the value add that information technology is bringing to economics—introducing both efficiency and benefits. And business around the globe have been investing heavily in the IT hardware and software infrastructure. As communication within companies and users occurs more rapidly, with more customised information, greater security, and interactively and timeliness than before, business strategies and even the structures of companies and industries are, being transformed.

Meaning

Information technology consist of electronic devices capable of performing a number of complex operations with in one time. They have internal storage, a stored program and program modification capacities. They are basically an automatic information convertor. They can transfer raw and unusable data into a meaningful information. Thus, information technology are utilised for processing of set of information.

Charactertics of Information Technology

(1) **Speed:** Its internal speed is virtually instantaneous

(2) **Storage:** It can store certain amount of information in the internal memory

(3) **Accuracy:** The accuracy of IT is consistently can do almost any task

(4) **Variability:** It seems capable of performing almost any task

(5) **Automatisn:** In IT once the process has begun, it would continue without the need for human intervention until completion.

6) **Diligence:** It does not suffer from the human traits of tiredness and lack of concentration.

IT Revolution in India

India - the world's largest democracy and home to a billion people is also rapidly emerging as a leader in the field of IT. The IT revolution has become the new mantra in the economic landscape here. The high potential of IT to generate wealth, foreign exchange and employment has already caught the imagination of India's businessmen, citizens, economists, bureaucrats and politicians.

A gradual shift towards the usage of IT is happening in the Government, public as well as the private sector all over the country. And in the last two decades, software engineering, web-based services and E-Commerce solutions have emerged as the new jewels of the Indian economy. The year 1999 - 2009 particularly witnessed a concerted effort to trickle the benefits of IT to the common masses in the country. India has many advantages that can enable it to become an important player in the global IT industry. By marshalling its vast human, industrial and technological resources, especially in the area of software. India can raise the productivity of domestic manufacturing and services. And this obviously will lead to IT in governance, IT in industry and IT for every citizen of the country.

Information Technology in LIC

The major growth drivers of the insurance business include the need for insurance companies world wide to reduce costs and focus on their insurance trade competencies to face increased global competition, global slowdown and increased speed of change brought about by technology. Information technology has been around for a longtime now. LIC of India is a pioneer financial institution in leveraging information technology as its front line tool to better its overall efficiency in all area of its activities. MIS—Management Information Strategies a leading international magazine in its issue of Dec.2000 reported that LIC is the second largest user of computer and information technology in India. LIC was one of the first organisation to computerise its operations to provide better services to customer. Today LIC has data pertaining to over 10 crores policies being held in computers. It has the largest dedicated network among all organisations in the country and has connected about 1500 branches all over India through Metro/Wide Area Net- work. LIC has launched a comprehensive any where enquiry and computer service system through which payment can be made and support obtained countrywide with the help of next generation connectivity.

Objectives of Information Technology in LIC

The main purpose of introducing information technology in LIC is to gather co- ordinated, systematic and continuous flow of relevant information. Information Technology is an organised set of procedures and routine. In brief, the following are the important objectives of information technology in LIC:

1. Information Technology makes available only the required information and is less time-consuming in making decisions.
2. To the top executives, information technology provides fast and accurate insurance marketing informations.
3. The operation and design of the system is handled by specialists, who gather information's and deal with it to meet the desired objectives.
4. It facilitates in taking suitable and quick decisions promptly.
5. To ensure to prepare an error-file for updating.
6. It provides the latest status of the master record resulting in happy customers, confident employees and above all maintenance of policy master files with high degree of purity and consistency.
7. To ensure better and prompt customer servicing.
8. It facilitates actively involved in routine work design and the work process.
9. It enables the employees acquiring multiple skills and getting empowered to deal with all type of situations.
10. It helps to achieve the maximum overall efficiency in all areas of its activities.

Moduling Systems

Office automation is changing the equipment and work habits of today's end users. Of course, none of us would like to work in an office where all information processing activities are done manually. Office automation systems are computer based information systems that collect, process, store and transmit electronic messages, documents and other form of communications among individuals, work groups and organisations.

For better and prompt customer servicing, LIC has a multi-channel approach of using information technology taking the optimum benefits of the latest technological advantages. The following modules are used:

1. Front End Application Programs
2. New Business Module
3. Cash Counter Module
4. Policy Servicing Module
5. Net Working.

1. Front End Application Programmes

The development of networking has been a landmark in the world of computers. A module is a representation of a real-world element (such as object, concept or event) or a group of elements and the relationships among them. Modules help us frame our thinking about items in the world. The field of life insurance also uses many modules. Modules may be classified in many ways. One way concerns how general or specific the modules are. General Modules that can be applied to a wide variety of settings, whereas specific modules are those that apply to a specific situations. All the 2048 Branches of LIC are equipped with in house developed programs covering all policy servicing aspects to give prompt computerised services from new policy introduction, acceptance of renewal premium, revivals, loans etc. to final claim settlement.

2. New Business Module

Organisation face problems during their operations and come across opportunities which could be converted into profitable solutions. Whenever there is an opportunity and/or problem in the existing system or when a system is being developed for the first time, the organisations considers designing a new system for information processing. Accordingly New Business Module aims to redesign the various activities into one integrated process of Branch New Business Department and thereby to shorten the turn-around/response time. The New Business Module generates the following outputs:

a. Proposal Introduction Register
b. New Business Adjustment Sheet
c. New Business Adjustment Sheet-For SSS/GSS
d. Agent's Introduction and completion Register
e. Agent's and Development Officer's Index Card
f. Policy Bonds
g. First Premium Receipt
h. MIS statements, Medical Examiners Bill

i. Newly created policy Master records

J. First/FYR premium commission Transaction

k. Proposal Deposit Schedule and List of pending proposals.

3. Cash Counter Module

Cash Counter Module aims to redesign the process of services at cash counter. Instead of the current practice of issuing preprinted receipts, receipts are generated on-line, thereby, eliminating the need to issue special premium receipts etc. and use multiple stationary formats. The system prints cashbooks, facilitates reconciliation of cheque and cash totals and dispenses with manual posting of premiums in ledger and obviously invoice posting and related tasks would not be required. The cash counter module takes care of the following items of income:

a. Renewal premium

b. Proposal Deposit

c. Policy Deposit

d. SSS Collection

e. Loan repayment and Loan interest

f. Miscellaneous receipts

g. Revenue stamps reconciliation lists

h. List of premia received through collecting Bank.

4. Policy Servicing Module

The business function of insurance marketing is concerned with planning, promotion and sale of insurance products in existing markets and the issue of new products and new markets to better serve present and potential customers. Thus, insurance marketing performs vital functions in the operation of LIC. Customer Service Strategy Module has been catalyst in the development of insurance information technology.

The objective of this module is to enable policy-servicing department, in particular, to handle expeditiously the most common requests. For example,

a. Change of Address

b. Revival Quotation

c. Policy Status Reports

d. Surrender Value Quotation

e. History of accounting transactions under a policy

f. Exit Transaction on:

Surrenders, Foreclosures, Cancellantions, Transfer outs, Death claims, Transfers to SSS.

The first policy service Info Centre was commissioned at Mumbai in March 2002. The centre is equipped with state of the art technology and manned by trained persons. People desiring any information regarding their life insurance needs and about their policies, can get the same by calling the Info Centre telephone number.

5. Networking

The Internet and the Worldwide Web are the latest in the series of milestones that mark the progress of technology. Ranking on par with discovery of fire, the invention of the wheel, the development of the steam engine and the proliferation of telephone lines — the advent of the worldwide web promises to change the way human beings communicate, educate, entertain and do business in a way that is perhaps unprecedented in the history of the human race. The term Internet refers to "consists of a huge number of computers connected together as a gigantic network."

LIC's wide area network covers 100 Divisional centres connecting about 1500 branches through a Metro Area Network. It is expected to cover all the remaining branches by the end of this year. This helps the customer to pay his insurance premium in any of the Branches connected to the network. The customer can get a status report on his policies in these branches as well as quotations for revival, loan and surrender. The Metro Area Network infrastructure also helps in various officies talking to each other through hotlines at no extra cost. The same infrastructure will be leveraged for setting up of call centres for customers to contact LIC.

Advantages of Information Technology

(1) Information Technology helps the management by providing necessary informations for effective decision making.

(2) It assists the executives to select a alternative course of actions and then provide feedback on the success of the implemented decisions.

(3) Information systems can help managers to exercise their effective control with in the organisation. They also monitor the strategic performance of the organisation and its overall direction.

(4) It helps to increase the operational efficiency of the concern, i.e., performing routine tasks better, faster and cheaper.

(5) It provides better insurance services to customers or clients and good enough to take care of customers satisfaction.

(6) It helps to keeping accurate financial and non-financial records of insurance companies up-to-date.

(7) It facilitates more effective communication's system and reduce the costs of creating, reviewing, revising etc.

(8) It helps to increase productivity of executives, development officiers and agents.

(9) It helps in assessing the viability of an insurance product and making a visible marketing commitment.

(10) It helps to know about competitive edge in the market with diversified product launch by competitors.

Questions

1. Explain the important objectives and various schemes of LIC Housing Finance Ltd.
2. What is meant by Mutual Fund?
3. What do you understand by LIC Mutual Fund and its importance?
4. Explain briefly the types of LIC Mutual Fund Scheme.
5. Explain the role of LIC Mutual Fund in the national economy.
6. What are the objectives of Information Technology in LIC?
7. What do you understand by Information Technology in LIC?
8. Write short notes on:
   a. Individual Housing Schemes.
   b. Non-Individual Housing Schemes.
   c. LIC Mutual Fund.
   d. Open–Ended Fund Scheme.
   e. Close–Ended Fund Scheme.
   f. Front End Application Programs.
9. Discuss the advances against Life Insurance Policies.
10. Discuss about LIC Housing Finance Ltd.
11. What are the benefits of LIC's Mutual Funds Scheme?
12. What are the factors which determine the LIC's Mutual Funds?
13. Discuss the Moduling Systems used in LIC.

PART V : ROLE OF DEVELOPMENT OFFICERS AND INSURANCE AGENTS

Chapter 17

Role of Development Officer

Introduction

The Development Officer is born, but not made. It is true to a certain extent, Development Officers are very important in the modern ever-widening insurance market by making distribution of insurance products easy and smooth. They create time, place and possession utility. Development officers concentrate their effort on insurance products through agents. He has real concern and care for the agent. He has to improvise a lot and find his own style of operation, draft his own plans, devise his own strategies for the development insurance business.

The role and importance of the Development Officer for the growth of insurance business are discussed briefly.

Importance of Development Officer:

In the present day, the Development Officer plays an important part in the growth of insurance business. The Development Officer is th immediate friend, philosopher and guide to the agent. The present e liberalisation of insurance business, is one of anticipating of high demar The insurance market expands along with high competition. This ma selling of insurance products difficult and a complex factor in the face competition. The expansion of the insurance market and grow competition etc., make the role of a development officer very importar

Development Officers by virtue of their specialisation, experience and contract, can perform the insurance marketing functions more economically and effectively than the insurance executives. The Development Officer has to work as the 'eye and ear' for the insurance companies. He is the creator of insurance demand.

To capture the new insurance market, Development Officers encourage savings among the public. In order to achieve the organisation objectives, the Development Officer has to bear testimony to the doctrine of insurance by appointing agents, appealing or advertising about various insurance schemes issued by the Insurance Company to meet the needs of the entire public. To fulfil these objectives, a Development Officer organising a team of agents performs the functions through them. Because of these reasons his role and responsibilities are of prime importance.

Duties of Development Officers

Performance of a function or service by an individual is called duty; activities that an individual is required to perform are a duty to him. Authority is a right or power required to perform a job on the basis of duty assigned to one. The Development Officer is like an authorised person who is empowered to do the assigned job. The various duties of the Development Officer can be discussed under the following heads:

I. Appointing Agents

An important duty of a Development Officer is to find or select suitable persons to work as agents. Appointing agents is an art of acknowledging the potentiality in the other and accepting the fact that no one can achieve everything being an island. Thus, the Development Officer should make an arrangement for appointing suitable persons on the basis of their educational qualifications, abilities, experience, written test and interviews etc.

II. Training of Agents

The training programmes are organised procedure methods through which knowledge as well as skill, for a definite purpose is acquired. By training, an agent can increase knowledge in an insurance field. The agent is not born but can be made effective through training.

Thus, the Development Officer should give training or repeated training to the agents. This is essential to keep the agents, with up-to-date knowledge, in respect of new and latest insurance products. Training is a systematic approach which gives scope for improvement.

III. Motivation of Agents

Agents are the backbone of an insurance business. A good agent makes poor selling insurance products into a progressive one. The success or failure of an insurance company depends upon the ability and initiation of insurance agents. The will and willingness to work is a matter as it is a motivation factor. Thus, the Development Officer should perform the following duties with regard to motivation of agents.

(1) Development Officer should help the agent to meet his physiological, safety and social needs.

(2) He should arrange conventions and meetings with agents for exchange of ideas and opinions.

(3) Development Officer should give a proper recognition and honour to his agents. This will greatly encourage the agents to do more hard work.

(4) He should give satisfactory solutions to the agent's problems or discuss them to arrive at satisfactory solutions.

(5) He should give a favourable report to the Branch Managers about the agent's abilities and experience for promoting his remuneration, status, and self respect etc.

(6) If necessary, the Development Officer should permit the agent to do his job in his own pattern.

IV. Fixing the Targets

In addition to appointing and training the agents, fixing the targets are the important duties of the Development Officer. A few of them are:

(1) Find out opportunity in the working area for fixing the targets.

(2) Find out the capabilities of agents according to the targets.

(3) Estimating the facilities and time allotment to the agents for determination of targets.

(4) Evaluate position and degree of competition prevailing in the insurance markets for fixing the targets.

(5) Prospecting, i.e., searching for new insurance market for estimating the targets.

(6) Allocating of agents and fixing the targets.

V. Duties of Communication

(1) He must arrange for the display of new schemes issued by th insurance company.

(2) He must provide information to the Branch Manager and Agents–Co–ordination.

(3) He should fully inform the agents about the Insurance Company, Insurance Products, Policies and Procedures etc.

(4) He should keep all the records for demonstrations.

(5) Arrange for effective advertising and publicity.

(6) He must inform the agents regarding day to day activities.

VI. Field Supervision

(1) He should know whether the agent is doing his job in the best way.

(2) Find out deficiencies if any in the field.

(3) Make suggestions for further improvement to the agents for development of insurance business.

(4) Check the procedure of fixing the targets for agents.

(5) To evaluate the performance of the agents.

(6) Provide spot motivation to agents.

(7) To study and secure maximum coverage of the insurance markets.

(8) He should compare the performance of agents and business opportunity.

VII. Achieving the Targets

(1) He should assist the agents in the sale of insurance products (insurance schemes).

(2) He should handle any complaints from the agents and policy holders.

(3) He should help the agents in planning the market campaign to achieve the targets.

(4) He should encourage the agents for sales promotion activities.

(5) To achieve the targets, he should be continuously working with agents.

(6) Selecting the right persons and approaching them as much as possible.

(7) He should follow an efficient monitoring mechanism for achieving the targets.

Characteristics or the Qualities of a Successful Development Officer

Quality of a successful Development Officer are the sum total of the impression made on people with whom one comes into contact. The impression is the result of many qualities that one possesses. There are a number of qualities which make a Development Officer successful. To become a successful Development Officer, he must master all the traits. Quality of a successful Development Officer are based on the following factors, such as personality of a Development Officer, knowledge of the insurance products, fixing the targets, planning the work, knowledge of the agents and their performance etc.

The following are some of the important qualities of a Development Officer. We discuss them in brief.

1. Quick Action

A Development Officer must be alert and quick in action. He has to face many prospects of different temperaments. He must have the mentality to face any situation and be ready to answer any questions. He should not be an absent-minded man. He must have quick thought of answering. What to say? how to tell? how to tackle the situation? etc., without throwing away the agents and policy holders.

2. Imagination

Imagination is a key to success in handling agents and selling insurance products. If one possesses a rich imagination, it is a great help in solving problems. He must have a creative mind.

3. Self Confidence

A confident man never fails. He has to have the confidence in his work, capacity and power. Confidence makes him optimistic and enthusiastic. He can meet any situation in the insurance product line. He engages or talks with agents, makes them believe and the agents act on his suggestions. Confidence makes him to meet any situation with courage. Experience and knowledge are the base for confidence.

4. Enthusiasm

It makes the work of a Development Officer pleasant. Enthusiastic talk is always listened to by prospects. It gains interest and confidence of agents and in turn more insurance business, thereby savings and investment enhancement, apart from satisfaction of the insurance company and entire public.

5.Initiative

A Development Officer must have initiative. He must learn the tricks of his insurance trade and must have the knowledge of various schemes of insurance products. An active initiator is a self starter. His job can be successfully carried out. He must have skill and be able to face and tackle situations intelligently.

6. Observation

A Development Officer should have a keen observation. He must have up-to-date knowledge about different types of insurance products, assignment, nomination, settlement of claims, changes in rules and regulations, attitude of the competitors and Government etc. With all the latest information, he can easily make suggestions to insurance agents and help them in achieving their targets.

7. Courtesy

Using polite and courteous words, a Development Officer can turn a prospect into an agent. Courtesy in dealing with agents, by using pleasing words like 'thank you', 'please', 'excuse me' etc., will win the heart of the insurance agents.

8. Tactfulness

When a delicate situation is faced, a tactful Development Officer deals with it in a proper way, in time and in an appropriate manner. He always tries to avoid unwarranted happenings. Through tactfulness, one can avoid obstacles, troubles, calamities etc.

9. Helpfulness

He must have a helping attitude whenever agents are in need of information. The Development Officer must expose the merits and demerits of the topic relating to insurance products.

10. Co-operation

Co-operative attitude is essential for the success of a Development Officer. He must co-operate with the insurance agents. Progress of insurance company depends on the mutual co-operation of all the employees.

11. Determination

A Development Officer must make constant effort and have patience in his profession to improve further. It is the will to succeed. He must stick to his profession. Practice makes the man perfect. Ceaseless practice, as a game, a player or a professional wrestler, makes the Development Officer to come up to the top.

12. Sincerity

It is an added quality. He must be sincere towards his assigned duties. By sincerity, one can win friends, enroll new customers, retain old ones and win similar other favours. Dependability is increased through sincerity.

13. Integrity

It denotes honesty, trust and purity. Trust talks and behaviour of a Development Officer must be believed, trusted, honoured and agreed by the insurance agents; thus agents and policy holders are satisfied. This is more essential for the progress of the insurance business and for keeping good relations with agents and the public.

14. Courage

This is the quality that enables one to meet danger without giving way to fear. One must have enough bravery or boldness. In insurance business, there arise various situations, such as happening of tactless deals, unfulfilled promises, errors committed, carelessness shown etc. In all these situations, a Development Officer should not fear but must face them courageously and frankly.

15. Self Management

Everyone works to achieve an aimed target of insurance business. A self-governed Development Officer can easily achieve his target through his agents. This is because he plans his work in advance and works according to the plan. Such a Development Officer finds enough time and has a feeling of self-assurance.

Questions

1. What do you understand by a Development Officer?
2. Explain the Role of a Development Officer in insurance business in India.
3. What are the important duties of a Development Officer?
4. What are the essential characteristics required for a successful Development Officer?
5. Explain the importance of a Development Officer in insurance business.

Chapter 18

Role of Insurance

Introduction

Numerous changes are captivating the consumers in the Financial Market, Banks, Mutual Funds and Financial Institutions that are increasing their presence in new areas. Financial planners and consultants are emerging to offer a variety of services in a number of places. Insurance industry itself is subjected to a closer scrutiny at public level.

The growth of insurance business to a large extent will be dependent on the skills and the ability of the well trained agents to attract the public to its fold. It is the responsibility of the industry to strengthen the hands of the agents to handle the problems linked with increasing complexity of insurance products, rapid changes in the market place scenario, sophistication etc.

Meaning and Definition of Agents

The term 'Agent' has a wider application than the meaning used loosely in insurance practice to describe one who introduces business to the insurer.

Sec. 182 of the Indian Contract Act defines the word 'Agent' and 'Principal'. An agent is a person employed to do any act for another or to represent another in dealing with a third person. The person for whom such act is done or who is so represented is called the principal.

In insurance industry, the term 'agent' is ordinarily applied to a person engaged by the insurer to procure new business.

Under Section 183 of the Act, any person who has reached the age of maturity according to the law to which he is subject and who is of sound mind can employ an agent. Sec. 184 provides that as between the principal and third person, any person may become an agent.

According to the Insurance Act, 1938 defines "Insurance Agent" as insurance agent licensed under Section 42 being an individual who receives or agrees to receive payment by way of commission or other remuneration in consideration of his soliciting or procuring insurance business including business relating to the continuance, renewal or revival of policies of insurance.

Who can become or Agent?

A person is eligible for an agent or can be appointed as an agent if he :

1. is a citizen of India.
2. is at least 18 years of age on the day of appointment
3. has not been found to be of unsound mind by a court or competent jurisdiction
4. has not been found guilty of criminal misappropriation
5. possess the minimum educational qualification of a pass of 12th.

Recruitment and Selection of Agents

Recruitment is concerned with the identification of sources from where the personnel can be employed and motivating them to offer themselves for the employment. Selection takes care of choosing the most suitable personnel for employment. In other words recruitment and selection are the indentification of source of manpower supply.

In the Insurance industry, appointing agents is an art of acknowledging the potentiality in the other and accepting the fact that no one can achieve everything by being an island.

Sources of Recruitment of Agents: Normally, insurance companies consider the following sources to be identified for recruitment of their agents.

(1) Advertisement

(2) Employment Agencies

(3) Public Employment Agencies

(4) Private Employment Agencies

(5) Life Insurance Agency Career

(6) Colleges, Clubs and Other Educational Institutions

(7) On Campus recruitment

(8) Employee recommendation

(9) Labour Unions

(10) Gate Hiring.

Selection of Agents: The selection process involves a number of steps. The basic solicit maximum possible informations about the candidate to ascertain their suitability for appointment as agent. As per Insurance Regulatory Authority norms, the following standard section process has been adopted by the Insurance Companies for selection of professional agents.

(1) Screening the Applications

(2) Selection Tests

(3) Interviews

(4) Checking of References

(5) Physical Examination

(6) Approval by the Appropriate Authority

(7) Placement.

Training of Agents

The term training is concerned with imparting specific skills for particular purposes. According to Flippo training is defined as "the act of increasing the knowledge and skills of an employee for doing a particular job."

In Insurance, the necessary knowledge, skill and attribute are acquired through systematic training and thereby making an agent capable of rendering valuable service to the entire community for reward and satisfaction.

The importance of training an insurance agent, lies in developing his personality through regular planning, prospecting and good work habits.

Training Methods: The following training methods have been adopted by the insurance companies for making an agent capable of rendering valuable service to the insurance company and to the policy holders.

1. On-the-Job Training

(a) Sharing experience

(b) Coaching

(c) Under-study

(d) Special lecturers

(e) Carrier agent schemes
(f) Vestible school
(g) Systematic training programmes
(h) Time management
(i) Arranging group meetings
(j) Narrating experiences.

2. Off-the-Job Training

(a) Special courses and lectures
(b) Conferences
(c) Case analysis
(d) Role playing
(e) Brain storming
(f) Sensitive training
(g) Transactional Analysis
(h) Field force analysis.

Duties of the Agents

The duties of the agent clearly reveal their importance in the insurance business. While performing their duties, they render the following valuable services to the insurance company, policy holders, Government and the society.

The following are the duties of the agents:

(1) He should perform his duties in order to achieve the objectives of the insurance companies.

(2) An agent should develop a close relationship with policy holders and the Development Officer.

(3) The agent should create mutual trust between each other, i.e., policy holders and insurers.

(4) An agent should render continuous service to the policy holders.

(5) The agent should give personal help and guidance relating to savings and investment plan of the policy holders.

(6) The agent should motivate the policy holders to renew the policy in case the policy lapses.

(7) An agent should help the policy holders in emergency for a loan or surrendering the policy.

(8) The agent should help the policy holder for appointment of a nominee or for the execution of an assignment.

(9) Death claim cheques should be personally delivered by the agent.

(10) He should do the market research and establish contacts with industries and institutions to explain various schemes of insurance companies and tax benefits granted by the Central Government.

(11) He should be ready to solve any servicing problems of existing policy holders.

(12) He should explain his ways of prospecting servicing and record keeping in the branch meeting.

(13) The agent must act with reasonable care and skill and must comply exactly with any instructions given to him.

(14) Implement advertising about various insurance schemes in consultation with the Development Officer.

(15) An agent should make plan and organise for implementing various policies issued by the insurance companies.

(16) Feed back information should be given to the Development Officer and Branch Manager about insurance market potential.

(17) He should achieve the targets before the fixed period.

Code of Conduct for Agent

According to the Insurance Act, provisions have been laid down for a Code of Conduct for Agent. These include:

(a) Disclosing the licence to the prospect on demand.

(b) Explaining all available options to the prospect.

(c) Explaining the nature of information required in the Proposal Form.

(d) Impress upon the prospect and the need to disclose all information.

(e) Informing the insurer about any adverse habits and material facts of the persons to be insured.

(f) Revealing to the prospect the commission that he is likely to receive, if asked for.

(g) Advising policy holders to effect nomination.

(h) Not interfering with the proposals introduced by other insurance agents.

(i) Not demanding or receiving share of proceeds under an insurance contract.

Rights of the Agents

The following are the rights of the Agent:

(1) He can issue Renewal Notices on behalf of insurers directly.

(2) He can give receipts for premiums collected which are remitted to the office.

(3) He can introduce business on behalf of the insurers.

(4) He can collect premiums at the homes of the policy holders and obtain new business.

(5) He is entitled to the agreed payment (commission) for his duties.

(6) He is entitled to receive reimbursement of any payment properly made on behalf of his insurers.

Essential Qualities Required for a Successful Agent

The success of the agent depends upon his ability in attending to the varying needs and objectives of the insurance company and the community. A successful agent requires a number of qualities and personal traits on his part in the discharge of his duties and responsibilities, such as personal aptitude, enthusiasm, foresight, tactics, patience, business morality, firmness and courage etc. Besides, there are certain other requirements for an efficient agent. They are:

(1) Every agent should be as a resource of the insurance company.
(2) He has to be mentally prepared to face hazards of the profession.
(3) He must know the rules and regulations governing the profession.
(4) He has to come in the field fully prepared with self confidence to meet any shocks
(5) He must have a background of planning and prospecting, i.e., constant search and research activity in the insurance field.
(6) He must have good work habits, job knowledge and punctuality.
(7) He must take special efforts for achieving targets.
(8) He must have good knowledge the insurance market.
(9) He must be intelligent. He must properly utilise his time.
(10) He must create goodwill and have personal touch with policy holders and the insurers.
(11) He must be hard working with dedication.
(12) He must create credibility in his profession.
(13) He must be able to understand the insurance market.
(14) He must identify the needs of policy holders.
(15) He must render service to the needs of the policy holders with insurance products.
(16) He must be ready to provide comprehensive life insurance services to the community at large.

(17) He must be ready to solve the servicing problems of existing policy holders.

(18) He must have adequate knowledge about various schemes of insurance business, principles, rules and regulations, tables in current use, various branches of coverage and closely allied business etc.

Termination of Agents

An agent can be terminated in the following circumstances:

(a) In case of cancellation or non renewal of the agent's licence.

(b) In case of permanent incapacity of an agent.

(c) In case of an agent's conviction for any criminal misappropriation.

(d) In case of an agent involved for any criminal breach of trust.

(e) In case of an agent involved in cheating or forgery.

(f) An agent can be terminated by the insurer in terms of the appointment of the agency.

(g) In case of an agent's non-performance of minimum business expected from him.

(h) In case of any violation of the code of conduct.

Questions

1. What do you understand by the term Insurance Agent?
2. Explain the role of insurance agent in insurance business in India.
3. What are the rights and duties of insurance agents?
4. What are the essential qualities required for a successful agent?
5. Outline a suitable selection process of insurance agent for insurance companies?
6. Write short notes on:
   (a) Termination of an Insurance Agent.
   (b) Training of agents.
   (c) Definition of insurance agent.
   (d) Recruitment and selection of agent.
7. Who can become an agent?

PART VI : GENERAL INSURANCE BUSINESS

Chapter 19

General Insurance Business and Role of GIC

Introduction

Law Relating to General Insurance:

The Insurance Act 1938 was a well thoughtout legislation and was passed to perform the control of working and activities of the companies carrying on the business relating to life, marine, fire and accidents. But the Act has seen many amendments, since it was passed, required from experience in the implementation of the Act. In 1963, the Marine Insurance Act was passed to regulate the contract of marine insurance. In 1971, the Government nationalised the insurance business and passed a General Insurance Business (Nationalisation) Act in 1972. A provision was made in the 1972 Act relating to General Insurance (Fire, Marine and Miscellaneous) business being taken over by the Central Government.

General Insurance Business (Nationalisation) Act, 1972

Objectives of the Act

(1) To provide for the acquisition and transfer of shares of Indian insurance companies and undertakings of other existing insurers.

(2) To serve better the needs of the economy by securing the development of general insurance business in the best interests of the community.

(3) To ensure that the operation of the economic system does not result in the concentration of wealth to the common detriment.

(4) For the regulation and control of such business and for matters connected therewith or incidental thereto.

Establishment of General Insurance Corporation of India (GIC)

The General Insurance Business (Nationalisation) Act 1972 provides that the Central Government shall form a Government Company in accordance with the provisions of the Companies Act 1956 to be known as General Insurance Corporation of India for the purpose of superintending, controlling and carrying on the business of general insurance.

The objectives of GIC are to carry on the general insurance business other than life, such as accident, fire etc. to aid and achieve the subsidiaries to conduct the insurance business and to help the conduct of investment strategy of the subsidiaries in an efficient and productive manner.

Sources of Funds

Its sources of funds are paid-up capital, reserves, profits and premium income. It can also like the LIC, operate in the money and capital markets, earn on underwriting and making of long term loans and investments. Its investment policy is governed by the Insurance Act like the LIC and its investments are accordingly spread in specified proportions in Central and State Government Securities, semi government bonds, debentures, preference shares and equity shares of companies, deposits with companies and other loans and advances.

The authorised capital of Rs. 75 crores of the corporation out of which Rs. 5 crore is the subscribed capital wholly contributed by the Central Government.

GIC with its Subsidiaries

General Insurance was nationalised by the passing of the General Insurance Business (Nationalisation) Act 1972, under which all the shares of the Indian insurance companies on the appointed day (Jan.1, 1973) vested first in the Central Government and after that in the General Insurance Corporation of India. On nationalisation, General Insurance Corporation was formed with four subsidiaries, viz.,

(1) New India Assurance Co. Ltd. — Head Office — Mumbai

(2) United India Insurance Co. Ltd.— Head Office — Chennai

(3) Oriental Insurance Co. Ltd.— Head Office — New Delhi

(4) National Insurance Co. Ltd.— Head Office — Kolkata

All general business is transacted through the above four subsidiaries.

insurance business is now under the ownership and control of Central Government.

Organisational Structure

The GIC is a holding company with the predominant function of regulating and controlling the operations of its subsidiaries. It concentrated on reinsurance. Direct underwriting of insurance by it was restricted to aviation and crop insurance. The four subsidiaries involved themselves in direct underwriting of insurance business, competing with each other on an all India basis.

This structure was in contrast to the other sectors, which were nationalized. The aviation, the life insurance businesses, which were nationalised in the Fifties, saw the creation of monoliths to carry out the operations. Nationalisation of banks saw a different pattern emerging with individual banks being allowed to carry on with their identities. Perhaps, the above two experiences led to the Government deciding on a third pattern when general insurance business was nationalised.

The Organisational structure of General Insurance Corporation and its four subsidiaries has a four tier structure. They are as follows:

(a) Head Office (or) Central Office

(b) Zonal Office

(c) Divisional Office

(d) Branch Office

The Central Office performs the activities relating to investments, frames and administers the rules and regulations of the corporation. In the Branch Office, 90% of the functions relate to policy holders. There are ten Zonal Offices and more than 1,000 Divisional Offices, which are established on the basis of geographical areas. They discharging their co-ordinating functions and executive functions relating to the Central Office and Zonal Offices.

The following chart explains this clearly

Organisational Chart

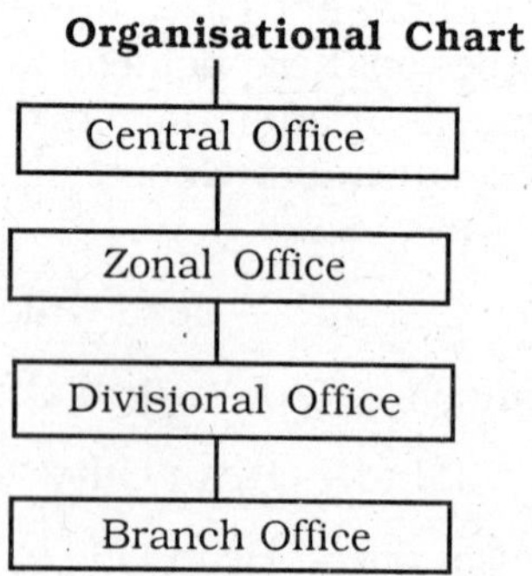

The primary functions of Divisional Offices relate to development of business and its administration including supervision of branches, if any, in their jurisdiction. The development function involves appointment of inspectors and agents and marketing, planning and procurement business. The administrative function involve issue of policies, settlement of claims, maintenance of accounts and general administration, e.g., personnel, establishment etc.

The functions of branch offices are similar except that they are not empowered to appoint inspectors and settle claims, except motor own damage, cattle claims and other claims within certain limits. Broadly speaking, the functions of the branches would include development of business direct and through inspectors and agents, collection of premium, issue of receipts, cover notes, policies etc., minor payments like commissions, rent etc., and maintenance of accounts in that respect and coordination and control over inspectors.

Functions of GIC

The functions of the Corporation shall include:

(a) carrying on of any part of the general insurance business, if it thinks it desirable to do so.

(b) aiding, assisting and advising the acquiring companies in the matter of setting up of standards of conduct and sound practice in general insurance business.

(c) rendering efficient service to holders of policies of general insurance.

(d) advising the acquiring companies in the matter of controlling their expenses including the payment of commission and other expenses.

(e) advising the acquiring companies in the matter of investing of their funds.

(f) issuing directions to acquiring companies in relation to the conduct of general insurance business.

(g) issuing directions and encouraging competition among the acquiring companies in order to render their services more efficiently.

Progress of General Insurance Business

In India, the general insurance business has grown tremendously over the last three decades. Accordingly, the public sector general Insurers – National Insurance, New India Assurance, Oriental Insurance and United India Insurance which had been the sole players in the market for over 25 years.

As a result of liberalisation, came with the setting up of the Insurance Regulatory Authority (IRA) and then the Insurance Regulatory and Development Authority (IRDA), which culminated in the entry of private players on the scenario, till then a state monopoly. Today, there are 11 private sectors operating in the general insurance market. The progress of general insurance business can be measured on the basis of gross premium income and net premium income during the period from 1997-98 to 2001-2002. The term gross premium refers to the total premium earned from the customs. Insurers normally avail reinsurance on their policies to hedge against huge losses impacting their financials. For this, they pay the reinsurance a portion of the premium earned. On the other hand, the term net premium refers to the premium after paying premium to reinsurers for their reinsurance protection. The table given below shows that the growth of premium income of Indian non-life insurers [including private sector] from 1997-98 to 2001-2002.

Growth of General Insurance Business from 1997-98 to 2001-2002

Year	Gross Direct Premium Rs. in Million	% to Total	Net Premium Income	% to Total Rs. in Million
1997-98	73,571	16.52	80,856	16.08
1998-99	84,025	18.11	91,575	18.22
1999-2000	93,634	21.16	99,822	19.85
2000-2001	1,02,721	23.21	1,07712	21.42
2002-2003	88,540	20.00	1,22,731	24.42
Total	4,42,491	100	5,02,696	100

Source: IRDA Journal

Source: (The Indian Insurance Industry (Non-Life) purchased by Interlink Reinsurance Consultant Pvt.Ltd., 2003)

The above table shows that the premium earned by the public sector insurers and private sector insurers. It is seen that the progress of both gross direct premium and net premium income is regular and constantly increasing. The percentage of gross direct premium income has increased from 16.52% in 1997-98 to 18.11% in 1998-99, and further to 21.26% in 1999-2000. It has increased to 23.21% in 2000-2001 and declined to 20.01% in 2002-03. On the other hand, the rate of net premium income as percentage to total net premium income has increased from 16.08% in 1997-98 to 18.22% in 1998-99. It has further increased to 19.85% in 1999-2000. Similarly, it has increased to 21.42% in 2000-2001 and further to 24.42% in 2001-2002. Thus, it is clear that there is positive growth in general insurance market. The above findings indicate that the high proportion of net premium to gross premium reveals high security and financial health.

Business Growth of GIC

On nationalisation, GIC was formed with four subsidiaries, *viz.*,

(1) New India Assurance Co. Ltd.

(2) United India Insurance Co. Ltd.

(3) Oriental Insurance Co. Ltd. and

(4) National Insurance Co. Ltd. All business is transacted through these four subsidiaries. General Insurance Corporation is the controlling body. Except crop insurance, aviation business of Indian Airlines and Air India, GIC does not involve itself directly in insurance business. Each of the subsidiaries has about 1,000 divisional offices and 40,000 operating offices spread all over India. The total manpower employed by the industry is 86,000, The main income and expenditure of the insurance companies is as follows. Income from (a) premium (b) interest on investment and other income. Expenditure on (a) claims (insured) (b) establishment and other expenses (c) commission to agents (d) dividends to shareholders. and 2002-2003 and number. of polices achieved in 2002-2003.

In 1970, the total premium income of 108 insurance companies was Rs. 105 crores. Today, the four nationalised insurance company's premium income totals up to Rs. 10,000 crores. The GIC and its four subsidiaries' gross premium and profit before tax from 1990-91 to 1998-99 are given below.

Statement of Gross Premium and Profit (1986-90 - 2000-01)

Year	Gross Premium Rs. in Crores	Profit (Before tax) Rs. in Crores
1989-90	2279	371
1990-91	2931	482
1991-92	3503	669
1992-93	4070	779
1993-94	4766	1082
1994-95	5271	503
1995-96	6377	8311
1996-97	7348	1084
1997-98	8066	1623
1998-99	9158	1467
1999-2000	9982	1153
2000-01	10772	729

Market share of the insurance business of GIC and its four subsidiaries is given below:

Company	Market share %
United	25
Oriental	22
National	20
New India	32
GIC	1

[Source: K.N. Bhandari "*Agenda for Insurance*" Economic Times 31, Jan 1999.]

Despite this, India remains one of the least insured countries in the world. While India ranks tenth in terms of corporate presence among the 78 industrial nations in the world, in terms of insurance covers it rank 51st.

The GIC not only does the mobilizing of resources and redistribute the funds to those who suffered losses but also as per the government guidelines the funds are invested for industrial development, social oriented sectors such as housing sector and State and Central Government Securities. In 1997, out of the total investment of Rs. 14,392 crores, the GIC subsidiaries invested Rs. 2,648 crores in Industry, Rs. 856 crores in State and Central Government Securities and Rs. 1,073 crores in housing sector.

Presently, the insurance industry contributes only 0.55% to GDP against 4% to 5% in developed countries like the USA, Canada and Japan etc. It is expected that current level of premium of 2 billion dollars in non-life sector, can easily be around 20 billion dollars in the next 10 years. Market liberalization will also bring new challenges.

The opening up of the insurance sector, therefore, would immensely help the Indian economy, particularly in mobilising substantial amounts of resources which could then be channelled into infrastructure development. But it is also true that insurance companies would command huge funds at their disposal which make reform critics to voice apprehensions for throwing open this sector to the private sector and foreigners, more so because these funds could be utilised to procure equity stake in Indian Companies as has been cone by the LIC and the GIC.

Role of Insurance in International Economy

Insurance plays an important role not only in the national economy but also in the international economy. Marine cargo insurance, for example, provides risks coverage for shippers and importers and the banks which finance international trade. This role becomes all the more important in the context of an active government policy to encourage exports.

Indian insurers operate in more than 30 countries through agencies, branches and subsidiary/associate companies. These operations earn foreign exchange and represent invisible exports. The U.K. insurers, for example, earn more premium overseas than from their domestic operations.

The Indian insurers have also an international presence through an active reinsurance exchange programme with insurers in over 100 countries. Another dimension of international insurance found in regional co-operation is reinsurance. Asian Reinsurance Corporation (of which India is a member) with head quarters in Bangkok, Thailand is one example. Large industrial and infrastructural project set up in India through joint ventures or otherwise with overseas finace need tailor made specialized insurance covers.

Performance of Public Sector and Private Sector Insurers

In an industry like general insurance, premium income growth indicates the efficiency and quality of financial strength of insurance companies. The following table shows the performance of public sector insurers and private sect or insurers of non-life insurance business based on gross direct premium income earned during 2001-2002-2003 and No. of Policies achieved in 2002-2003.

The above table indicates that there had been a significant growth of total gross direct premium income earned by the public sector insurers and private sector insurers went up from 1,22,730.69 millions in 2001-2002 to Rs. 1,42,794.11 millions in 2002-2003. It is seen from the table that the public sector insurers still lead the pack, both in premium and number of policies issued. Among the total insurers, New India has captured a top rank market share holder by 34.20% in 2001-2002 and it has declined to 27.51 % in 2002-2003. The share of gross direct premium income of United India has declined from 22.66% in 2001-2002 to 20.80% in 2002-2003. Similarly, the share of premium income of Oriental Insurance has gone down from 20.35% in 2001-2002 to 19.48% in 2002-2003. On the other hand, in National Insurance, it has increased from 19.87% in 2001-2002 to 20.25% in 2002-2003. During the year 2002-2003, the share of number of policies has been achieved by public sector Insurers — New India 39.55%; United India 22.71%; National Insurance 19.77% and Oriental 19.02% respectively. It is clear indication that the public sector insurers are doing the ensure that their commanding position in the insurance market. At the same time, public sector Insurers face major challenges in the coming days.

In private insurers where the share of total gross direct premium of insurance market accounted from below 1% in 2001-2002 to less than 3% in 2002-2003. The similar trend in number of policies achieved by less than 1% of total number of policies in 2002-2003 has been observed in Private Insurers. This indicates that Private Insurers have began to strengthen their strengths and eliminate their weakness. The growth of the private sector has not hampered the public sector Insurers in their quest for business.

Performance of Public Sector Insurers and Private Sector Insurers of Non-Life business during 2001-02 and 2002-2003						
	Gross Direct Premium					
Insurance Companies Both Public Sectors Insurers & Private Sectors Insurers	2001-2002 Rs. in Millions	% to Total 2002-2003	2002-2003 Rs. in Millions	% to Total	No. of Policies	% to Total
National	24394.05	19.87	28891.59	20.25	8275203	19.77
New India	41980.65	34.20	39290.99	27.51	14461798	34.55
Oriental	24986.36	20.35	27824.11	19.48	7963873	19.02
United India	27814.75	22.66	29712.20	20.80	9506487	22.71
Royal Sundram	711.30	0.57	1817.72	1.27	312339	0.74
TATA AIG	784.57	0.63	2219.29	1.56	183772	0.43
Reliance	774.65	0.63	1849.48	1.29	28631	0.06
ICICI Lambard	705.13	0.57	2141.28	1.49	146559	0.35
IFFCO-TOKIO	271.13	0.22	2152.15	1.50	98293	0.23
Bajaj Allianz	308.10	0.25	2892.84	2.03	819190	1.95
Cholamandalam	NA	NA	147.77	0.10	27133	0.06
HDFC Chubb	NA	NA	94.39	0.07	17562	0.04
ECGe	NA	NA	3760.30	2.64	10779	0.25
Total	122730.69	100	142794.11	100	418511619	100

Performance of Major Business Segments

Market share of the major business segments pertaining to general insurance business and the increase in the activities of the non-life insurance market in India have significantly influenced the development of general insurance business. This is an indicator of the financial strength and solvency of the Insurers. The table given below shows the market share of Public Sector Insurers and Private Sectors Insurers in major non-life business segments during the year 2002-03.

General Insurance: Major Business Segements in 2002-2003

Line of Business	Public Sector Rs.in Crores	% to Total	Private Sector	% to Total	Combined Rs.in Crores	% to Total
Fire	2557	20	412	31.52	2969	21.39
Marine	1123	8.92	83	6.35	1206	8.69
Motors	5038	40	382	29.23	5420	39.06
Engineering	590	4.69	128	9.79	719	5.18
Health	963	7.66	82	6.27	1045	7.53
Others	2301	18.33	220	16.84	2520	18.15
Total	12572	100	1307	100	13879	100

Source : IRDA Journal - 2003

It is seen from the table that the market share of Public Sector Insurers in 2002-2003 has mainly been in major business segments such as Motor Insurance 40%; Fire Insurance 20%; other areas of Insurance 18.33%; Marine Insurance 8.92%; Engineering Insurance 4.69% and Health Insurance 7.66% respectively. Similarly, the market share of Private Sector Insurers during the year 2002-2003 has to be seen against the growth of its market such as Fire Insurance 31.52%; Motor Insurance 29.23%; other areas of Insurance 16.84%; Engineering Insurance 9.79%; Marine Insurance 6.35% and Health Insurance 6.27% respectively. Thus, it is clear indication that the satisfactory performance of both Public Sector Insurers and Private Sector Insurers and their growth are mainly in Motor Insurance, Fire Insurance and other areas of insurance. In areas such as engineering, cargo transit insurance and health insurance, their presence is very low.

Questions

1. Discuss the role of General Insurance Corporation of India in insurance business.
2. Explain the functions of General Insurance Corporation.
3. Explain the features of General Insurance Corporation of India.
4. Describe the administration of General Insurance Corporation.
5. Explain the progress of General Insurance business in India.
6. What are the important types of General Insurance Products or Policies?

Chapter 20

Nature of Marine Insurance Contract

Definition

A contract of marine insurance is defined by the Marine Insurance Act, 1963 as "an agreement whereby the insurer undertakes to indemnify the insured, in the manner and to the extent thereby agreed, against losses incidental to marine adventure. It may cover loss or damage to vessels, cargo, or freight.

An instrument containing the contract of marine insurance is entered into, between the insurer and the assured is called a marine policy or sea policy. The consideration for the policy is called the premium. The insurer in marine insurance is known as the underwriter.

Arnold defines, "Marine insurance as a contract whereby one party for an agreed consideration, undertakes to indemnify the other against loss arising from certain perils and sea risks to which a shipment and other a marine adventure may be exposed during a certain voyage or a certain time".

Characteristics:

1. It is a contract of indemnity
2. It is a contract based upon the utmost good faith
3. Doctrine of Subrogation and Contribution apply

4. A marine policy is invariably subject to average clause
5. All marine insurance contracts are subject to certain express and implied warranties.

Insurable Property

Insurable property means any ship, goods or other moveables exposed to maritime perils Section 2(c). Insurable property is also called the subject matter of insurance. It must be designated in the policy with reasonable certainty.

Marine Adventure

There is a marine adventure, when —

(1) any insurable property is exposed to marine perils,

(2) the earning or acquisition of any freight, passage money, commission, profit or other pecuniary benefit, or the security for any advances, loans or disbursement is endangered by the exposure of insurable property to maritime perils,

(3) any liability to a third party may be insured by the owner of, or other person interested in or responsible for, insurable property by reason of maritime perils Sec.2(d).

Maritime Perils

Maritime perils are also called as "Perils of the Sea". It means the perils consequent on, or incidential to the navigation of the sea, that is to say, perils of the sea, fire, war perils, rovers, thieves, captures, seizures. restraints and detainments of princes and people, jettisons, barratry and any other perils which are either of the like kind or may be designated by the policy. The term "Perils of the Sea" refers only to fortuitous accidents or casualties of the sea, and does not include the ordinary action of the winds and waves.

The following losses have been held to be perils of the sea:

(1) Loss caused because of collision against a sunken rock.

(2) Loss caused because of collision with another ship.

(3) Loss caused because of heating due to the closure of ventilators to prevent the immersion of sea waters.

(4) Loss caused because rats made a hole in the bottom of a ship and sea water entered the ship through the hole and damaged the cargo.

However, perils do not cover

(1) Loss caused by rats

(2) Loss caused to timber by worms

(3) Loss caused by natural action of salt water of the sea

Marine Policy

The instrument in which the contract of insurance is effected is known as the "Marine Policy" or "Sea Policy". It is a document which incorporates the details of terms and conditions on which the contract of insurance is entered into between the parties. A contract of marine insurance is evidenced by the policy and the clauses attached to it. It is the clauses which specify the risk covered, risk excluded and other terms and conditions of insurance.

Contents of Marine Policy: The policy contains the following particulars:

(1) Name of the insured

(2) Policy Number

(3) Sum Assured

(4) Premium

(5) Stamp Duty

(6) Steamer (or) Other Conveyance

(7) Voyage or Journey

(8) Number or Date of Bill Lading or Lorry or Registered Post or Air Freight Receipt (as the case may be)

(9) Interest to be insured

(10) The subject matter insured and the risk insured against

(11) Place where claims are payable

(12) Place of issue of policy and date

(13) Signature of the authorised person signing on behalf of the insurers.

Every Marine Policy must be stamped in accordance with provisions of the Indian Stamp Act.

Essential Elements of Marine Insurance

The marine insurance has the following essential features which are also called fundamental principles of marine insurance.

(1) Fundamental features of general contract

(2) Insurable interest to exist at the time of loss

(3) Utmost Good Faith or *uberrimae fidei*

(4) Contract of indemnity

(5) Subject to Principles of Subrogation and Contribution

(6) Warranties

(7) Proximate Cause

(8) Assignment and Nomination of Policy

(9) Return of Premium.

1. Features of General Contract

A marine insurance policy must fulfill all the essentials of a valid contract, namely offer, acceptance, agreement, competent parties, free consent, lawful consideration and legal object. Here, the insured or proposal may be offered by a ship owner or a cargo owner or a freight receiver. When the insurer accepts their proposal, it becomes an agreement. The insurer is known as "Underwriter". The premium is determined on assessment of the proposal and is paid at the time of the contract.

2. Insurable Interest

The insured must have an insurable interest in the subject matter insured at the time when the loss occurs. It is not necessary that insurable interest must exist at the time of effecting the insurance. According to Marine Insurance Act 1963, it states that "every person has an insurable interest who is interested in a marine adventure."

The following persons have insurable interest in Marine Insurance:

(1) Ship owner

(2) Cargo owner

(3) A creditor who has advanced money on a ship or cargo to the extent of his interest in such ship or cargo

(4) Mortgager

(5) Mortgagee

(6) Master and Crew in respect of their wages

(7) Bottomry bond holder

(8) Person who pays advance freight if freight is recoverable on loss

(9) Shippers and their agents

(10) Persons with defeasible or contingent interest such as the buyer, though the goods may be at seller's risk and though he may have the right to reject the goods

(11) Trustee

(12) Bailee

(13) Insurer ¾ he can reinsure

(14) Assignee of the Bill of Lading.

3. Utmost Good Faith

Marine Insurance is a contract of *Uberrimae fidei* or Utmost Good Faith. The insured must observe utmost good faith in a contract of marine insurance. He must disclose all those relevant facts to the insurer which are likely to affect his willingness to undertake the risk.

If full facts are not disclosed by either party, the contract can be voided by the other party.

4. Contract of Indemnity

The essence of a marine insurance contract is that it is a contract of indemnity. This means that by this contract the underwriter agrees to indemnify the insured against losses by sea risks to the extent of the amount insured. As a result, the insured can recover only the actual loss suffered. He will not be allowed to make a profit of his loss. The insured in return for this undertaking pays an agreed amount known as the premium.

5. Principles of Subrogation and Contribution

The principles of subrogation and contribution are applicable to the marine insurance contract. After meeting the loss agreed, the insurer steps into the shoes of the insured and becomes entitled to all the rights and remedies available to the insured against third persons.

The doctrine of contribution also applies in the case of marine insurance. Where the subject matter has been insured with more than one insurer, each insurer has to meet only the rateable proportion of loss. If he has paid more than his share of loss, he is entitled to recover the excess paid from his co-insurers.

6. Warranties

The principles of warranties applies to a marine insurance contract. According to the Marine Insurance Act, a warranty means a stipulation or term of breach which entitles the insurers to avoid the policy altogether and this is so even though the breach arises through circumstances beyond the control of the warrantor. Warranties may be express or implied.

Express Warranties: Express warranties may be in any form of words from which the intention to warrant is to be inferred. It must be included in or written upon the policy or must be contained in some document referred to in the policy.

The usual express warranties are as follows:

(1) The ship is safe on a particular day

(2) The ship and goods are neutral and shall continue to be so

(3) The ship will proceed to its destination without any deviation

(4) The ship will sail on or before a certain day.

Implied Warranties: There are certain warranties which are implied in every contract of marine insurance unless they are expressly excluded. These are:

(a) Warranty of sea-worthiness

(b) Warranty of non-deviation

(c) Warranty as to the legality of the voyage

(d) Proper documentation of the ship.

(a) Warranty of sea-worthiness: In a voyage policy the insured, at the time of effecting the insurance is supposed to give a warranty of sea worthiness, i.e., the ship concerned is in every respect fit for the voyage on which it is sailing.

The Warranty of sea–worthiness may be:

[a) The ship must be sound as regards her hull.

(b) The gear must be sufficient and must be fully equipped, officered and manned.

(c) She must not be overloaded.

(d) If the voyage is to be performed in stages, the ship must be seaworthy at the commencement of each stage.

(e) Seaworthiness also include cargo-worthiness, it must be fit to carry the cargo.

(b) Warranty of Non-deviation: In the case of a voyage policy where a voyage is contemplated between any two given ports there is an implied warranty of non-deviation on the part of the insured, by which the insured is supposed to give an undertaking, that he shall take the usual route taken by navigators, and shall not deviate there from except in cases where it is excusable by the law. If the ship, without lawful excuse, deviates from the voyage contemplated by the policy, the insured is discharged from liability as from the time of deviation. It is immaterial in such a case that the ship may have regained her route before any loss occurs.

Such a deviation exists:

(a) Where the course of the voyage is specifically designated by the policy, and that course is departed from, or

(b) Where the course of the voyage is not specifically designated by the policy, but the usual and customary course is departed from.

(c) Where several ports of discharge are specified by the policy. The ship must proceed to them in the order designated by the policy; if she does not, there is a deviation.

(d) Where the policy is to ports of discharge within a given area, which are not named, the ship must proceed to them in their geographical order, if she does not, there is a deviation.

When is Deviation excused? Deviation means change of the prescribed route or where no route is prescribed, change of the usual or customary route. One of the implied warranties in a contract of marine insurance is that there should not be deviation. The intention to deviate is immaterial. There must be deviation in fact to discharge the insurer from his liability under the contract.

However, deviation or delay is excused (justified) under the following circumstances:

(a) Where it is authorised by the contract (or)

(b) Where caused by circumstances beyond the control of the master and his employer (or)

(c) Where reasonably necessary for the safety of the ship or subject matter insured (or)

(d) Where reasonably necessary in order to comply with an express or implied warranty (or)

(e) When it is necessary to save life or to help a ship in distress (or)

(f) When it is necessary for containing medical or surgical aid for any person on board the ship (or).

(g) When it is necessary to avoid being captured or destroyed by the enemy of the government.

(h) Where caused by the barratrous conduct of the master or crew if barratry be one of the perils insured against.

(c) Legality of the Voyage: There is an Implied Warranty on the part of the insured that the adventure insured is a lawful one, and that, so far as the assured can control the matter, the adventure shall be carried out in a lawful manner. This warranty implies that the ship must not be used for undertaking any voyage e.g., trading with enemy, smuggling etc.,

(d) Proper Documentation of the Ship: Where there is an Express Warranty that the ship shall be neutral (in the case of a wartime adventure) there is an implied warranty that the ship carries all the papers necessary to prove her neutrality.

7. Proximate Cause

According to the Marine Insurance Act, subject to the provisions of the Act and unless the policy otherwise provides, the insurer is liable for any loss proximately caused by a peril insured against, but subject to as afore said, he is not liable for any loss which is not proximately caused by a peril insured against.

8. Assignment and Nomination of Policy

A marine insurance policy is assignable unless it contains terms expressly prohibiting assignment. It may be assigned either before or after loss. A marine policy may be assigned by indorsement thereon or on other customary manner.

9. Return of Premium

Premium is the consideration for the risk run by the insurers, and if the risk insured against is not run, then the consideration fails, the policy does not attach, and as a consequence the premium paid can be recovered from the insurer. The general principle applicable to the claim for the return of premium is that if the insurers have never been on the risk, they cannot be said to have earned the premium. But where the insurance is voided by the insurers on the ground of breach of warranty, the premium can only be recovered if it is shown there was breach *ab initio.*

Double Insurance

Double insurance arises: Where two or more policies are effected by or on behalf of the assured on the same adventure and interest or any part there of, and the sums assured exceed the indemnity allowed by the Marine Insurance Act, the assured is said to be over insured by double insurance.

According to Section 34, the requisites of double insurance are:

(1) There must be two or more policies.

(2) The policies must be effected by the same assured.

(3) The policies must relate to the same adventure and interest or any part oneward thereof

(4) The sums insured must exceed the indemnity allowed by this Act.

Reinsurance in Marine Insurance Schemes

According to Marine Insurance Act, the insurer under a contract of marine insurance has an insurable interest in his risk, and may reinsure in respect of it. This is called Reinsurance. It is also termed as insurance of insurance.

There are various reasons why an underwriter may deem it prudent to re-insure part or all of a risk for which he has accepted liability. For example, he may find that his commitments on any one vessel or in any locality have become too burdensome. Declarations under open covers or floating policies and acceptances by his agents in other markets may give him an accumulated liability considerably in excess of his usual retention. He may have accepted a line on "all Risk" terms and then desire to reinsure in respect of total loss only. Further, there may be a possibility of placing the risk in some other market at a profit or he may ultimately decide after due consideration that his acceptance of a particular risk was an error of judgment.

The right to re-insure is conferred by the Marine Insurance Act which, it may be seen, gives the original assured no right or interest in respect of the re-insurance unless the policy otherwise provides.

An underwriter may re-insure:

1. Facultative
2. By means of an open cover
3. By means of a re-insurance treaty.

1. Facultative Reinsurance

Facultative re-insurance is the direct reinsurance of individual risks through the medium of a broker in precisely the same way as original insurances are placed. The reinsurance underwriter may fix the rate of premium or, if the re-insurance is affected on the identical conditions of the original policy, he may be content to accept the original premium of the re-insured. The speculative re-insurance of an overdue vessel or a vessel, which is known to have met with some casualty, may be affected in this way.

2. Open Cover Re-insurance

Open cover Re-insurance is often used by underwriters in respect of their cargo business, say, to reinsure their interest on particular voyages, commodities, or types of vessels, Such open covers may be effected on free from particular average conditions at lower rates of premium than the original insurances effected on more comprehensive terms.

3. Re-insurance Treaties

Re-insurance Treaties can be used for either hull or cargo re-insurance.They are generally very elaborate contracts between insurance companies providing for the cession of some proportion of the whole of the re-assured's business to the re-insuring company at the original premiums less an overriding commission.

Whichever of these three methods of re-insurance is employed, the original underwriter has a choice of re-insuring on a first interest basis, a quota-share basis, or an excess basis.

Mutual Insurance:

According to the Marine Insurance Act, mutual insurance is:

(1) Where two or more persons mutually agree to insure each other from marine losses, there is said to be a mutual insurance.

(2) The provisions of the Act relating to the premium do not apply to mutual insurance, but a guarantee, or such other arrangement as may be agreed upon, may be substituted for the premium.

Questions

1. What is a contract of marine insurance? State its essential features.
2. Write short notes on Maritime Perils and Perils of the Sea.
3. Define and explain a contract of marine insurance.
4. Write short notes on insurable interest in connection with marine insurance contract: Who are deemed to have insurable interest in a marine insurance contract?
5. What is warranty in a contract of marine insurance? What are express and implied warranties?
6. What is deviation in a marine insurance? How does it differ from a change of voyage?
7. When is deviation excused?
8. What is marine policy? State its contents.
9. Explain and illustrate the rule of causa proxima in marine insurance.
10. Explain the important characteristics of marine Insurance contract.
11. Define a contract of marine insurance and explain how it differs from other forms of insurance.
12. Discuss fully the implied warranties in a contract of marine insurance.
13. When can the non-compliance with a warranty be excused?
14. What are the perils of the sea?
15. What does seaworthiness of a ship mean?
16. Wrote short notes on:
    (a) Double Insurance
    (b) Assignment of Marine Insurance Policy
    (c) Insurable Interest.

Mini Cases

Case 1. X got his ship insured against losses due to collision. The ship was carrying eatables. On account of collision, the ship was delayed and the eatables were spoiled. Is the insurer liable for this loss to X?

Ans: An insured can recover damages from the insurer only in those cases when (i) the loss has been caused by an insured peril and (ii) the cause has been immediate or proximate to the loss. In the instant case, collision is not the proximate cause of the loss. The loss has been caused because of delay of ship which does not seem to be an insured event. Thus, the insurer is not liable for loss.

Case 2. A ship is insured against loss due to enemy's action. The enemy had sunk a ship in the ocean and the insured ship suffered damage on account of the collision with the sunk ship. Is the insurer liable?

Ans: Yes. Sinking of the ship was due to the enemy's action and the insured ship happened to collide with the ship. Enemy's action is, therefore, a proximate cause of the loss.

Case 3. A cargo of oranges was insured against loss due to collision. The ship actually collided resulting in delay and mishandling of the shipment which made oranges unfit for human consumption. The insurer refuses to admit the claim. Decide.

Ans: In order to make the insurer responsible for loss, it is necessary that the loss should be caused by an insured peril and such peril should be the proximate cause of loss.

In the instant case, after collision of the ship a new and independent cause "delay and mishandling" had arisen resulting in spoilage of oranges. Since this was not an insured peril and, therefore, the insurer could not be held responsible for the loss suffered by the owner of the cargo.

Case 4. A, the owner of a ship by fraudulently representing the ship to be seaworthy induces 'B' an underwriter to insure the ship. Can 'B' obtain the cancellation of the policy?

Ans: A contract of insurance is a contract of "*Uberrimae fidei,* i.e., absolute good faith". It is, therefore, expected from the insured to disclose all facts regarding the subject matter of insurance correctly to the insurer. According to Section 19 of the Marine Insurance Act 1963, if utmost good faith is not observed by any party, the contract may be voided by the other party. Moreover, under Section 22 of the said Act, every material representation made by the insured to the insurer during negotiations for the contract and before the contract is concluded, must be true. If it is untrue, the insurer may void the contract. On account of the above reasons, B can obtain cancellation of the policy.

Chapter 21

Kinds of Marine Insurance Policies

Various Kinds of Marine Policy

Though commonly in one form, Marine Policies are known by different names according to their manner of execution and the nature of risks covered. The following are the various kinds of marine insurance policies as contained in the Marine Insurance Act 1963.

(1) Voyage Policy

(2) Time Policy

(3) Voyage and Time Policy (or) Mixed Policy

(4) Valued Policy

(5) Unvalued Policy (or) Open Policy

(6) Floating Policy

(7) Wagering Policy (or) PPI Policy

(8) Construction (or) Builders Risk Policy

(9) Open Cover Policy (Blanket policy)

(10) Port Risk Policy

(11) Named Policy

(12) Single Vessel and Fleet policy

(13) Currency policy

(14) Interest policy

(15) Composit policy.

1.Voyage Policy

This is a policy in which the limits of the risks are determined by place of particular voyage. For example, Chennai to Singapore; Chennai to London. Such policies are always used for goods insurance, sometimes for freight insurance, but only rarely now-a-days for hull insurance.

2.Time Policy

This is designed to give cover for some specified period of time, say, for example 1st Jan. 2003 to noon, 1st Jan. 2004. Time Policies are usual in the case of hull insurance, though there may be cases where an owner prefers to insure his vessel for each separate voyage under voyage policy.

3.Voyage and Time Policy or Mixed Policy

This is a combination of Voyage and Time Policy. It is a policy which covers the risk during a particular voyage for a specified period. For example, a ship may be insured for voyages between Chennai to London for a period of one year.

4.Valued Policy

This is one which specifies the agreed value of the subject matter insured, which is not necessarily the actual value. Such agreed value is referred to as the insured value. A policy may be, say, for Rs. 10000 on Hull and Machinery etc., valued at Rs. 2,00,000 or for Rs. 7,000 on 100 cases of Whisky valued at Rs. 7,000. Once a value has been agreed, it cannot be reopened unless there is proof of fraudulent intention. It remains binding on both parties. These policies are not common now-a-days.

5.Unvalued Policy

In the case of an Unvalued Policy, the value of the subject matter insured is not specified at the time of effecting insurance. It is taken for a specified amount and the insurable value is ascertained in the case of loss. Here, the insurer is liable to pay only up to actual loss incurred to the policy amount. It is also known as Open Policy.

6. Floating Policy

This policy provides another method of obtaining a long term contract for goods insurance, which may be used instead of or in addition to an open cover. A floating or open policy describes the insurance in general terms, leaving the names of the ship or ships to be defined by subsequent declaration. Such policy has the advantage of being a valid marine policy, in all respects fully complying with the requirements of the Marine Insurance Act. The declaration may be made by endorsement on the policy or in any other customary manner. Unless the policy otherwise provides. declaration must be made in the order of shipment. They must comprise all the consignments within the terms of the policy and values must be honestly stated. Errors and omissions however, may be rectified even after a loss has occurred, if made in good faith. When the total amount declared exhausts, the amount for which the policy was originally issued. it is said to be "run off" or "fully declared". The assured may then arrange for a new policy to be issued, to succeed the one about to lapse, otherwise the cover terminates when the policy is fully declared.

7. Wagering Policy

This policy is issued without there being any insurable interest, or a policy bearing evidence that the insured is willing to dispense with any proof of interest. If a policy contains such words as "Policy Proof of Interest" ((PPI) or "Interest or No Interest", it is Wagering or Honour Policy. Under Section 4 of the Marine Insurance Act, such policies are void in law but such policies continue to be common.

8. Construction or Builder's Risk Policy

This is designed to cover the risks incidental to the building of a vessel, usually giving cover from the time of laying the keel until completion trials and handing over to owners. In the case of a very large vessel, the period may extend over several years.

9. Open Cover Policy (Blanket Policy)

In order to arrange their marine insurance in advance and to be assured to cover at all times, and also to avoid the effects of possible rapidly fluctuating rates, it is the practice of regular importers and exporters to avail themselves of some kind of "Blanket Insurance". One way, and the most popular one of achieving this is by means of "Open Cover". An open cover is an agreement between the assured and his underwriters under which the former agrees to declare, and the latter to accept, all shipments coming within the scope of the open cover during some stipulated period of time.

10. Port Risk Policies

This is to cover a ship or cargo during a period in port against the risks peculiar to a port as distinguished from voyage risks. This kind of policy is probably very rarely used now-a-days.

11. Rent Policy

This policy protects the building owners against the loss of rent. If a tenant does not pay rent because of fire, the insurance company will pay such loss. Such an insurance my constitute a separate policy, or can be included within other forms of cover and may be effected either by the owner, or by the tenant or owner-occupier.

12. Transit Policy

A Transit policy covers goods in course of transit from one place to another by rail, road, air or sea transport. Under the policy the insurance company promises to make up for the loss or damage to merchandise while it is being moved.

13. Building's Risk Insurance

These policies are issued by fire insurance companies to protect against loss to buildings, including machinery and equipment, in the course of construction and to materials incidental to construction. This policy is also known as contract's risks or contract works risks policy.

14. Excess Policy

This policy is suitable to those businessmen who deal in different stocks of goods in their usual course of business and whose value of stocks also fluctuate from time to time Such businessmen take two policies such as (i) Loss Policy and (ii) Excess Policy. Under 'loss policy' the minimum value of stock which is held always. In the case of 'excess policy' it is taken for the excess value of stocks which may be held any time over the minimum stock within a stipulated period.

15. Sprinkler Leakage Policies

This policy insures destruction of or damage due to accidentally discharged or leakage water, from automobile sprinkler installation in the insured premises. However, the discharge or leakage of water due to heat caused by fire, repair or alteration of building or sprinkler installation, earthquake, war, explosion are not covered by the policy.

16. Blanket Policy

This policy is issued to cover several different properties or all assets fixed as well as current of the insured under one insurance. It is a policy which covers more than one type of property in one location or one more type of property at several locations.

17. Maximum Value With Discount Policy

A policy is taken for a maximum amount and full premium is paid thereon. At the end of the year, in case of no loss, one third of the premium paid is returned to the policy holder. This type of policy is not issued on all types of commodities and is confined only to selected commodities.

Questions

1. Describe the different kinds of Marine Insurance Policies.
2. Define Contract of Marine Insurance. Explain briefly the various kinds of Marine Insurance Policies.
3. Write short notes on the following:
   (a) Voyage Policy
   (b) Floating Policy
   (c) Wagering Policy
   (d) Valued Policy.
4. Define Marine policy. Explain the essentials of a valued policy.

Chapter 22

Important Clauses in Marine Policy

Clauses Incorporated in a Marine Policy

The clause makes it lawful for the assured and his servants where there is a danger that the subject matter insured may suffer loss or damage for which the underwriter would be liable, to take such steps as may be reasonable to avert or minimise the loss or damage and at the same time it binds the underwriters to pay their share of the expenses incurred.

Important Clauses

The following are the usual clauses that may be incorporated in a marine policy:

(1) Assignment Clause

(2) Lost or Not Lost

(3) At and From Clause

(4) Warehouse to Warehouse Clause

(5) Deviation Clause (or) Change of Voyage Clause

(6) Touch and Stay Clause

(7) Inchmaree Clause

(8) Running Down Clause

(9) Sue and Labour Clause

(10) Reinsurance Clause

(11) Memorandum Clause

(12) Continuation Clause

(13) Perils of the Sea Clause

(14) Waiver Clause

(15) All Risks Clause

(16) Foreign General Average Clause (F.G.A.)

(17) Free of Capture and Seizure Clause (F.C.S.)

(18) Free of Particular Average (F.P.A.)

(19) Bottomry Bond

(20) Respondentia Bond

1. Assignment Clause

This clause makes it clear that the marine policy is assignable unless it contains terms expressly prohibiting assignment, and may be assigned either before or after a loss. The assignee who has acquired the beneficial interest in the policy is entitled to sue thereon in his own name, and the defendant is entitled to make any defence arising out of the contract which he would have been entitled to make if the action had been brought in the name of the person by or on behalf of whom the policy was effected. Assignment may be endorsement or in other customary manner. Where the assured has parted with or lost his interest in the subject matter insured, and has not, before or at the time of so doing expressly or impliedly agreed to assign the policy, any subsequent assignment is incorporative.

2. Lost or Not Lost Clause

Where the subject matter is insured "lost or not lost" and the loss has occurred before the contract is concluded, the risk attaches unless, at such time the assured was aware of the loss, and the insurer was not.

3. At and From Clause

The risk starts as soon as the contract of insurance is concluded provided the ship is in good safety at that time. If the ship is not in good safety at that time, the risk will begin on her till arriving in good safety at the port of departure. Where freight, other than chartered freight is payable without special conditions and is insured "at and from" a particular place, the risk attaches *pro rata* as the goods or merchandise are shipped, provided that if there be cargo in readiness which belong to the shipowner, or which some other persons had contracted with him to ship, the risk attaches as soon as the ship is ready to receive such cargo.

4. Transit Clause or Warehouse to Warehouse Clause

This clause provides with respect to goods, for the risk to attach "from the loading thereof aboard the said ship" and for the insurance to continue until the goods are discharged and safely landed at the port of discharge. Modern trading conditions call for a policy which provides cover during the entire period of transit, for which reason this clause, designed to extend the period of cover from the time the goods leave the exporter's warehouse until they are delivered to the importers warehouse at the named destination, or to any other warehouse, whether prior to or at the named destination, which the assured elect to use either for storage or for allocation or distribution, or on the expiry of 60 days after discharge from the overseas vessel at the final port of discharge whichever first occurs.

5. Change of Voyage Clause (or) Deviation Clause

The Marine Insurance Act, provides that where there is a change of voyage then, unless the policy otherwise provides, the insurer is discharged from liability as from the time of the change. Through this clause the policy does provide otherwise, and the event is held covered at a premium to be arranged.

6. Touch and Stay Clause

In the absence of any further licence or usage, the liberty to "touch and stay at any port or place whatsoever" does not authorise the ship to depart from the course of her voyage from the port of departure to the port of destination.

7. Inchmaree Clause (or) Negligence Clause

This is designed to extend the underwriters' liability to cover risks of a kind which are not included within the ordinary meaning of maritime perils. It provides for the insurance to cover loss or damage to hull or machinery directly caused by:

(a) Accident in loading or shifting cargo or fuel explosions on shipboard or elsewhere
Bursting of boilers
Negligence of Master, Officers
Negligence of repairs provided such repairers are not assured hereunder.

(b) Contact with aircraft
Contact with any land conveyance, dock or harbour equipments or installation
Earthquake, volcanic eruption or lightning.

8. Running Down Clause

In an ordinary marine policy, the assured is covered in respect of the damage sustained by his own ship in the case of collision, but such cover does not extend to his liability for the damage done to the other ship. This clause provides a supplementary contract whereby the assured is given some protection against such third party damages. It provides that if the insured vessel collides with another vessel, the underwriters agree to pay three–quarters of the amount of damages to which the assured becomes liable.

9. Sue and Labour Clause

This clause explains in detail the extent of underwriter's liability for such expenses. In particular, it provides that liability shall not exceed the proportion that the amount insured bears to the value of the vessels has been previously mentioned that in the absence of this provision, underwriters would be liable for the full amount of sue and labour charges even where there was under-insurance.

10. Re-insurance Clause

There are various reasons why an underwriter may deem it prudent to reinsure part or all of a risk for which he has accepted liability. For instance, he may find that his commitments on any one vessel or in any locality have become too burdensome. Declarations under open covers or floating policies and acceptances by his agents in other markets may give him an accumulated liability considerably in excess of his usual retention. He may have accepted a line on 'all risk' terms and then desire to re-insure in respect of total loss only.

11. Memorandum Clause

This clause is meant to provide a minimum limit to the underwriter's liability regarding claims for particular average by exempting him from such claims.

12. Continuation Clause

This clause refers that the vessel shall continue to be covered even after completion of voyage under the policy at a *pro rata* premium to her port destination provided previous notice was not given.

13. Perils of the Sea Clause

The term "perils of the sea" refers only to fortuitous accident or casualties of the seas. It does not include the ordinary action of the winds and waves.

14. Waiver Clause

This is really supplementary to the 'Sue and Labour' clause, provided simply to assure that, in the event of a causalty, either party to the contract may take such steps, or incur such expenses, as are contemplated under the Sue and Labour Clause, to minimise a loss without prejudice to the rights of the assured on the one hand and the underwriter on the other.

15. All Risks Clause (for All Risks Policy)

This provides that the insurance is against all risks of loss or damage to the subject matter insured and that claims are payable irrespective of percentage.

16. Foreign General Average Clause (F.G.A.)

Foreign General Average clause means that the arrangement in case of a General Average Claim which may arise under the policy, the average settlement made in a foreign country will be adopted as the basis for settlement.

17. Free of Capture and Seizure (F.C.S)

This clause is generally inserted in times of war, it means that the underwriters will not be liable for loss or claim arising from seizure of ship as a prize of war. In times of war, this clause is inserted unless the insured pays the underwriter additional premium for war risks.

18. Free of Particular Average Clause (F.P.A)

This clause restricts the liability of the underwriter and the underwriter is liable only for total loss and not for particular average or partial loss.

19. Bottomry Bond

It is a bond representing monetary loan raised by the master of the ship so as to meet certain urgent expenses like repairing a ship on the security of a ship or ship and cargo. It is repayable after a certain agreed number of days after the arrival of the ship as specified in the bond. If the vessel is lost before the arrival at destination, the lender loses his money.

20. Respondentia Bond

Like Bottomry Bond, Respondentia Bond also represents a monetary loan borrowed by the master of a ship to meet certain urgent expenses. The loan is raised on the security of the cargo only. The loan is to be repaid within a certain number of days after the arrival of the cargo at the destination as specified in the Respondentia Bond. If the cargo is lost on its way, the lender loses his money.

Questions

1. What is marine insurance policy? State its main clauses.
2. Explain the important clauses of a marine policy.
3. Write short notes on:
   (a) Bottomry Bond
   (b) Respondentia Bond
   (c) Inchmaree Clause

(d) Lost or Not Lost Clause

(e) At and From Clause

(f) Assignment Clause.

Mini Cases

Case 1. A ship, which was insured under a 'time policy' was sent to sea unseaworthy in two respects; her hull was in an unfit state for voyage and her crew was insufficient. The assured knew of the insufficiency of the crew but not of the unfitness of the hull. Is the insurer liable to pay for the loss?

Ans: Yes, the insurer is liable to pay for the loss. In a time policy, there is no implied warranty of seaworthiness provided the loss is not attributable to the unseaworthiness of which the assured was having the knowledge.

Case 2. A ship was insured against 'perils of the sea'. The ship deviated to assist another in distress, but instead of merely saving the crew, she attempted to earn salvage by towing the distressed vessel into a nearby port, and in the attempt, went ashore herself and was lost. Is the insurer liable?

Ans: No, the insurer is not liable. Deviation to aid a ship in distress where human life may be in danger is always excused, but deviation to save property as such, with a view to earn salvage is not allowed. Hence, in the instant case, there is a breach of warranty of 'non-deviation' without a lawful excuse; as a result the insurer is discharged from liability.

Chapter 23

Marine Losses and Abandonment

Introduction

According to the provision of the Marine Insurance Act, unless the ›licy otherwise provides, the insurer is liable for any loss proximately used by a peril insured against, but, subject to as above said, he is not ble for any loss which is not proximately caused by a peril insured against. particular, the insurer is not liable for any loss attributable to the wilful sconduct of the assured but, unless the policy otherwise provides, he is ble for any loss proximately caused by a peril insured against even though .e loss would not have happened but for the misconduct or negligence of .e Master or Crew.

Unless the policy otherwise provides, the insurer is not liable for ordinary wear and tear, ordinary leakage and breakage, inherent vice or nature of the subject matter insured, or for any loss proximately caused by rats or vermin or for any injury of machinery not proximately caused by maritime perils.

Kinds of Marine Losses

The losses of insurance may be divided broadly into two classes (a) Total Loss and (b) Partial Loss. And the Total Losses are again sub-divided into (a) Actual Total Loss and (b) Constructive Total Loss. Partial Loss may be (a) Particular Average Loss and (b) General Average Loss.

Marine losses can be classified as shown in the following chart.

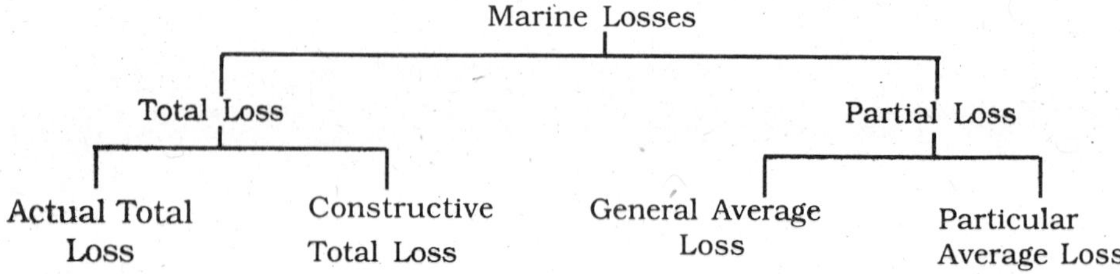

Total Loss

When the subject matter of insurance (the ship, cargo, or freight) is totally lost, it is called Total Loss. A Total Loss may be either an Actual Total Loss, or a Constructive Total Loss.

Actual Total Loss: Actual Total Losses arises —

(1) Where the subject matter insured is destroyed or so damaged as to cease to be a thing of the kind insured (or).

(2) Where the assured is irretrievally deprived, there is an Actual Total Loss. In the case of actual total loss, no notice of abandonment need to be given.

(3) Where the ship concerned in the adventure is missing, and after the lapse of a reasonable time no news of her has been received, an actual total loss may be presumed.

In the case of an actual total loss, the underwriter has to pay either the insured amount or the actual loss whichever is less. But the cause of loss must be one of the perils insured against.

Constructive Total Loss: Is defined in general:

Where the subject to any express provision in the policy, there is a Constructive Total Loss where the subject matter insured is reasonably abandoned on account of its actual loss appearing to be unavoidable or, because it could not be preserved from actual total loss without expenditure which would exceed its value when the expenditure had been incurred.

Constructive Total Loss is defined in particular:

(1) Where the assured is deprived of the possession of his ship or goods by a peril insured against and

 (a) it is unlikely that he can recover the ship or goods, as the case may be (or)

 (b) the cost of recovering the ship or goods, as the case may be, would exceed their value when recovered (or)

(2) In the case of damage to the ship, where she is so damaged by the peril insured against that the cost of repairing the damage would exceed the value of the ship when repaired.

(3) In the case of damage to goods, where the cost of repairing the damage and forwarding the goods to their destination would exceed their value on arrival.

Effect of Constructive Total Loss: Where there is a constructive total loss, the assured may either treat the loss as a particular loss or abandon the subject matter insured to the insurer and treat the loss as if it were an actual total loss.

Abandonment:

The term Abandonment refers to surrounding of the insured property along with all proprietary rights to the insurance company in order to claim total loss for the same.

Notice of Abandonment

Notice of abandonment is a notice by the assured to the insurer that he abandons all interests in the subject of insurance unconditionally to the insurers. Section 62 speaks of the rules regarding abandonment which are as follows:

(1) Subject to the provisions of this section, where the assured elects to abandon the subject matter insured to the insurer, he must give notice of abandonment. If he fails to do so, the loss can only be treated as a partial loss.

(2) Notice of abandonment may be given in writing, or by word of mouth or partly in writing and partly by word of mouth, and may be given in any terms which indicate the intention of the assured to abandon his insured interest in the subject matter insured unconditionally to the insurer.

(3) Notice of abandonment must be given with reasonable diligence after the receipt of reliable information of the loss, but where the information is of a doubtful character the assured is entitled to a reasonable time to make inquiry.

(4) Where the notice of abandonment is properly given, the rights of the assured are not prejudiced by the fact that the insurer refuses to accept the abandonment.

(5) The acceptance of an abandonment may be either express or implied from the conduct of the insurer. The mere silence of the insurer after notice is not an acceptance.

(6) Where the notice of abandonment is accepted, the abandonment is irrevocable. The acceptance of the notice conclusively admits liability for the loss and the sufficiency of the notice.

(7) Notice of abandonment is unnecessary where, at the time when the assured receives information of the loss, there would be no possibility of benefit to the insurer if notice were given to him.

(8) Notice of abandonment may be waived by the insurer.

(9) Where an insurer has reinsured his risk, no notice of abandonment need to be given by him.

Effect of Abandonment

Where there is a valid abandonment the insurer is entitled to take over the interest of the assured in whatever may remain of the subject-matter insured, and all proprietary rights incidental thereto.

Difference between Actual Total Loss versus Constructive Total Loss

Actual Total Loss	Constructive Total Loss
(1) It arises because of physical impossibility. (2) Notice of abandonment is not necessary.	(1) It arises because of commercial impracticability. (2) Notice of abandonment is necessary.

Partial Loss

In marine insurance, the term 'average' means loss or damage resulting from loss or damage to ship, cargo or freight.

Partial loss is any loss other than a total loss. The partial loss may be classified into:

(1) Particular Average Loss

(2) General Average Loss

1. Particular Average Loss

When the subject-matter is partially lost or damaged by a peril insured against, it is called Particular Average Loss.

A Particular Average Loss must fulfil the following conditions:

(a) Only a particular subject-matter should have been lost or damaged.

(b) The loss should be accidental.

(c) It should be caused by a peril insured against.

(d) The damage should not have been suffered for the general benefit.

Particular Average on Ship: The loss on account of partial damage to the ship from the peril insured against is called Particular Average On Ship. A particular average loss falls directly upon the party interested in the subject-matter. In the case of accidental or fortuitous damage to the ship, it is the shopowner or, to the extent that he is insured against such loss, underwriters who must bear the loss.

When a ship meets with several accidents, the insurer is liable to pay successive losses to the extent of the insured amount even though the total amount of such successive losses may far exceed the amount of the policy.

Where there is a partial loss of freight because of the peril insured against, it is called Particular Average On Freight. Subject to any express provision in the policy, where there is a partial loss of freight, the measure of indemnity is the proportion of the sum fixed by the policy, as the case of valued policy, as the proportion of freight lost by the assured bears to the whole freight at the risk of the assured under the policy.

Particular Average on Cargo: A claim for particular average on cargo arises where the cargo has been either partially damaged by the peril insured against or when a portion of the cargo is totally lost.

Salvage Charges: It is the reward paid under maritime law to the salvor for saving or helping to save property at sea or property of life. No salvage will be awarded if the services of the salvor are of no material consequence.

Further, the salvor must be a stranger to the adventure. In other words, he should not have been connected with the adventure. The salvage charges are recoverable from the insurers as partial loss. If the salvage charges become necessary because of the unseaworthiness of the ship, the underwriter on the hull is not liable for any portion of the remuneration awarded to the Salvor.

The salvor who has saved the property has a possessory right on it in respect of his reward for the services. However, if the property is not in his possession he enjoys, what is called a Maritime Lien, i.e., a claim which he can enforce by legal process in the Court of Admiralty.

2. General Average Loss

A General Average Loss occurs where any extraordinary sacrifice or expenditure is voluntarily and reasonably made or incurred in time of peril, for the purpose of preserving the property involved in a common adventure. The rule with regard to general average loss is that it must be borne rateably by the parties interested in the common adventure.

For example, when a cargo ship caught fire, water is thrown to extinguish fire by which cargo is damaged. The loss caused by cargo is a general average loss.

A Few More examples: A few more examples of General Average Losses are given below:

(1) Jettisoning cargo to lighten ship in distress.

(2) Throwing of water on board of ship to extinguish fire.

(3) Money paid to pirates for the purpose of saving ship and cargo.

(4) Expenses incurred in taking vessel to its destination with outside help.

(5) Loss arising on account of sale of cargo by the Master to raise funds when other means of obtaining funds have failed.

(6) When the Master of the ship has to cut away the masts of the ship for the safety of the cargo, passengers etc. the loss caused is general average.

(7) Interest on loans obtained by way of Bottomry or Respondentia Bond.

York-Antwerp Rules

As General Average causes many difficulties particularly where adjustments have to be made in foreign courts, an international code has been compiled known as the York -Antwerp Rules to facilitate matters. This code admits as general average certain losses, e.g. masts, sails or rigging cut away for the common safety during a storm; loss of cargo or freight through jettison; damage done to cargo by water used to extinguish other cargo on fire, etc.

In 1864, the Association for the Reform and Codification of the Law of Nature held a meeting at York, England, and another meeting at Antwerp in 1877, when a code of rules as mentioned above was adopted which was known as the "York-Antwerp Rules". In 1890, the Association met again in Liverpool and revised this code. The rules were further revised in 1924. This was the origin of the "York-Antwerp Rules" and insurance policies can provide that General Average would be adjusted in accordance with these rules. These rules deal only with certain specific matters relating to general average, and further provide that in the case of matters not included in the rules they should be dealt with according to the law and practice of the port of destination.

Difference Between General Average Loss versus Particular Average Loss

General Average Loss	Particular Average Loss
(1) It is incurred for the benefit of all the interested.	(1) It is in connection with any of the interested.
(2) It is always voluntarily and resonably incurred.	(2) It is accidental or fortuitous.
(3) General average is shared by all those who is benefited by the average act.	(3) Particular average is paid by the insurer.
(4) It includes expenditure and sacrifice along with loss.	(4) Particular average loss is resulting from an accident or normal perils of the sea.
(5) It is an extraordinary character or emergency nature.	(5) No such extraordinary or emergency losses.
(6) The cause relating into a general average loss cannot be duly insured as it cannot be anticipted.	(6) It must be caused by peril against which the property is duly insured.

General Average Contribution: Where there is a general average loss, the party on whom it falls is entitled, subject to the conditions imposed by maritime law, to a rateable contribution from the other parties interested. Such a contribution is called a General Average Contribution. All who have benefited by the general average act must share the loss, or the expenditure, i.e., they must all contribute to the same. This liability extends to owners of the ship, the cargo and the freight but not to wages of the seamen.

Claims Documents

Claims under marine policies have to be supported by certain documents which vary according to the type of loss as also the circumstances of the claim and the mode of carriage.

The documents required for particular average claims are as under:

(1) Original Policy - (Certificate of Insurance)

(2) Bill of Lading - (evidence that the goods were actually shipped)

(3) Invoice - (evidence for the terms of sale)

(4) Survey Report - (Shows the cause and extent of loss)

(5) Debit Note - (Claim bill)

(6) Copy of Protest - (Protest on arrival at destination before a Notary Public)

(7) Letter of Subrogation - legal document which transfers the right of claimant against third party to the insurer.

Rights of Insurer on Payments

Sec. 79 and 78 deal with the rights of the insurer on payment.

After making payment on Marine Insurance Policy, the insurer has the following rights:

1. **Right of Subrogation:** By this right of subrogation, he becomes entitled to all the rights of the insured in whatever remains of the subject matter for which he made the payment. He is also entitled to all the rights and remedies available to the assured from the time of loss.

2. **Right of Contribution:** Where the subject matter has been over insured by double insurance, each insurer is bound to contribute only rateably to the loss. In other words, each insurer has to bear the loss only to his proportion to the amount for which he is liable under the contract. If any insurer pays more than his share of loss, he is entitled to contribution from coinsurers.

3. **Right in the Case of Under Insurance:** Where the assured is insured for an amount less than the insurable value or in the

case of a valued policy, for an amount less than the policy valuation, he is deemed to be his own insurer in respect of the uninsured balance

Questions

1. Write a note on abandonment in marine insurance and the rules relating to Notice of Abandonment.
2. What is actual total loss?
3. What is meant by abandonment in case of constructive total loss?
4. What is a particular average loss?
5. What do you mean by general average loss?
6. What is the difference between actual and constructive total loss?
7. What are the rights of the insurer on payment in marine insurance?
8. Discuss in detail the various kinds of marine losses?
9. What is the difference between general average loss and particular average loss?
10. Write short notes on the following:
    (a) Salvage Charges
    (b) York-Antwerp Rules
    (c) Claim Documents in Marine Policies
    (d) General Average Contribution
    (e) Notice of Abandonment.

Mini Cases

Case 1. A's cargo was damaged on account of fire on board a ship. During the course of putting out the fire by water, the cargo of 'B' was also damaged. Can A or B claim contribution from owners of their interests on the basis of **General Average Loss?**

Ans: 'A' cannot but B can. B's loss is caused in common interest.

Case 2. A ship is insured for a sum of Rs. 1,00,000. It meets two successive partial losses. The actual cost of repairs being Rs. 20,000 in each case. Later on, the ship is totally lost. State the liability of the insurer.

Ans: In case of a **particular average loss,** the amount of claim is the reasonable outlay for repairs. However, the insurer's liability is limited to the amount of policy so far as any one accident is concerned. In case a vessel meets several accidents, the insurer is liable for successive losses though the total amount of losses may far exceed the amount of policy.

On the basis of the above provision, in the instant case the insurer is liable for particular average loss of Rs. 40,000 and also for the total loss of the ship.

Case 3. A cotton bale is insured for Rs. 10,000. It is damaged in transit and is expected to realise Rs. 6.000 gross. If the bale had reached safely, it would have fetched Rs. 12,000. Calculate the amount of **particular average loss.**

Ans: In those cases where the goods insured are of greater value than the sum assured, the liability of the insurer is restricted as follows:

$$\frac{\text{Amount of Loss} \times \text{Insured Amount}}{\text{Value of the Goods}}$$

In the instant case, the amount of Particular Average Loss would therefore be calculated as follows:

$$\frac{6{,}000 \times 10{,}000}{12{,}000} = \text{Rs.}5{,}000.$$

Case 4. The captain of a ship, which was on the point of capture threw overboard a quantity of the cargo lest it should fall into enemy hands. The marine policy covers the 'general average loss'. The ship ultimately escaped capture. Is the insurer liable to the owners of the cargoes, whose cargoes were thrown overboard?

Ans: No, the insurer is not liable as the loss in the instant case cannot be called as a general average loss because the sacrifice was neither prudently made nor the object of the sacrifice can be said to be the preservation of the property in peril in common adventure and enabling the ship to proceed safely with her journey. However, the captain or the owner of the ship is liable to indemnify the owners, whose cargoes were thrown overboard.

Chapter

24

Nature of Fire Insurance Contract

Introduction

Many provisions of the Insurance Act 1932 and the General Insurance Business (Nationalisation) Act 1972 relates to fire insurance business in India. From Jan. 1, 1994, fire insurance business is being transacted only by the General Insurance Corporation of India, and its four subsidiaries.

Definitions

A contract of fire insurance may also defined as "a contract by which the insurer undertakes, for a consideration in the form of a payment of money either in lump sum or instalments, to indemnify the insured against the consequences of a fire, or the loss or injury as arising therefrom during an agreed period and upto a certain amount. The contract is to be found embodied in a document known as the "policy of the fire insurance" and usually for a period one year and renewed each year.

A few notable definitions are also reproduced below:

(1) "A contract whereby the insurer in consideration of the premium paid undertakes to compensate the insured for any loss that may result due to occurrence of fire."

(2) "Fire Insurance is a contract of indemnity against loss or damage to property arising from fire during an agreed period of time. Here, the insurer undertakes to indemnify the insured against financial loss caused directly as a result of fire."

(3) "A contract of fire insurance is a contract by which the insurer undertakes, for a money consideration, to indemnify the insured against the consequences of a fire during an agreed period upto the amount stated in the policy."

Fire: The term "fire" in a contract of fire insurance is used in its popular and literal sense. It means the production of light and heat by combustion. Combustion occurs only at the actual ignition point. Hence, there is no fire without ignition. Loss or damage which occurs as a result of putting out the fire would also be covered by the fire risks. Fire policies are not covered through fire caused by earthquakes, riots, civil commotion, foreign enemy, rebellion etc.

Example: A,B, and C are three continuous houses insured against fire. An earthquake caused A to fall and as a consequence fire broke out and spread to B where an explosion occurred whereby C was wrecked.

Is the insurer liable for the loss caused to C?

Answer: Fire risks do not cover loss caused only by explosion. However, where explosion actually causes ignition which spread into fire, the loss would be taken as a loss by fire. A simple fire insurance policy covers loss by explosion incidental to fire unless specifically excluded.

In the instant case, the insurer will be liable for the loss caused to house C if (i) the explosion was caused by fire and (ii) the insurer has not excluded his liability for explosion by a special clause in the fire policy.

Subject Matter of Fire Insurance

Subject matter of fire insurance may be of any kind of moveable and immoveable property having pecuniary value. The property intended to be insured must be properly described. As per fire insurance, it is governed by Tariff, the following are the example of insurable property such as:

(1) Building

(2) Electrical installation in buildings

(3) Contents of building such as machinery, plant and equipment, accessories etc.

(4) Goods (raw materials, work in progress, semi finished goods, finished goods, packaging materials) in factories and godowns

(5) Goods in open

(6) Contents in dwellings, shops, hotels, etc.

(7) Furniture, fixture and fittings

(8) Pipelines (including contents) located inside or outside the compound etc.

Fundamental Principles of Fire Insurance

The following are the fundamental principles essential for a valid contract of fire insurance.

(1) A contract of indemnity

(2) Insurable interest to exist both at the time of effecting the insurance as well as at the time of loss

(3) Utmost good faith or *Uberrimae fidei*

(4) Loss through fire (*Causa Proxima*)

(5) A contract from year to year

(6) Subject to the principles of subrogation and contribution.

1. **Contract of Indemnity:** Its object is to place insured as far as possible in the same financial position after a loss as that occupied immediately before the loss. The insured can recover only the amount of actual loss subject to the sum assured.

The following have been held to have insurable interest in the subject matter—

(1) Owner

(2) Mortgagee

(3) Trustee

(4) Executor

(5) Warehouseman

(6) Common

(7) Bailee

(8) Pledgee

(9) Person in lawful possession

(10) Finder

(11) Insurer

(12) Commission Agent where the agency is coupled with interest and

(13) Tenants who are liable to pay rent after a fire.

It should however, be noted that persons can insure only to the extent of such limited interest.

2. **Insurable Interest:** In fire insurance, the insurable interest must exist at the time of effecting the insurance as well as the time of the loss. The interest, however, may be legal or equitable or may arise under a contract of purchase or sale.

3. **Contract of Good Faith:** The contract of fire insurance is a contract of *Uberimae fidei*, i.e., a contract based upon absolute good faith, and therefore, the insured must make full and detailed disclosure of all material facts likely to affect the judgement of fire officials in determining the rates of premium or deciding whether the proposal should be accepted.

The description of the property, when asked for, should be correctly given, and all information that may be required as to the class of goods and articles that are kept on the premises or in the surrounding neighbourhood, should be accurately supplied.

4. **Loss Through Fire:** Loss resulting from fire or some other cause which is the proximate cause is the risk covered under a fire insurance contract. But where the fire is caused by the insured himself or by the operation of a peril specifically excluded under the policy like earthquake, the loss will not be covered.
5. **A Contract from Year to Year:** A fire insurance policy is usually for one year only and can be renewed after that.
6. **Principles of Subrogation and Contribution:** Subrogation is a doctrine applicable to both fire and marine insurance by which the insurer or underwriter, becomes entitled to on his paying compensation to the insured, to claim the advantage of every right of the insured against third parties who may be proved to be responsible for that loss, owning to such third parties negligence, default etc.

   Where the subject matter has been insured with more than one insurer, each insurer has to meet the loss only rateably. If he has paid more than his share of loss, he is entitled to recover the excess paid from his co-insurers. Thus, the principle of contribution applies in the case of fire insurance.

Fire Policy

It is a document containing the written contract between the insurer and the insured setting forth the terms and conditions under which the insurance is issued, the particulars of the property insured, risks and hazards covered, the sum assured, the cost or the rate of premium and the period.

The Risk

The risk on the fire policy commences from the moment of time, the cover note or the deposit receipt, or the interim protection note is given and continues for the term covered by the contract of insurance. It is the practice to allow a certain number of days as days of grace within which a fire policy may be renewed after the expiration of the term. In such a case, if a fire should occur within this time the insured would be entitled to recover damages. The days of grace only apply when the insured has the intention to renew the policy, failing which, the policy expires on the day the period runs out. If however, it is expressly stipulated in the policy that unless the renewal premium is paid and the renewal risk is accepted the insurance would expire, the insured would not be able to recover in the case where a fire occurs after the expiration of the term and before the acceptance by the fire insurance company of a proposal for further insurance.

Distinction between Life Insurance and Fire Insurance

Basis of distinctions	Life Insurance	Fire Insurance
1. Types of contract contract of certainty	The contract is a indemnity	It is a contract of
2. Occurence of event (Risk)	Death will certainly occur	The fire may or may not occur
3. Period of insurance	Life Insurance policies are generally issued for 10 to 20 years duration	Maximum period covered under fire policy is usually one year
4. Insurable interest	Insurable interest exists at the time of taking policy	It must exist from the date of the proposal to the date of completion of the contract.
5. Protection and	It includes the elements of protection and investment	It includes only element of protection
6. Premium	Permium rates are fixed on the basis of nature of risk	Premium is determined according to the type of risk involved
7. Payment of premium	Premium may be paid in monthly, quarterly, half yearly or yearly instalments	Premium is paid in lump sum at the time of taking the policy
8. Surrender Value	The life policy can be surrendered and the insured gets the surrender value	Fire insurance policies cannot be surrendered at all.
9. Moral Hazard	It is very nominal is maximum	Degree of moral hazard
10. Value of policy	In the case of life insurance one can get policy of any amount	In the case of fire insurance the amount of policy cannot exceed the total value of goods or properties insured
11. Indemnity of loss	The law of indemnity does not apply to life insurance as loss of life cannot be indemnified in money terms.	Fire insurance contract is a contract of indemnity as the actual loss caused by uncertain event is compensated.

Questions

1. Define fire insurance contract. What are the characteristics of a fire insurance contract?
2. What is the meaning of 'fire' in a fire insurance policy?
3. What is the subject matter of fire insurance?
4. Discuss the essential elements of a contract of fire insurance?
5. "A fire insurance is a contract of indemnity." Explain.
6. Explain the insurable interest in a fire policy.
7. Discuss the differences between life insurance and fire insurance.
8. What are the differences between fire insurance and marine insurance?
9. Explain the causes of fire.

Chapter 25

Types of Fire Policies

More Common Types of Fire Policies

There are various types of fire insurance policies which are issued to meet the varying needs of the individual persons.

The following are some of the more common types of fire policies:

(1) Specific Policy

(2) Valued Policy

(3) Average Policy

(4) Floating Policy

(5) Replacement Policy or Reinstatement Policy

(6) Declaration Policy

(7) Comprehensive Policy

(8) Consequential Policy

(9) Adjustable Policy

(10) Rent Policy

(11) Transit Policy

(12) Builder's Risk Insurance

(13) Excess Policy

(14) Sprinkler Leakage Policies

(15) Blanket Policy

(16) Maximum Value with Discount Policy.

1. Specific Policy

A specific policy is one where the insurer undertakes to make good the loss upto the amount specified in the policy, irrespective of the value of the property. For example, if a property worth Rs. 2,00,000 is insured for Rs. 1,00,000 but the actual loss is only Rs. 1,50,000 he can only recover the actual loss if it is equal to or less than the value of the policy, but if his loss is more than the sum insured, he can recover only the amount of policy.

2. Valued Policy

A valued policy is usually taken where it is not easy to determine the value of the property. For example, works of art, pictures, sculptures etc., whose value cannot be determined easily. In the case of total loss in the valued policy, the insurer undertakes to pay the value of the property as mentioned in the policy, or the declared value, irrespective of its actual or market value. Such policies are, however, not very common in fire insurance.

3. Average Policy

A fire policy containing an average clause is called an Average Policy. Under this policy, the insured is penalised for under-insurance of the property. In other words, the insured is considered to be a self insurer to the extent of under insurance.

For Example: Where the property worth of Rs. 80,000 is insured for Rs.60,000 and the loss caused by fire is Rs. 40,000 then the amount of claim to be paid by the insurer will be

$$\frac{60,000}{80,000} \times 40,000 = \text{Rs. } 30,000$$

It must be remembered that average clause applies only where there is under insurance and partial loss. If the loss is total, the insured amount will be paid. For instance, if in the above example, the entire property is lost, then the claim that will be admitted is

$$\frac{60,000}{80,000} \times 80,0000 = \text{Rs. } 60,000$$

4. Floating Policy

A floating policy covers loss on goods which are lying in different places. For example, a dealer may take out only one floating policy, instead of separate specific policies for all his goods, some of which may be in warehouses, others in railway stations, shop counters etc. This policy is useful when the insured is in a position to declare only the total value at risk and not separate values in separate risks.

5. Replacement Policy (Reinstatement Policy)

Replacement policy is otherwise termed as Reinstatement policy. This policy is issued in respect of building, plant and machinery, furniture and fixtures and fittings etc. Under this policy, the insurer undertakes to pay the cost of replacing the property instead of paying compensation to the insured for the property destroyed. In short, the damaged.property is replaced by a new property.

6. Declaration Policy

Declaration Policy may be granted only in respect of stock of inventories (stock of raw material, stock of work in progress and stock of finished goods) of the insured. Generally, levels of stock which are subject to frequent fluctuations in value or in volume, present a special problem for insurance. In such a case, the businessman takes a policy for a maximum expected amount and the premium is paid. Every month the insured must declare in writing the stock covered under the policy to the insurance company. At the end, the premium is adjusted accordingly.

7. Comprehensive Policy

This policy undertakes full protection not only against the risk of the fire but combining with the risk against burglary, riot, civil commotion, theft, damage from pest, lightning. The policy is also termed as All Insurance Policy. Here, the comprehensive does not mean that every type of risk is covered. Such policies are not common in our country.

8. Consequential Loss Policy

Under this policy, the insurer agrees to indemnify the insured for the loss of profits which he suffers due to dislocation of his business as a result of fire. This type of policy is also called as "Loss of profit policy". Thus, this policy covers:

(1) loss of goods or property damaged

(2) loss of net profits

(3) outstanding expenses (interest on debenture, salaries, rent on building etc.)

(4) prepaid expenses etc.

9. Adjustable Policy

This policy is nothing but an ordinary policy on the stock of the businessman with liberty to the insured to vary at his option. The premium is adjustable *pro-rata* according to the variation of the stock. The adjustable policy is granted to remove the disadvantage of declaration on policy. This is issued for a definite term on the existing stock. The premium is calculated in the ordinary manner and is paid in full at the inception of the policy. Whenever, there is variation in the stock, the insured informs the insurer. As soon as the information of variation is received, the policy is suitably endorsed and the premium is adjusted on a *pro-rata* basis. The policy amount will, thus, be changeable from time to time.

Difference Between Declaration Policy versus Adjustable Policy

Declaration Policy	Adjustable Policy
(1) Insurer's liability is the insured's last declaration made.	(1) Insurer's liability is the value of the last declaration made on the amount
(2) Periodical declarations have no direct bearing on the measurement of indemnity.	(2) Periodical declarations have direct bearing on the measurement of indemnity.
(3) Maximum amount insured would be considered risk during the period of policy.	(3) Risk cover is always for the declared value.
(4) Declaration is meant only for the purpose of ascertaining the average of the actual cover given throughout the year to arrive at the figure to which the actual premium will be calculated.	(4) In the case of adjustable policy, declaration is on the basis of policy amount adjustment by endorsement.
(5) High premium is fixed at the beginning for the maximum cover of risk. If any excess, actual premium will be returnable at the end of the year.	(5) Premium is calculated according to the variation of the risk and the liability of the insurer.

Double Insurance in Fire Policy

When more than one policy is taken to cover the same risk, it is called "Double Insurance." Any person is free to insure his goods or property against fire, under more than one policy but in such case the insured cannot recover more than the insured value of the property from his insurers. Suppose a house worth Rs. 20,000 has been insured against fire under two policies, each for Rs. 20,000. The house is destroyed in fire, the insured cannot claim Rs. 20,000 from each of the policies.

Reinsurance

It is an arrangement whereby an original insurer who has insured insures a risk insures a part of that risk again with another insurer. It is a contract of insurance between two underwriters and the assured does not come into the picture at all. The insurer who transfers a part of the business is called the principal and the insurer to whom the business is transferred is the "Reinsurer".

A contract of reinsurance like any fire insurance contract is a contract of indemnity. It also requires utmost good faith.

Assignment of Fire Policy

A fire policy can according to English Common Law, be assigned only with the consent of the insurer or the insurance company. It is said to be contract of a personal nature, and therefore, a policy of insurance does not pass with the sale or assignment of the property on which it is effected. A transfer or assignment with the consent of the insurance company, as stated above, would give an effective right to the assignee.

Section 135 A of the Transfer of Property Act requires only an endorsement or any other writing in the case of an assignment of immovble property which has been insured against fire. Notice is only necessary to make the insurer liable to the assignee if the insurer pays the insurance money to the insured after receiving notice of the assignment. This notice is not necessary for a valid assignment of a fire policy.

Section 49 of the Transfer of Property Act deals exclusively with immovble property. Here, our Indian law differs from the English. Here unlike English law, the policy virtually passes to the purchaser on the transfer of the insured property since a transferee for value of an immovable property insured against fire is empowered to compel the transferor to apply any money received by him under a fire policy, to reinstate the property.

Payment of Claims

In case of an outbreak of fire, the first care that the insured must take is to give notice to the insurance company. The policies generally provide for notice within a specified time of the occurrence which clause should be strictly complied with. The claim to be made out should be for the exact value of the goods damaged, or destroyed at the date of the fire. In case of goods partly destroyed or damaged, details as to their value in good condition and in damaged condition ought to be made out and furnished to the insurance company. In the case of damaged buildings, the basis of the claim should be the cost of repairs of the damage, with due allowance for the greater value of the new premises over the old. This is, of course, applicable where the policy covers the full value of the property, but in fire insurance the peculiarity is, unlike marine insurance, that the insurance company cannot, where the property is partially insured, claim to pay only a proportional loss, i.e., loss in proportion in which the amount insured stands to the full value of the property.

Average Clause

The clause is usually inserted in all general insurance contracts to discourage under insurance. The clause limits the liability of the insurer to that proportion of the actual amount of loss which the insured amount bears to the actual value of the property.

Example: 'A' gets his house worth Rs. 5,000 insured for Rs. 1,000 only. The policy contains an average clause. The house is completely destroyed by fire. How much **can** *'A'* recover by way of compensation from the insurance company?

Answer:

The average clause comes into pay only in those cases where it is proved that the loss sustained by the insured is less than the sum insured where the loss is more than the sum insured, the insured can recover the whole amount of loss inspite of the average clause.

Thus, in the instant case, A will recover the full amount of loss of Rs. 1,000 from the insurance company.

Rights of Insurer

The following are the rights of the insurer:

1. Rights to Avoid the Policy: An insurer has a right to void the policy where the subject matter is not specified honestly or wilful fire is caused by the insured or with his connivance.

2. Rights of Entry Control Over the Property: Where any loss or damage of property insured arising of an outbreak of fire, the insurance company has rights to enter the premises and take possession of the building or property. It is essential for the insurer to ascertain the cause of loss or damage to minimise the loss and to protect the salvage.

3. Right of Reinstatement: An insurer has a right of reinstatement or replacement of damaged property under which insured instead of paying the amount of loss or damage in money. Here, the insured has no right to claim reinstatement.

4. Right of Subrogation: Subrogation is the principle by which the insurer on paying the loss to the insured, becomes entitled to all the rights and remedies available to the insured in respect of the subject matter insured against. This principle holds goods in fire insurance. For example, when loss is caused by the wrongful act of a third party, the insurer can proceed against the third party after paying the insured his loss.

5. Right to Contribution: This doctrine of contribution also applies to fire insurance contracts of indemnity. According to this principle, in case a person has taken out more than one policy against the same risks, the insurers are to share the loss in proportion to the amount assured by each. If an insurer pays more, he can recover the excess from his co-insurers to contribute proportionately towards the loss.

6. Right to Salvage: In the case of any loss due to fire, it is the duty of the assured to hand over to the salvage to the insurance company. The insurer has right to ascertain the claim to be made should be for the exact value of the goods damaged or destroyed at the date of fire.

Questions

1. Explain the various kinds of fire policies.
2. "Fire insurance is a personal contract." Explain.

3. How should a claim under a fire policy be made?
4. What is the effect of average clause in a fire policy?
5. What is a comprehensive policy of fire insurance?
6. Discuss the rights of the insurer under a fire policy.
7. What is the value of an average clause in a policy of a fire insurance?
8. What are the differences between Declaration policy and Adjustable policy?
9. Write short notes on:
   (a) Average clause in a fire insurance policy
   (b) Specific Policy
   (c) Floating Policy
   (d) Declaration Policy
   (e) Double Insurance
   (f) Reinsurance
   (g) Rent Policy
   (h) Builder's Risk Insurance
   (i) Blanket Policy
10. What types of losses are covered by a fire policy? Mention the types of losses not covered under fire policy.
11. Define fire insurance and explain the different types of fire insurance policies.

Mini Cases

Case1. A godown contained bags of potatoes insured against fire. The potatoes were spoiled on account of great heat caused by the closing of the ventilators. Is the insurance company liable for the loss?

Ans: The insurance company is not liable for the loss since the loss is not on account of fire. The loss by heating alone cannot be taken as loss by fire unless the subject matter has been actually burnt by fire.

Case 2. P got his goods lying in a godown insured against fire with Q. The goods were destroyed by fire. Precovered full compensation for goods from Q. P then sued the godown keeper and recovered a sum of Rs. 1,000 from him. Q claims this amount from P. P refuses to pay. Decide.

Ans: P cannot make a profit out of a contract of fire insurance. It is a contract of indemnity. He must pay Rs. 1,000 to Q.

Case 3. A insured her jewellery against fire and hid it in her grate under the coal. Later having forgotten this, she lit the fire and the jewellery was damaged. Can she recover damages under the fire policy?

Ans: The cause of fire is immaterial unless it has been due to the wilful misconduct of the insured herself. The insurer continues to be liable on a fire insurance policy for losses by fire even if the insured goods are inadvertently set fire by the insured herself.

Hence, in the instant case, the insurance company shall be liable for the loss since the fire was caused by the *bonafide* mistake of the insured herself. The fire was of course, intentionally lit but there was no intention to cheat the insurance company.

Case 4. Mr. X got his goods insured against fire. Afterwards Mr. X and his wife quarrelled and she set fire to the goods. The goods were destroyed. Is Mr. X entitled to recover the loss from the insurer?

Ans: Yes, Insurer may proceed against Mr. X's wife after paying compensation to Mr. X.

Case 5. R's car was insured against fire but not against collision. While he was driving, a fire started in the dashboard caused by a short circuit in the electrical connections. While trying to put it out, Mr. R lost control of the car and it collided with a tree. After the collision, the fire spread and engulfed the whole car. It was assessed that the loss due to the collision was Rs. 10,000 and due to the subsequent fire was Rs. 4,000. How much can R claim from the insurers?

Ans: Mr. R can claim from the insurers total loss of Rs. 14,000 loss of Rs. 10,000 on account of collision and Rs. 4,000 on account of fire because losses caused due to the efforts made to arrest or extinguish fire are also recoverable as losses caused by fire. Collision took place while R was trying to put out fire in the dashboard of the car. In case of loss by fire, cause of fire is not material unless it is fraudulent. Therefore, R can claim compensation from the insurers for both the losses.

Case 6. A got his house insured against fire with X Insurance Co Ltd. B, a miscreant set fire to A' s house. The insurance company compensates A for the loss. State the rights of the insurance company against B.

Ans: In all contracts of indemnity, the indemnifier having indemnified the indemnity holder, acquires all his rights against a third party in respect of the loss indemnified. This is on account of the doctrine of subrogation. In the instant case, the insurance company has already compensated A for the loss suffered by him.

It can, therefore, now proceed against B on the basis of subrogation and make him responsible for the loss.

Case 7. Mr. A got his property worth of Rs. 40,000 insured for Rs. 30,000. The policy contains average clause. The house is destroyed by fire and the actual loss is estimated at Rs. 24.000. How much can A recover by way of compensation from the insurance company?

Ans: The average clause comes into play only in those cases where it is proved that the loss sustained by the insured is less than the sum assured. In other words, the average clause applies only where there is under insurance and partial loss.

In the instant case, the claim will be settled at Rs. 18,000.

$$\text{i.e., } \frac{30,000}{40,000} \times 24,000.$$

Thus, A can recover the loss amount of Rs. 18,000 from the insurance company.

Case 8. A house covered by a fire policy catches fire. In the confusion that followed a theft is committed. Discuss the liability of the insurer.

Ans: Loss by theft during or after the occurrence of a fire is not covered by a fire policy. As such, the insurer is not liable for the loss.

Case 9. A insured his house against loss by fire. Later, while insane, he killed his wife, severely injured his only son and set fire to the house. Is he entitled to recover?

Ans: Yes, the son is entitled to recover on the policy, for the insured caused the fire when he was insane, and not deliberately.

Case 10. Mr. R injured his house worth Rs. 30,000 for Rs. 20,000 against risk by fire. There is an average clause in the policy. In a fire, the house was burnt to ashes. Mr. R claimed the whole insured amount. The insurer pleaded the "average clause". Decide.

Ans: Mr. R. is entitled to recover the whole insured amount of Rs. 40,000, because the "average clause" does not come into operation in the case of total loss. This clause comes into play only if there is a partial loss.

Chapter 26

Fire Insurance Claims

Introduction

Fire, in the business premises of any firm, destroys a number of assets such as building, machinery, furniture, stock etc. In addition, the normal working of a firm is affected for a number of days or months, resulting in loss of sale and loss of profits. Besides, it is very difficult for the business to replace the lost asset because of the limited working capital. So it is the interest of a business unit to take fire insurance policy to indemnify the loss of stock and other assets resulting from fire.

A fire insurance claim is lodged with the insurance company for the loss of stock and other assets by fire. The insurance company usually employs experienced Assessor to investigate the causes of fire and the extent of the damages. As per the report of the Assessor, the insurance company settles the claim made against it for loss due to fire.

Types of Losses

Losses due to fire are of two types such as:

I. Loss of Assets or Stock

II. Loss of Profit

I. Claims for Loss of Stock

Business units which have insured their godown or stores against the risk of loss of stock by fire are eligible to lodge loss of stock claims when a fire causes loss of their stock.

Salvage

Fire may destroy some items of stock completely. Some other portion of stock may be damaged and some items of stock may not be affected at all. The damaged stock and undamaged stock are separately valued and are called salvage value or stock salvaged. To lodge claim for the loss of stock by fire, the value of stock in trade on the date of fire has to be estimated.

Procedure for Calculating Claim for Loss of Stock

The following are the various points to be considered for calculating claim for loss of stock:

(1) In order to lodge the claim, it is essential to calculate (a) Total stock in the firm on the date of fire, and (b) Stock salvaged.

(2) Ascertain the actual loss of stock due to fire; the claim for loss of stock depends upon actual loss of stock due to fire.

(3) The actual loss of stock is equal to "Total stock on the date of fire less stock salvaged."

(4) Total stock is equal to stock in the beginning plus purchases (from the beginning of accounting year to the date of fire) less cost of stock sold (from the beginning of accounting year to the date of fire).

(5) Cost of goods sold is calculated by deducting gross profit from sales.

(6) The next step is to prepare Memorandum Trading Account of the current year upto the date of fire on the basis of opening stock purchases and sales from the beginning of the year upto the date of fire and estimated gross profit on the basis of last year's gross profit ratio. The balancing figures on the credit side of the Memorandum Trading Account reveals the value of stock on hand on the date of fire.

Specimen Form:

Memorandum Trading Account

Particulars	Amount	Particular	Amount
By Opening Stock By Purchases By Wages By Gross Profit C/d		By Sales By Stock on the date of fire (Balancing figure)	
	xxx		xxx

Note:

Value of stock hand on the date of fire	xxx
Less: Salvaged Stock	xxx
Claims to be lodged	xxx

(7) When ledger account for stock is not maintained, Gross Profit can be calculated with the help of sales and rate of gross profit. The following relevant points are to be considered

(a) $\text{Gross Profit Ratio} = \frac{\text{Gross Profit}}{\text{Sales}} \times 100$

(b) Previous Accounting year's gross profit and sales can be used for gross profit ratio

(c) Rate of profit is given sometimes "on sales" and sometimes "on cost".

(d) In case, it is given 'on cost' then it must be converted to "on sale"

(e) In case, it is not given then it must be calculated by preparing the trading account of the preceding year or years.

However, it must be remembered that the effect of abnormal happenings Examples:

(a) Variation in the practice of stock valuation

(b) Selling a part of goods either at a loss or at a rate of, profit which is different from that normally followed

(c) Charging productive or direct expenses as indirect expenses must be nullified at the time of preparing the trading account for the calculation of rate of gross profit.

This is necessary because the rate of gross profit has a direct impact on the calculation of claim for loss of stock. Higher the rate of gross profit more is the stock at the end (because it is a balancing figure) and more is the claim. Therefore, insurance company is very particular about the rate of gross profit used for the calculation of claim. The insurer has to ensure that it is not higher than what it should be.

Average Clause

A fire insurance policy usually includes an average clause to discourage under insurance of stock or of any asset. The effect of this clause is that if the value of stock or any asset insured on the date of fire, is more than the amount of policy taken, the full value of stock or any asset destroyed does not become payable to the insured but the insurance company pays the proportion of the loss which the amount of policy taken bears to the total value of stock or any asset in hand on the date of fire. It can be explained as below:

$$\text{Actual value of stock destroyed} = \text{Stock on the date of fire} - \text{Salvage Value}$$

$$\text{Claim to be lodged} = \frac{\text{Value of Insurance Policy}}{\text{Value of stock on hand on the date of fire}} \times \text{Value of stock destroyed}$$

Example:

Value of Policy	Rs. 1,00,000
Stock in hand in the godown on the date of fire	Rs. 1,25,000
Stock destroyed by fire	Rs. 50,000

$$\text{Claim to be lodged} = \frac{\text{Value of Insurance Policy}}{\text{Value of stock on hand on the date of fire}} \times \text{Value of stock}$$

$$= \frac{1,00,000}{1,25,000} \times 50,000$$

= Rs. 40000

Therefore, insurance claim admitted will be proportionately reduced to Rs. 40000 and the total value of stock destroyed by fire (i.e., Rs. 50000) will not be admissible to the insured.

Illustration No.:1

A fire occurred on September 30, 2003, in the godown of Mr. Anand. From the following figures ascertain the claim to be lodged.

	Rs.
Stock on January 1,2003	17,000
Purchases from Janurary 1,2003, to date of fire	1,70,000
Wages and other manufacturing expenses	17,000
Sales from January 1,2003, to date of fire	2,00,000
The rate of gross profit is 25% on cost.	
The stock salvaged was valued at	4,000

Solution:

Memorandum Trading Account upto Sept. 30,2003

Particulars	Amount Rs.	Particular	Amount Rs.
To Opening Stock	17,000	By Sales	2,00,000
To Purchases	1,70,000	By Closing Stock	44,000
To Wages and Manufacturing Exp.	17,000	(Balancing Figure)	
To Gross Profit 25% on Cost $\left(2,00,000 \times \frac{25}{125}\right)$	40,000		
	2,44,000		2,44,000

	Rs.
Value of Stock on hand on the date of fire (Balancing Figure)	44,000
Less: Stock Salvaged	4,000
Claim to be lodged	40,000

Illustration No.:2

Fire occurred in the premises of Mr. Anand on 1st April, 2003 and a considerable part of the stock was destroyed. The stock salvaged was Rs. 5,600. A fire insurance policy for Rs. 34,200. was taken to cover loss of stock by fire. You are required to ascertain the insurance claim which the company should claim make from the insurance company for the loss of stock by the firm from the following particulars:

	Rs.
Purchases for the year 2002	1, 87, 600
Sales for the year 2002	2,30,000
Purchases from 1st Jan.2003 to 1st April 2003	36,400
Stock on 1st January 2002	28,800
Stock on 31st December 2002	48,400
Wages paid during the year 2002	20,000
Wages paid during 1st January, 2003 to 1st April 2003	3,600
Sales from 1st January 2003 to 1st April 2003	48,000

Fire also broke out on 21" December, 2002 and destroyed stock of the estimated cost of Rs. 1000. There was a practice in the concern to value the stock at cost less 10%, but all of a sudden this practice was changed and stock on 31st December, 2002 was valued at cost plus 10%.

Solution:

Memorandum Trading Account of Mr. Anand Upto 1st April 2003

Particular	Amount Rs.	Particulars	Amount Rs.
To Opening Stock (1.1.2003)	44,000	By Sales	48,000
To Purchases	36,400	By Closing Stock (Balancing figure)	45,600
To Wages	3,600		
To Gross Profit (20% of Rs. 48,0 00)	9,600		
	93,600		93,600

Working Notes:

1. **Calculation of stock destroyed by fire:**

	Rs.
Value of Stock on 1st April, 2003	45,600
Less: Stock salvaged	5,600
Stock destroyed by fire	40,000

2. **Calculation of insurance claim to be lodged:**

The average clause will apply as the value of stock on the date of fire. Rs. 45,600, is more than the sum assured of Rs. 34200. Therefore, the insurance claim to be lodged will be:

$$\text{Claimto be loged} = \frac{\text{Valueof policy}}{\text{Value of Stock}} \times \text{Valueof stockdestroyedon the Dateof fire}$$

$$= \frac{34,200}{45,600} \times 40,000$$

$$= \text{Rs. } 30,000$$

(3) Calculation of Gross Profit through Trading Account: Trading Account of Mr. Anand For the Year Ending 31st December, 2002

Particulars	Amount (Rs.)	Particulars	Amount (Rs.)
To Opening Stock (1.1.2002)		By Sales	2,32,000
		By Closing Stock	
$\left(28{,}800 \times \frac{100}{90}\right)$	32,000	$\left(48{,}400 \times \frac{100}{110}\right)$	44,000
To Purchases	1,87,600	By Stock destroyed	
To Wages	20,000	by Fire	10,000
To Gross Profit	46,400		
	2,86,000		2,86,000

(4) Calculation of Percentage of Gross Profit to Sales:

$$\text{Gross Profit Ratio} = \frac{\text{Gross Profit}}{\text{Sales}} \times 100$$

$$= \frac{46{,}400}{2{,}32{,}000} \times 100$$

$$= 20\%$$

Stock destroyed on 31st December, 2002 has been shown on the credit side of the Trading Account for the year 2002 to ascertain the correct percentage of Gross Profit.

II. Claim for the Loss of Profit

In the event of fire, it not only destroys the properties but also affects the earning capacity of the business. This results in partial or total stoppage of business leading to the reduction in the profit which is called "loss on profit". An ordinary fire insurance policy covers the loss on account of stock or properties destroyed by fire, but it does not cover such loss of profit. In order to give complete protection to the insured, a new type of insurance called as "Consequential Loss Insurance" or "Loss of Profit Insurance".

Under Consequential Policy, the insurer indemnifies the policyholder against losses arising from the suspension, wholly or partly of the activities of the business caused by fire.

Loss of Profits insurance covers the following risks consequent upon fire:

(a) Loss of Profit due to inability to produce

(b) Loss of Profit due to short sales

(c) Loss due to non-recovery of standing charges such as salaries, rent and rates, taxes etc.

(d) Increased working expenses incurred by the insured during the indemnity period in order to maintain normal business activity.

Important Terms

Before the claim, it is better to be conversant with the following important terms:

(1) Indemnity Period: Any period not exceeding twelve months from the date of damage during which the results of the business shall be affected due to fire is known as indemnity period. This is the period for which insurance policy is taken against the risk of fire.

(2) Standing Turnover: Standing Turnover refers to the turnover during that period in the twelve months immediately before the date of the damage, which corresponds with the indemnity period.

(3) Annual Turnover: Annual Turnover indicated Annual Sales during the twelve months immediately before the date of damage.

(4) Loss due to Short Sales: This is the difference between the standard Turnover and the Actual Turnover.

(5) Standing Charges: These are the fixed expenses, which have to be paid whether work is carried on or not, like salaries, rent and rates, taxes, postage etc.

(6) Insured Standing Charges: Any fixed expenses, which are mentioned in the policy taken by the insured firm.

(7) Uninsured Standing Charges: This is an additional expenditure incurred by the insured in order to carry on the business during the indemnity period.

(8) Saving in Standing Charges: Any saving in expenses will have to be deducted before arriving the claim for loss of profit and increased working expenses.

(9) Average Clause: As it has been explained already, the insured is entitled to get only a proportion of his claim. Where the policy covers a portion of the loss, this is ascertained by first calculating the amount of profit for which the insurance policy ought to have been taken and then allowing the claim only proportionately.

Steps in the Preparation of Claim under Loss of Profits

The following steps are followed for the calculation of claim for the loss of profit:

Step 1: Claim for reduction on Turnover or Short Sales:

Claim for Reduction Turnover = Short Sales × Gross Profit Ratio

$$\text{(a) Gross Profit Ratio} = \frac{\text{Net Profit} + \text{Insured Standing Charges}}{\text{Turnover}} \times 100$$

(b) Where there is a Net Loss the Formula will be:

$$\text{Gross Profit Ratio} = \frac{\text{Insured Standing Charges} - \text{Net Loss}}{\text{Turnover}} \times 100$$

(c) Where the amount of loss is arrived at as follows when only a portion of the standing charges are insured:

$$\text{Gross Profit Ratio} = \frac{\text{Net Loss} \times \text{Insured Standing Charges}}{\text{All the Standing Charges}}$$

Step 1 indicates that the calculation of loss of profit on sales by applying the rate of gross profit

Step 2: Claim for increased Cost of Working:

The claim for increased cost of working is restricted to the lowest of the following amounts:

(a) Actual increased working expenses

(b) If all standing charges are not insured:

$$\frac{\text{Net Profit} + \text{Insured Standing Expenses}}{\text{Net Profit} + \text{All Standing Expenses}} \times \text{Actual Increased cost of working}$$

(c) Gross Profit on Sales resulting from the increased working expenses.

Step 2 indicates that deduct the amount of expenses saved as a result of fire from the total claim and the resultant figure will be the amount of gross claim for the loss of profit.

Step 3: Application of Average Clause:

If the policy amount is less than gross profit on annual turnover, the gross claims as calculated in Step 3 is subject to the Average Clause follows:

Claim to be made =

$$\text{Total Claim} \times \frac{\text{Policy Amount}}{\text{Gross Profit on Adjusted Annual Turnover}}$$

Amount to be Insured =

Adjusted Turnover for the 12 months before fire × Rate of Gross Profit

Illustration: 3

There was a serious fire in the premises of M/s Nancy & Co. on 1st September 2003. Their business activities were interrupted until 31.12.2003, when normal trading conditions were re-established. M/s Nancy is insured under the loss of profit policy for Rs. 4,20,000 the period of indemnity being six months.

You are able to ascertain the following information

(a) The net profit for the year ended 31.12.2002 was Rs. 2,00,000.

(b) The annual insurable standing charges amounted to Rs. 3,00,000 of which Rs. 20,000 were not included in the definition of insured standing charges under the policy.

(c) The additional cost of working in order to mitigate the damage caused by the fire amounted to Rs. 6,000 and but for this expenditure, the business would have had to shut down.

(d) The saving in insured standing charges in consequence of the fire amounted to Rs. 15,000.

(e) The turnover for the period of four months ended April 30, August 31 and December 31 in each of the year 2002 and 2003 was as under.

	Rs.	Rs.	Rs.
2002	6,50,000	8,00,000	9,50,000
2003	7,00,000	8,00,000	1,50,000

You are required to compute the relevant claim under the terms of the loss of profit policy.

Solution:

Set I – Claim for reduction in turnover or short sale:

Computation of short sales:

Standard Turnover	
(for the 4 months ending with 31.12.2002)	9,50,000
Less: Actual sales for the indemnity period	
(for the 4 months ending with 31.12.2003)	1,50,000
Short sales	8,00,000

Computation of Gross Profit Ratio:

$$= \frac{\text{Net Profit + Insured Standing Charges}}{\text{Accounting Year Turnover}} \times 100$$

$$= \frac{2,00,000 + 2,80,000}{24,00,000} \times 100$$

= 20%

Gross Profit on short sales or claim for reduction in Turnover:

$$= 8,00,000 \times \frac{20}{100}$$

= Rs. 1,60,000

Step II–claim for increased cost of working:

[a] Additional cost of working in order to mitigate the damage Rs.6,000

[b] Since all the standing charges are not insured, the amount of claim will be:

$$= \frac{\text{Net Profit + Insured Standing Charges}}{\text{NetProfit + All Insurable Standing Charges}} \times \text{Actual Increased Cost}$$

$$= \frac{2,00,000 + 2,80,000}{2,00,000 + 3,00,000} \times 6000$$

= Rs. 5,760

Gross Profit on Saved Turnover

$$= 1,50,000 \times \frac{20}{100}$$

= Rs. 30,000

Claim for increased cost (lowest of a, b, and c) Rs. 5,760

Step III – Calculation of Claim:

Claim for Reduction in Turnover	=	1,60,000
Add: Claim for increased cost (stepII)	=	5,760
		1, 65, 760
Less: Savings in standing charges	=	15,000
Total claim for loss of profit	=	1,50,760

Step IV – Application of Average Clause:

$$= \frac{\text{Sum Assured}}{\text{Gross Profit on Annual Turnover}} \times \text{Total Claim}$$

Annual Turnover = Sale for 12 months ending with 31.8.2003

= Rs. 24,50,000

$$\text{Gross Profit on Annual Turnover} = 24{,}50{,}000 \times \frac{20}{100}$$

= Rs. 4,90,000

$$\text{Amount of Claim admissible} = \frac{4{,}20{,}000}{4{,}90{,}000} \times 1{,}50{,}760$$

= Rs. 1,29,223

Questions

Indicate the correct answer:

(1) Consequential loss policy indemnifies

(a) Capital losses (b) Revenue losses

(c) Budgeted losses (d) Normal losses

(2) Fire insurance policy provides cover for

(a) Tangible Assets (b) Intangible Assets

(c) Fictitious Assets (d) Current Assets

(3) The average clause in a loss of profits policy protects the

(a) Insured

(b) Insurer

(c) Workers

(4) The difference between Standard Turnover and Actual Turnover during the indemnity period is ______________

(a) Short Sales (b) Estimated Sales

(c) Increased Sales (d) Quota Sales

(5) The minimum period for which indemnity is to be sought by the insured is ____________ in the case of a consequential loss policy.

(a) 6 months (b) 3 months (c) 2 months (d) 4 months

(6) A fire insurance policy is taken up to indemnify

(a) Capital losses to tangible property

(b) Revenue losses to tangible property

(c) Capital losses to ill tangible property

(d) Discourage under insurance

(7) The loss of profit policy covers loss of profits due to:

(a) Loss of sales

(b) Non-recovery of standing charges

(c) Loss of sales as well as loss of insured standing charges.

(8) The objective of inserting average clause in loss of stock policy is to:

(a) Encourage under insurance

(b) Discourage full insurance of stock

(c) Encourage full insurance of stock

Answers:

(I) b (2) a (3) b (4) a (5) b (6) a (7) c (8) a

(9) Explain the accounting procedure for ascertaining the loss of stock by fire.

(10) What do you understand by the Average clause in the policy?

(11) What is a consequential loss? How is it computed?

(12) Write shore notes on:

(a) Gross profit Ratio

(b) Short sales

(c) Average clause

(d) Standing charges

(e) Indemnity period

Practical Problems

1. Fire occurred in the premises of Ram & Co. on 20th February 2003. The company has taken out a fire insurance policy of Rs. 1,00,000 covering its stock in trade and the policy was subject to average clause. From the following particulars ascertain the claim to be lodged.

	Rs.
Stock on 1st January 2002	90,000
Purchases during the year 2002	**3,65,000**
Purchases Returns during the year 2002	**5,000**
Stock on 31st December, 2002	**1,26,000**
Sales for the year 2002	**4,10,000**
Sales Returns during the year 2002	10,000
Purchases from 1.1.2003 to date of fire	84,000
Sales from 1.1.2003 to due of fire	1,03,000
Value of stock saved 19,800	

It was the practice of the concern to value stock at cost less 10%

Ans: [Rs. 86,326]

2. A fire occurred on 1.9.2003 in the goon of Mr. Ramesh. From the following particulars find out the claim to be lodged:

	Rs.
Stock on 1.1.2003	25,300
Purchases from 1.1.2003 to date of fire	50,400
Sales from 1.1.2003 to date of fire	1,.56,000
Manufacturing expenses and wages	60,000
Goods taken by Ramesh at cost	2,500
The rate of gross profit on cost is	30%
Value of salvaged stock	3,600

Ans: [Gross Profit 30% on cost or 30/130 on sales]

3. A fire occurred in the premises of a merchant on June 15,2003 and a considerable part of the stock was destroyed. The value of the stock saved was Rs. 4,500.

The books disclosed that on April 1 2003 the stock was valued at Rs. 36,750, the purchases to the date of fire amounted to Rs. 1,04,940 and the sales to Rs.1, 56,500. On investigation it is found that during the past five years the average gross profit on sales was 36%.

You are required to prepare a statement showing the amount the merchant should claim from the insurance company in respect of stock destroyed by the fire.

Ans: [claim Rs. 37,030]

4. A merchant's godown caught fire on Nov. 3,2003 at night causing serious damage to stock. The following information is obtained from the books and records salvaged.

	Rs.
Stock on 31.12.2001	45,000
Stock on 31.12.2002	50,000
Purchases during 20024,	75,000
Sales from Jan. to Nov.3, 2003	4,00,000
Purchases from Jan. to Nov. 3, 2003	4,40,000
Sales during 2002	5,87,500

Assuming that the rate of gross profit on sales has been the same in 2003 as in 2002, estimate the value of stock in the godown at the time of fire.

Ans: [G.P. in 2002–20%, Stock on date of fire Rs. 1,70,000.]

Chapter 27

Miscellaneous Insurance

Personal Accident Insurance

Definition

Lord Macnaughten defines an accident as "an unlooked mishap or an untoward event which is not expected or designed." In the term accident some violence, casualty or *vis-a-vis* major is necessarily involved. Accident insurance consists of three branches:

(a) Personal Accident Insurance, including insurance against sickness.

(b) Property Insurance including Burglary, Fidelity, Insolvency etc.

(c) Liability Insurance including Motor Insurance and Workmen's Compensation Insurance.

Now we can discuss Personal Accident Insurance briefly.

Personal Accident Insurance

A contract of personal accident insurance is a contract whereby a sum of money is secured to the assured or his legal representative in the event of his disablement or death by accident. It is a contract against injury or death resulting from accident. Personal Accident Insurance akin to life assurance is not a contract of indemnity. The insurer usually undertakes to pay specified sums in the event of temporary or permanent disability, whether partial or total. Other sums are agreed to be payable in the event of death or loss of limb etc. as the result of an accident.

For example, the insurer may agree to pay Rs. 10,000 for the loss of both eyes, and Rs. 5,000 for the loss of one eye or Rs. 50,000 for permanent disablement and Rs. 1,000 for temporary disability plus Rs. 10 per week during the period of disability and so on.

Rating

The rate of premium charged depends mainly on the type of cover desired and the insured person's occupation. This is non–tariff business. The same rate of premium charged by various insurers for the same risks. The risks associated with occupation vary according to the nature of work performed. It is difficult to fix the rate of premium for each profession or occupation. Hence, occupation is classified into groups, each group reflecting, more or less, similar risk exposure.

Classification of Occupation

Risk Group I: Accountants, doctors, lawyers, architects, consulting. engineers, teachers, bankers, persons engaged in administration functions, persons primarily engaged in occupation of similar hazards.

Risk Group II: Builders, contractors and engineers engaged in superintending functions only, veterinary doctors, paid drivers of motor cars and light motor vehicles.

All persons engaged in manual labour (Except those falling under Risk Group III), cash carrying employees, garage and motor mechanics, machine operators, sportsmen etc.

Risk Group III : Persons working in underground mines, those exposed, to explosives and magazines, workers involved in electrical installations with high tension supply, jockeys, circus personnel etc.

Proposal Form: Under Personal Accident Insurance, the Proposal Form consists of the following information:

(1) Personal details, i.e., age, height and weight, full description of occupation and average monthly salary

(2) Physical conditions

(3) Habits

(4) Other or previous insurance

(5) Previous accidents

(6) Selection of benefits and sum assured

(7) Declaration.

Claims

For the settlement of insurance claims under Personal Accident Insurance, the following procedure is required to be adopted —

(1) On the receipt of notice of damage or loss against personal accident, the insured is requested to submit the Claim Form

along with Medical Certificate, Medical Examiner's Report, Receipt/Discharge Form, Death Certificate, Prescription, Bills and Receipts etc.

(2) On the receipt of the Claim Form, the Insurance Company **investigates the relevant facts and necessary documents in addition to the Claim Form.**

(3) After the process of investigation, the Claim Form enclosed with necessary documents is sent to the claim department for approval of claim to the insured person,

(4) On the basis of investigation and inspection, the Insurance Company determines the extent of its liability and the loss is indemnified.

Accident Cover and Compensation

Personal Accident insurance is non-tari8/ff, which provides cover for accidental bodily injury resulting in death or disablement. On payment of additional premium, generally the policy may be extended to cover medical expenses. The following are the accident cover and related compensations for individual and family:

Accident Cover and Compensation

Accident cover	Compensation
A. Individual Cover:	
1. Death only	100% of capital sum assured
2. Loss of two limbs, two eyes or one limb and one eye	100%
3. Loss of one limb or one eye	50%
4. Permanent total disablement from injuries other than named above	100%
5. Permanent partial disablement	As per the scale incorported in the policy
6. Temporary total disablement	@1% of capital sum assured upto 104 weeks, maximum weekly benefit not exceeding Rs. 3,000/-
7. Reimbursement of medical/surgical/ capital hospital/nursing/home expenses necessarily incurred.	Subject to a limit of 10% of sum assured or 25% of valid claim, whichever is less.
B. Family Package cover:	
1. Earning member (person insured) and spouse if earning	100% of capital sum assured each
2. Spouse (if not earning)	50% of capital sum assured or Rs. 1 lakh whichever is less
3. Children (between the age of 5 years and 19 years)	25% of capital sum assured or Rs. 50,000 whichever is less per child

Questions

1. What do you understand by Personal Accident Insurance?
2. What are risks covered under Personal Accident Insurance? Explain the procedure of effecting Personal Accident Insurance.
3. Explain the special features of Personal Accident Insurance.
4. What are the legal requirements for settlement of insurance claim under Personal Accident Insurance?

Chapter 28

National Agricultural Insurance Scheme

Crop Insurance Scheme

This insurance scheme is also known as Rashtriya Krishi Bima Yojana. It came into existence in India from 22nd June 1999. The primary objective of the insurance is:

(a) To provide a measure of financial support to farmers in the event of crop failure due to drought, flood etc.

(b) To restore credit eligibility of farmers after a crop failure, for the next crop season.

(c) To support and stimulate production of pulses and oil seeds.

Salient Features of Crop Insurance

1. **Crops to be covered**

   (a) Rice, wheat and millets

   (b) Oil seeds and pulses

   (c) Cotton, sugarcane and potato.

2. **Farmers to be Covered**

   (a) Dwelling hut/house and contents

   (b) Cattle (indigenous)

(c) Agricultural pumpset

(d) Bullock cart

(e) Gramin Personal Accident (Insured and Spouse).

3. Risk Covered against

(a) Natural fire and lightning

(b) Storm, cyclone

(c) Flood and landslide

(d) Drought, dry spells

(e) Pests, diseases.

4. Extentions of Schemes

The scheme extends to all States and Union Territories.

5. Sharing of Risk

The coverage in respect of crops insured in any State, the loss or damage will be shared between General Insurance Corporation of India and the State Government. The sharing of risk between GIC and State Government will be in the ratio of 2: 1.

6. Area Approach

The scheme will operate in defined areas for each crop as may be notified by the Union Ministry of Agriculture. A defined area may be a District, Taluka, Block, or other smaller identified areas.

7. Sum Insured

The sum insured, per insured farmer shall be 100% of the loan sanctioned to him for growing the crop in the defined area during the insured season, with effect from the year 1999. The sum insured is restricted to Rs. 10,000 for each farmer for all crops put together in the revised scheme.

8. Threshold Yield of Crop for 'Defined Area'

The sum assured is fixed with reference to the Threshold Yield (TY) for a crop based on past three years average yield in case of rice and wheat and five years in case of other crops, for a defined area. This is multiplied by level of indemnity, *viz.*, 90%, 80%, and 60%, corresponding to low risk, medium risk and high risk.

Basis of Indemnity

If there is a shortfall in the actual average yield per hectare of the insured crop, each of the insured farmers growing that crop in the defined area will eligible for indemnity in the following manner —

$$\frac{\text{Short fall in Yield}}{\text{Threshold Yield}} \times \text{Sum Insured}$$

Central Crop Insurance Funds

To meet the catastrophic losses a Corpus Fund is created with contribution from the Central Government and State/Union Territory on 50:50 basis.

The Main Objectives of Central Funds

(a) To receive crop insurance premium from the financial institutions and issue policy

(b) To settle claim promptly

(c) To notify crop-wise areas and premium rates well in advance of the season

(d) To maintain communications with financial institutions regarding notified crops, areas, premium rates etc.

(e) Strenghten crop estimation survey machinery in order to furnish accurate yield estimates.

(f) To keep the excess of crop insurance charge over indemnity claim in good crop years so as to enable GIC to draw from the fund to meet additional indemnity claims in bad crop years.

State Crop Insurance Funds

The State Government will set up State Crop Insurance Fund. The initial fund of Rs. one to two crores to be equally contributed by the State Government concerned and the Central Government. The size of the State Crop Insurance Fund for each State would be decided in consultation with the State Government, Ministry of Finance and Ministry of Agriculture of the Central Government.

Agricultural Pumpset Insurance

This policy applies to centrifugal and submersible pumpsets for agricultural purpose only up to 25 HP only. Under this policy indemnifies the insured against the unforeseen and sudden physical damage to the pumpsets caused by fire or lightning, theft/burglary, mechanical/electrical breakdown, riot, strike, malicious damage landslide and terrorism. Food risk can be covered by payment of additional premium at the rate @ of 2% of sum assured per annum and 1% for submersible pump. The minimum premium is Rs.50 for electric pumpsets and Rs.70 for diesel pumpsets. In the case of total loss in company's liability is 50% of sum assured.

Important Exclusion

(a) Normal wear and tear gradual deterioration due to atmosphere conditions or otherwise.

(b) Wilful act or gross negligence of insured or his representative.

(c) Faults existing at the time of commencement and know to the insured or his representative.

(d) Loss or damage for which the manufacturer or supplier is responsible either by law or under contract.

(e) Cost of dismantling transport to workshop and back, as also cost of re-erection.

Sum assured

100% market value at the time of issue of cover new replacement value of pump sets (including provision for packaging, freight and erection charges and customs duties if any).

No claim discount:

Claim Application for	**The renewable premium at the rate of**
(i) If no claim arises for 1 year	10%
(ii) If no claim arises for 2 consecutive years	15%
(iii) If no claim arises for 3 consecutive years	20%
Long Term Discount available	
(i) If taken for 2 years policy	15%
(ii) If taken for 3 years and up 5 years	25%
(iii) If taken 6 years upto 9 years policy	30%
Group Discount Applicable	**Group Discount at the If No. of Pumpsets**
2,500 to 5,000 sets	10%
5,001 to 25,000 sets	15%
25,000 to 10,000 sets	20%
Above 50,000 sets	25%

Horticulture/Plantation (Input) Insurance

Horticulture and plantation insurance scheme is applicable to the following horticulture and plantation crops.

(a) Horticulture Crops: (I) Grape (2) Citrus (Orange, Lime, Sweet lime) (3) Chikoo (4) Pomegranate (5) Banana

(b) **Plantation Crops:** (1) Rubber (2) Eucalyptus (3) Peepal (4) Teakwood (5) Oil Palm Plantations (6) All types of trees (7) Sugarcane (8) Tea (9) Coffee (10) Apple

This policy indemnifies the insured to the extent of loss of input due to loss or damage to the insured tree/fruits (whichever is applicable depending on the crop insured) occasioned by operation of any one or more of the following perils either in forest fire and bush fire) lightning, storm, hailstorm, cyclone, typhoon, tempest, hurricane, tornado whilst in direct and immediate operations over the insured area flood and inundation (inspection report in necessary to cover these risks) riot, strike and malicious damage and the acts of terrorism. These perils are also applicable for all types of insured fruits crops and plantation crops. Under this policy, an insured may be an individual farmer whether owner or tenant engaged in cultivation of above mentioned items. However, a policy may be issued in the name of an association or an organized and registered body of form engaged in cultivation of the specified crops. Under this policy, sum assured is determined on the basis of cultivation or input cost, i.e., cost of raising/development of insured trees. The policy will be issued for fixed sum assured which is given separately under each crop.

Period of Insurance

Crop duration of twelve months (one year) whichever is shorter subject to the following:

(a) This policy is valid for one season. The policy period is taken from the date of payment of premium until crop in that season is harvested. For fruit crops having season more than one year, appropriate additional premium will be charged. For citrus fruits, policy period will be one year from the date of issue of policy.

(b) Period of insurance in respect of sugarcane crop shall be extendable from 12 months to 18 months.

(c) In respect of rubber, eucalyptus and peepal and other trees where plants are first required to be raised in nurseries and then fields, the period of insurance shall commence after expiry of twelve months of transplanting and policy for these crops can be issued on annual basis.

Premium Rates

Premium rates shall be charged for difference insurable crops at the following rates:

Insurable Crops	Premium rates
(a) Horticulture Crops Citrus, Fruits (Orange, Lime, Sweet lime) Chikoo, Pomegranate, Banana (Standard Cover)	5% Sum Assured
Grape Crop (Optional Cover: losses due to unseasonal rains and frost)	Additional Premium @ 1.5% of sum assured

(b) Plantations:
Rubber, Eucalyptus, Peepal, Teakwood — 1.25%of sum assured

(c) Sugarcane — 1.25% of sum assured

(d) Oil Palm
Part "A" — 1.50% of sum assured
Part "B" — 2.00% of sum assured

Under this policy, no claim shall be payable if the amount of claim assessed does not exceed 10% of sum assured per acre or Rs. 1,000 – per affected acre whichever is lower. This rule is not applicable for the fire losses under the sugarcane policy. The assured shall be deemed to be his own insurer for first 20% of the claim assessed per acre, only 80% of claim assessed shall be paid under the policy.

Hut Insurance - Individual

This insurance scheme is applicable to dwelling huts in rural areas constructed with financial aid from banks, co-operatives and Government institutions. In maximum, 200 huts situated in one contiguous area are covered under this plan. Separate rating applicable to a larger number on reference General Insurance Corporation. Hut insurance policy indemnifies the insured against all accidental losses or damages due to fire, earthquake, storm, tempest, impact damage, riot strike and malicious damage. Under this policy, the maximum sum assured is Rs. 6,000. The minimum premium is Rs. 15 per policy. This applies only in cases where individual huts are covered. The rate of premium is Rs. 3 per mille per annum. The limit of liability is Rs. 6,000.

Hut Insurance Group/State Governments

Hut Insurance Group policy indemnifies the insured against all accidental losses or damages due to fire, lightning, storm, flood etc.

Salient features

(1) This group cover is given to state Governments only in respect of huts/semi-rural areas of the state, provided all huts are covered.

(2) The amount of sum assured should not be more than Rs. 5,000 for fire and allied perils.

(3) The premium rate is Rs. 3 per mille per annum.

(4) 50 per cent of the premium share by the Government.

(5) The total aggregate claim amount shall be limited to (a) Rs. 2 crores per event and (b) Rs. 10 crores in any one year during the currency of the policy.

(6) For ordinary claims the State Government may nominate claim enquiry cum settlement officer

(7) For major claims – the insurer will constitute a task force to survey and assess major flood and fire claims

(8) The hut insurance business will be shared by the leader and other companies in the ratio of 40 : 20 : 20 : 20.

(9) The scheme provide compensation not exceeding Rs. 1,000 for a hut and Rs. 500 for belonging therein the entire premium cost is being borne by the Central Government.

Questions

1. Explain the salient features of Crop Insurance.
2. State what is Crop Insurance Fund. Explain.
3. What do you understand by Crop Insurance Scheme?
4. Write an explanatory note on National Agricultural Insurance Scheme.
5. What are the advantages and disadvantages of Crop Insurance Scheme?
6. Explain the operations of Crop Insurance Schemes.
7. What do you understand about Agricultural Pumpset Insurance?
8. Explain the features of Agriculture/Plantation Insurance.
9. What is Hut Insurance? Explain its features–

Chapter 29

Fidelity Guarantee Insurance

Meaning

In this insurance, the insurer undertakes to indemnify the assured (employer) in consideration of certain payments, upto certain specified amount insured against for loss arising through the fraud, or embezzlement on the part of the employees. This kind of insurance is also known as 'fidelity guarantee' insurance and is frequently adopted as a precautionary measure in cases where new and untried employees are given positions of trust.

Types of Policies

The following types of policies are in general demand.

(a) Individual Policy

(b) Collective Policy

(c) Floating or Floater Policy

(d) Positions Policy

(e) Blanket Policy

(a) **Individual Policy:** This type of policy is used where only one Individual is to be guaranteed. Name of the employee, occupation/ duties and the sum insured must be clearly stated.

(b) **Collective Policy:** This policy embracing all employees falling within certain categories, or alternatively, the whole staff, has become very common.

(c) **Floating Policy or Floater:** This is an extension of the collective form of contract in which the names and duties of the individuals to be covered are inserted in a schedule, but instead of individual amounts of guarantee, a specified sum of guarantee is 'floated' over the whole group. Under the floating policy and claim, in respect of one employee will reduce the guarantee by the amount thereof until renewal unless such amount is reinstated proposals for floating policy should be discouraged. When acceptance has to be considered for business reasons, the proposal should first be referred to the regional office for approval before acceptance.

(d) **Positions Policy:** This is similar to a Collective Policy with the difference that instead of using names, the 'position is guaranteed for a specified amount, so that a change in the person holding the position does not affect cover. This policy covering persons holding a particular position (e.g. persons holding the position of cashier with its organisations) or the entire staff of a firm.

It is to be noted that the liability of the insurers in respect of each position remains limited to the amount guaranteed for the position, irrespective of the number of person acting in that position.

(e) **Blanket Policy:** This policy covers the entire staff without showing names or positions. No enquiries about the employees are made by the insurers. Such policies are only suitable for an employer with a large staff and the organisation to make adequate enquiries into the antecedents of his employees.

Rating

The rate of premium depends upon the type of occupation, status of the employee, the system of check and supervision. Under individual and collective policies, the rate is a per cent of the amount of guaranteed, e.g., 1 per cent. The premium for a Floating Policy comprises a percentage charge and a per capita charge. The percentage charge is applied on the amount guaranteed and the per capita charge on the number of employees to be guaranteed.

Claims

For the settlement of insurance claims under Fidelity Insurance, the following procedure is required to be adopted.

The investigation of fidelity guarantee claims is entrusted to independent surveyors like Chartered Accountants. The Surveyor would conduct a detailed investigation into circumstances of the loss which would involve mainly the examination of the books of accounts of the insured employer.

The policy provides that the amount payable by the insurer in respect of the defaulting employee shall not exceed the, amount of indemnity stated in the schedule of the policy in respect of such employee. Any money which, but for fraud or dishonesty of an employee, would become payable to him, shall be deducted from the amount of the loss before a claim is made under the policy.

Questions

1. Explain the special features of Fidelity Guarantee Insurance.
2. Write a note on the types of Fidelity Guarantee Insurance.
3. What do you understand by Fidelity Guarantee Insurance?
4. Discuss the scope of Fidelity Guarantee Insurance.
5. Explain the procedure of Fidelity Guarantee Insurance.

Chapter 30

Property Insurance

Meaning

Property insurance includes fidelity, burglary and insolvency. Property insurance covers all loss of property by burglary, theft or house breaking by any other act which is a criminal offence.

Burglary Insurance

Burglary insurance is a major business in the miscellaneous class of insurance. The policy is available to commercial establishments, factories, godowns, shops etc. Property in any form including cash, in the business premises can be covered.

Types of Policies

The main type of policies are as follows:

(1) Business Premises Insurance Policy

(2) Private Dwellings Insurance Policy

(3) Jewellery and Valuables Insurance Policy.

(4) All Risks Insurance Policies.

1. **Business Premises Insurance Policy:** Business Premises Insurance Policy is designed to meet the cover against risks of burglary and house breaking only. Mere theft without the use of

force and violent entry into the premises is not covered. This policy is issued to 'commercial establishments' to cover against risks relating to damage to insured property or premises by burglars or house breakers.

2. **Private Dwelling Insurance Policy:** This policy is specially suitable for covering theft risk also in addition to burglary and house breaking risks. The sum assured under this policy must represent the full value. One policy may be issued for (a) furniture and household goods and personal effect and another for (b) jewellery and valuables.

3. **Jewellery and Valuable Insurance Policies:** Insurance of property under this policy is made for jewellery, plates, watches, personal ornaments and other valuables. This policy covers any loss or damage by any cause including fire, theft to the insured property, But policy does not cover loss or damage caused by the consequence of war, act of foreign enemy etc.

4. **All Risk Policies:** This policy is intended to cover risks in respect of jewellery, valuable, works of art, paintings and other similar articles. All Risks Policy is suitable for covering any damage or loss by fire or burglary or theft or by any other accident or fortuitous circumstances. The insurable value in these cases is decided on agreed value basis.

Questions

1. What you understand by Property Insurance?
2. Write a note on the types of Property Insurance Policies.

Chapter 31

Motor Vehicle Insurance

Meaning And Definition

Motor Vehicle Insurance had its beginning in the United Kingdom. Motor Insurance belongs to the miscellaneous class of Insurance. Motor Insurance has got great importance recently. Motor insurance accounts for a major portion of the miscellaneous premium income of insurance companies. In the older times, persons who were injured or killed through the negligence of the motorists could not get any compensation from the motorists because they did not have the financial resources to pay the compensation. And also there were no insurance schemes available at that time. In order to safeguard the financial hardship caused to the persons, the Motor Vehicles Act 1939 introduced Compulsory Motor Vehicle Insurance.

The Motor Vehicles Act 1938 was amended in 1988. As per the provision of this Act, it was made compulsory for the motorists to insure against the risk of liability to third parties. In other words, the insurance of motor vehicles against risk is not made compulsory, but the insurance of third party liability arising out of the use of motor vehicles in public places is made compulsory.

The rate of premium under Motor Vehicle Insurance is standardised because the business is tariff. No insurer can charge lower rates than the tariff rates and no insurer can grant benefits exceeding those prescribed by the tariff.

Classification of Motor Vehicles

For purpose of insurance, **Motor Vehicles** are classified into three broad categories—

(a) Private Cars (not used for commercial purposes)

(b) Motor Cycles and Motor Scooters

(c) Commercial Vehicles.

Commercial Vehicles can further be classified into —.

(1) Goods Carrying Vehicles

(2) Passengers Carrying Vehicles (e.g.) (motorised riskshaws, taxis, buses etc)

(3) Miscellaneous Vehicles (e.g.) (hearses, ambulances, cinema film recording and publicity vans, mobile dispensaries garbage dumping trucks, fire tenders etc.)

The following chart can make this more clear —

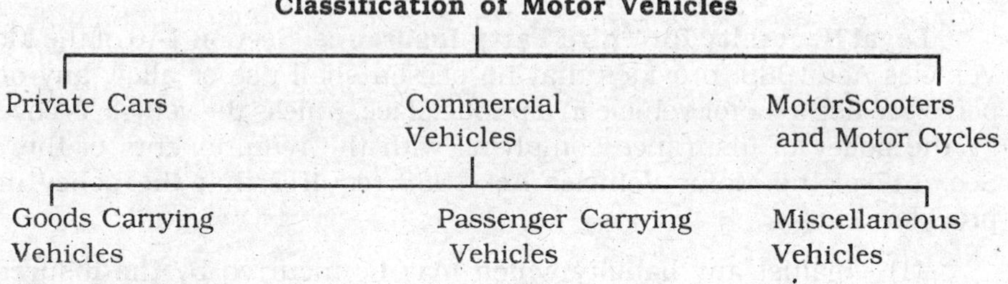

Kinds of Policies

To cover the losses arising in respect of motor vehicles, the following different kinds of policies are issued under Motor Vehicles Insurance:

(1) Act Liability Only (or) Act only Policy

(2) Third Party Only

(3) Comprehensive Policy

(4) Garage Insurance Policy

(5) Collision Insurance Policy.

1. Act Liability: This policy is designed to meet the requirements of Motor Vehicles Act 1988, which provides for compulsory insurance in regard to liabilities arising out of the use of motor vehicles in a public place. This policy is also called as Form 'A' policy. This policy applies uniformly to all classes of vehicles, whether private cars, commercial vehicles, motor cycles motor scooters.

2. Third Party Policy: This policy undertakes the liabilities of the third parties who suffered loss in connection with the damage of property and personal injury or death. Thus, the policy indemnifies the insured's liability for damage to property of third parties is limited to Rs. 6,000. But at the same time, liability for death or bodily injury to third party is unlimited.

This policy may be extended to include:

(a) Fire

(b) Theft risks

(c) Legal liability to persons employed in connection with the operation and or maintenence and or loading or unloading of motor vehicles.

The Private Car Policy extends to indemnify the insured (individual only) against legal liabilities incurred by him subject to limitations of indemnity while personally driving a private motor car. The private car policy covers legal liability of the insured to passengers (not for hire or reward) in the car. Liabilities arising while the motor car is being used in private places is covered. It covers bodily injury or death, property damage and medical expenses.

Legal Necessity for Third Party Insurance: Section 146 of the Motor Vehicles Act 1988, provides that no person shall use or allow any other person to use a motor vehicle in a public place, unless the vehicle is covered by the policy of insurance complying with the requirements of the Act. Sec. 147 of the Motor Vehicles Act 1988 requires that the policy must provide cover —

(1) Against any liability which may be incurred by the insured in respect of death or bodily injury to any person (or)

(2) Damage to any property of a third party (or)

(3) Against death or bodily injury to any passengers of a public service vehicle, caused by or arising out of the use of the vehicle in a public place.

3. Comprehensive Policy: This policy covers own damage, losses and act liability. The policy may extend to cover additional liabilities as provided in the Tariff. Comprehensive Policy is called as Form 'B' Policy.

The Comprehensive Policy has three sections, they are:

(1) First Section covering damage to the vehicles

(2) Second Section covering the insured liability to third parties

(3) Third Section which differs according to the class of the vehicles.

The Comprehensive Policy covers the following risks:

(a) Loss or damage (Own damage)

(b) Third party liabilities

(c) Repair charges, medical expenses

(d) Remover charges of repairer

(e) Damage to car parts or body.

4. Garage Insurance Policy: Under this policy, such motor vehicles risks are covered which are related to the motor vehicles standing in the motor garages or service stations. As such, all the risks which can affect the vehicles kept in the garage or at service stations and any loss caused to the motor vehicle is agreed to the indemnified by the insurance company.

5. Collision Insurance Policy: This policy is designed to meet the losses caused due to any collision or accident between two or more vehicles indemnified by the insurance company.

Procedure for Motor Vehicle Insurance

1. Proposal Forms

In Motor Insurance Contract, the Proposal Form is used, as a rule, it constitutes the means of communicating the offer to the insurers or for making proposal for motor insurance. It is also customary to indicate on the form a brief statement of the cover which is provided by the appropriate policy, or the terms and conditions which relates to motor insurance of:

(a) Identification of Vehicles (register number, horse power, shape, size etc.)

(b) Risk identification

(c) Declaration etc.

2. Rating of Insurance

After selecting an appropriate policy, the proposal form elicits all information necessary to determine the amount of premium and underwriting. Some examples of rating are given below:

(a) Private Cars: Rates are determined on the basis of the cubic capacity (Power of the engine as given by manufacturer, Insured Estimated value and the Zone of operation.

(b) Goods Carrying Vehicles: The rate or amount of premium is determined on the basis of Gross Vehicle Weight i.e., the total weight of the vehicle and load certified by the registering authority.

3. Tariff Rules

Some important tariff rules prescribed by the Tariff are as follows:

(1) Agreed value policies are not allowed except for vintage cars.

(2) Policies have to be issued in the name of the registered owner only.

(3) The prescribed cover note should be used when full details are not available. The cover note incorporates certificate of insurance.

(4) The Tariff prescribes the procedure for issue of a duplicate certificate when the original is lost, torn, defaced etc.

(5) The Tariff provides concessions, e.g., return of premium, restricted cover etc. when the vehicle is laid up in a garage and not in use for a period of two consecutive years or more.

4. Policy Form

As soon as the proposal form is accepted, Cover Note is issued. Policy forms, like proposal forms, vary within wide limits as between different classes of insurance, but they have certain features in common. The policy is not the contract itself, but the evidence of the contract. As soon as the policy is issued, the cover note is cancelled.

5. Term of Insurance

The Motor Insurance Policy is issued generally for one year. However, the policy can be issued for less than one year but the premium rate will be higher, e.g., the premium rate is three fourths of annual premium of the policy issued for six months.

6. Extra Benefits

During the currency of policy, after payment of extra premium, additional benefits can be added to the original policy. Thus, additional risks can be included to the original policy.

7. Change of Vehicle

The insured vehicles can be disposed of along with policy. The term of policy will remain the same. The policy will continue upto the unexpired period with the purchaser of the car. Similarly, the insured can replace another car under the same policy.

Settlement of Claims Under Motor Vehicle Insurance

For settlement of insurance claim under Motor Vehicle Insurance, the following claims usually occur in the following ways:

(a) Claims for own damage

(b) Claims for theft

(c) Claims for third party.

1.Claims for Own Damage

On receipt of notice of loss, the policy records are checked to see that the policy is in force and that it covers the vehicle involved. The loss is entered in the claim register and a claim form is issued to the insured for completion and return. The insured is also requested to submit a detailed estimate of repair charges.

Assessment or Survey Report: Independent Automobile Surveyors are assigned the task of assessing the cause and extent of loss. They inspect the damaged vehicle, and submit their survey report along with the copy of the policy, Claim form and estimate cost of repairs.

Claim Documents: Apart from claim form and survey report, the other documents required for processing the claim are:

(1) Driving Licence

(2) Registration Certificate Book

(3) Fitness Certificate

(4) Permit

(5) Police Report

(6) Financial Bill from repairs

(7) Satisfaction Note from the insured

(8) Receipted Bill from the repairer if paid by insured.

Settlement of Claim: On the basis of survey report and claim documents, the insurance company determines the extent of its liability and the loss is indemnified. The usual practice in the case of damage of motor vehicle, the insurance company may get the vehicle repaired instead of making cash payment to the insured.

2. Claims for Theft or Total Loss Claims

Total Losses can also arise due to the theft of the vehicle and its remaining untraced by the police authorities till the end. These losses will have to be supported by a copy of the First Information Report lodged with police authorities immediately after the theft has been detected. If the police authorities do not suceed in recovering the vehicle for theft claims, the insurer is requested to submit the certificates of SIDE No. or CR NO, certification of true and undetected, R.C. Books and Taxation certification of vehicle etc. along with documents related to vehicles and insurers. On the basis of investigation or inspection with valid documents, the insurance company determines the total loss or theft is indemnified.

3. Claims for Third Party

Section 165 of the Motor Vehicles Act 1988 empowers the State Government to set up Motor Accident Claims Tribunals, for adjusting upon third party claims.

On the receipt of notice of claim from the insured, or the third party or from the Motor Accident Claims Tribunals, the matter is entrusted to an advocate. The insured is requested to submit full information relating to accident along with the following documents:

(1) Driving Licence

(2) Police Report

(3) Details of driver's prosecution

(4) Death Certificate

(5) Coroner's Report

(6) Medical Certificate

(7) Details of age, income, no. of dependents etc.

On the basis of the written statement, the matter is then filed with Motor Accident Claims Tribunals by the Advocate, the MACT determines the amount of claims to the third party. Pending cases with the MACT where the liability under the policy is not in doubt are placed before the LOK Adalat or Lok Nyayalaya, for a voluntary and amicable settlement between the parties.

Questions

1. What do you understand by Motor Vehicle Insurance?
2. Explain the special features of Motor Vehicle Insurance.
3. Write about the types of Motor Car Insurance Policies?
4. What are the risks covered under Motor Insurance?
5. Explain the procedure of effecting Motor Insurance.
6. Mention the three main types of Motor Insurance Policies.
7. Explain the settlement of insurance claims under Motor Vehicle Insurance.
8. What are the advantages of a Comprehensive Policy?
9. Write short notes on:
   (a) Third Party Policy
   (b) Act Liability Only
   (c) Comprehensive Policy
   (d) Garage Insurance Policy.

Chapter 32

Health Insurance

Meaning

Policies under this insurance, the insurer undertakes to indemnify the assured in consideration of certain payment, up-to certain specified amount insured against for loss arising in respect of hospitalisation or injury sustained by the insured person.

Rapid population growth, contamination of food, water, and air etc., which makes to hospitalisation are more frequent. To cater to the varying and increasing needs, different forms of cover are available.

Types of Policies

The following types of policies are issued by the insurance corporation in order to meet the requirements of the public at large:

1. Individual Mediclaim Policy
2. Group Mediclaim Policy
3. Jan Arogya Bima Policy
4. Cancer Policy
5. Bhavishya Arogya Policy
6. Overseas Medical Policy
7. Videsh Yatra Mitra Policy.

1. Individual Mediclaim Policy: An individual is granted this cover under an Individual Mediclaim Policy. The policies under this plan provide reimbursement of hospitalisation/domiciliary expenses for illness/disease or accidental injury sustained during the policy period within India only. The liability in respect of all claims admitted during the period of insurance shall not exceed the sum insured for the person as mentioned in the schedule. Under this plan, person between the age of 5 years to 75 years can be covered without reduction in benefits, however children between the age of 3 months to 5 years can be covered provided one or both parents are covered concurrently. One can take sum assured ranging from Rs. 15,000 to 3,00,000. The premium of Rs. 15,000 is exempted under Income Tax Section 80D, if paid by cheque. Under this plan, claim with in 30 days are excluded except injury arising out of accident.

2. Group Mediclaim Policy: The policies under this plan are issued for group of individuals. The Group Mediclaim is available to any group/ association/institution/corporate body provided it has a central administration point and subject to a minimum number of persons to be covered. The coverage under the policy is the same as under Individual Mediclaim Policy with few differences. It is not permissible to issue any unnamed policy. There will be no family discount, cumulative bonus cost of health check up. The policy should not be issued through intermediaries. The maximum cover available upto Rs. 50,000 for maternity or the sum insured opted by the members of group, whichever is lower.

3. Jan Arogya Bima Policy: The coverage under this policy can be considered, to a certain extent, along the lines of Individual Mediclaim Policy except that cumulative bonus and mediclaim check up benefits are not included. The above plan covers the risks or reimbursement in respect of hospitalisation and domiciliary hospitalisation up-to Rs. 5,000 per person per annum. The salient feature of the scheme is that it is granted only for the benefit of the lower income sector of society and common masses.

4. Cancer Policy: This policy is designed to meet the risks or coverage for the members of the cancer patient aid association. There are two schemes available for Cancer policy:

(1) Indian Cancer Society

(2) Cancer Patients Aid Association.

This policy is introduced in collaboration with the Indian Cancer Society. Any person who has been admitted as a member of the society can avail of the benefit of this scheme. The policy lapses immediately if the insured ceases to be a member of the Cancer Society for any reason whatsoever. On payment of the prescribed membership fees, which is included in insurance premium, the membership will be allotted by the Society. If the insured during the currency of the policy suffers from cancer, the policy will pay up to Rs. 50,000 to meet the cost of diagnosis, biopsy, chemotherapy, radiotherapy, hospitalisation and rehabiliation.

5. Bhavishya Arogya Policy: This scheme has been designed so as to enable a person to provide himself for medical needs during an old age security. Under this policy, the medical expenses to be incurred over the balance life span after a predetermined age of retirement will be reimbursed up-to the amount of the sum insured with a limit of an amount per anyone illness or injury. The scheme is available to all Indian citizens provided his/her age at the time of taking policy is within the age group of 25 years to 55 years. The amount of maximum total benefit available under the basic policy is Rs. 50,000 during the life time of the insured commencing from the Policy Retirement Age and is not to exceed Rs. 20,000.

6. Overseas Mediclaim Policy: This policy was originally introduced in 1984 to provide for payment of medical expenses in respect of illness suffered or accident sustained by Indian residents during their overseas trips for official or holiday purpose. The insurance scheme since 1984 has been modified from time to time to provide for additional benefits such as inflight personal accident, loss of passport etc. In 1991, Employment and Study Policy was introduced. This policy is meant for Indian citizen temporarily working or studying abroad. Under this plan, the sum assured is 75,000 US dollar. Proposal inrespect of employment has to be referred to Head Office in advance with all relevant medical report and the premium should be collected in foreign currency. For period exceeding 180 days, the premium is quoted on, per month basis. All the policies are given only to the citizen of India and/or with valid permission of residence from concerned authority. All proposal over the age of 60 years under all plan and 40 years under this plan will have to submit detailed medical report including ECG, fasting blood sugar and urine strip test report. The medical certificate should be obtained from a cardiologist having M.D. qualification.

7. Videsh Yatra Mitra Policy: Videsh Yatra Mitra Policy is another Overseas Mediclaim Scheme introduced by General Insurance Corporation with effect from 1998. This policy provides the widest cover of personal accident, loss of checked baggage, loss of passport, medical expenses and repartiation, delay of checked baggage, personal liability etc. Insured person is that person named in the overseas policy schedule, for whom the appropriate premium has been paid. The policy is valued only from the first day of insurance and expires on the last day of the number of days specified in the policy schedule or on return to India whichever is earlier.

Questions

1. Explain the special features of Health Insurance.
2. Describe the types of Mediclaim Policies.
3. Write short notes on:
   (a) Cancer Policy
   (b) Bhavishya Arogya Policy
   (c) Videsh Yatra Mitra Policy.

Chapter

33

Cattle Insurance and Engineering Insurance

Cattle Insurance

The cattle insurance policy under market agreement with effect from 1.10.1997 amongst the subsidiaries of GIC of India in respect of Cattle Insurance business. The agreement shall be observed by the constutent companies with regard to the rates, terms and conditions prescribed by this agreement to underwrite the business of cattle insurance within India.

Age of Animals

Animal of age in years shown below shall be accepted under standards insurance scheme prescribed by this agreement.

(a)	Milch cows	2 years (or age at first calving) to 10 years
(b)	Milch buffaloes	3 years (or age at first calving) to 12 years
(c)	Stud bulls	3 years to 8 years or earlier
(d)	Bullock	3 years to 12 years
(e)	Indegenous, Cross-bred and exotic female calves/heifers	From 4 months upto the date of first calving or minimum age as in (1) and and b.

Cattle Insurance Policy

This policy provides cover against death of animals occurring during any period and if the animal is pregnant for less than four months, the indemnity will be restricted to 50% of sum insured or market value whichever is less. The policy is also extended to cover the risk of permanent total disability on payment of extra premium. The rate of basic premium and extra premium can be reduced by 15% and the deduction as shown on the face of the policy if there is no agency involved.

Premium Rate

The premium rates are separately applied for:

(a) Indigeneous animals

(b) Cross bred animals

(c) Exotic animals

The policy shall give indemnity only for death due to

(a) Accident (inclusive of fire, lightning, flood, inundation, storm, hurricance, earthquake, cyclone, tornado, tempest and famine)

(b) Diseases contracted or occurring during the period of the policy

(c) Surgical operations

(d) Riot and strike

The policy can also be extended to cover permanent total disability on payment of extra premium

(a) In the case of Milch cattle result in permanent and total incapacity to conceive or yield milk

(b) In the case of Stud bulls results in permanent and total incapacity for breeding purposes.

(c) In the case of bullocks and castrated amle buffaloes results in permanent and total incapacity for the purpose of use mentioned in the proposal firm.

In the event of death of scheme animals, the policy is agreed value policy, hence claim will be settled for 100% of sum assured. Under this policy, valuation of insurance is based on the market value of cattle which is examined by veterinary doctors. The sum insured will not exceed 100% of market value.

Claim Procedure

In the event of death of an animal, immediate intimation should be sent to the insurers and the following requirements should be furnished:

(a) Duly Completed Claim Form

(b) Death Certificate obtained from Veterinarian on Company's Form

(c) Post Mortem Examination Report if required by company

(d) Ear tag applied to the animal should be surrendered

(e) Complete treatment chart in case of permanent total disablement claim.

Exclusions

(a) Malicious or wilful injury or neglect, overloading, unskillful treatment or use of animal for purpose other than stated in the policy without the consent of the company in writing

(b) Accidents occuring and/or disease contracted prior to commencement of risk

(c) Theft and clandstine sale of the insured animal

(d) Any accident, loss destruction, damage or legal liability directly or indirectly caused by or contributed to by or arising from nuclear weapons.

(e) Consequential loss of whatsoever nature.

(f) Transport by air and sea.

Identification of Animal

All insured animals should be suitably identified by one or more of the following methods:

(a) Ear tag made of suitable materials be used

(b) Natural identification and colour should be clearly noted in the proporal form

(c) Photograph of animal may be insisted in case of high value animals

(d) Death certificate

(e) Veterinarian's report

Engineering Insurance

Meaning

This policy is designed to protect the interest of contractors and principals in respect of civil engineering projects, like building, bridges, tunnels etc., This policy provides an "All Risk" Cover. Every risk is covered which is not specifically excluded. This means that almost any sudden and unforeseen loss or damage occurring during the period of insurance to the property insured on the construction site is indemnified.

Types of Policies

Many types of engineering insurance policies likewise combine liability with property insurance. They are as follows:

(1) Boiler Insurance Policy

(2) Engine Insurance Policy

(3) Electrical Plant Insurance Policy

(4) Lifting Machinery Insurance Policy

1. Boiler Insurance Policy: A boiler policy covers damages to the boiler or other apparatus described in the schedule to the policy or to the other property of the insured and liability of the insured for fated or non-fated injury to third parties or for damage to their property, arising as a direct consequence of explosion or collapse of the boiler or other plant specified. This section includes the insurance of power boilers, heating and domestic boilers, and pressure vessels such as steam receivers and steam-jacketed pans.

2. Engine Insurance Policy: An engine insurance covers damages to the engine or machine breakdown, while third party liability and damage to property of the insured by flying fragments can be insured, if desired. Steam gas, oil and diesel engines, refrigerating plant and air compressors are within this section.

3. Electrical Plant Insurance Policy: The cover is similar to that of the engine insurance policy and it relates to dynamos, motors, turbo-generators and static plant such as transformers and rectifiers, etc.

4. Lifting Machinery Insurance Policy: This insurance policy is designed to cover the third party liability and other protection according to circumstances arranged for passenger and goods, lifts, cranes, hoists and lifting tackle generally.

Questions

1. Cattle Insurance – Explain.
2. Explain the procedure for settlement of a claim under cattle insurance.
3. What do you understand by engineering insurance?
4. Describe the different types of engineering insurance policies.

Chapter 34

Public Liability Insurance

Introduction

Under Public Liability Insurance Act (PLI Act) 1991, all the companies, individual and persons owning and dealing hazardous goods are required to take insurance policy satisfying the limits specified in the Act. Public Liability under the Public Liability Act is different from other legal liability in respect of 'negligence' or 'wrong doing' on the part of the owner or negligence in causing the accident is not required to be proved in case of PLI Act whereas in all other cases it is must.

Types of Public Liability Risk Insurance

For the purpose of insurance, public liability risk insurance is classified into:

I. Industrial Risk Insurance

II. Industrial All Risk Insurance

III. Non-Industrial Risk Insurance

I. Industrial Risk Insurance

This policy covers industrial risks as per the market agreement for public liability insurance and it has been effective from 1.1.88. This agreement applies to industrial and storage risks such as godowns, depots, tank farms etc. With aggregate limits of any one year during the policy upto Rs. 13 crore with in Geographical of India. Any proposal other than the above has to be submitted to market agreement committee prior to acceptance for rating, terms and conditions. Proposals shall not be accepted unless standard proposal form is filled in. Granting cover could be subject to duly signed declaration by the proposer that all the statutory requirements related to the business activities are complied with.

Scope of Cover

(a) Legal liability of the insured towards damages to the third party in respect of accidental death or bodily injury or disease and loss or damage to property arising out of such claims.

(b) Legal costs and expenses incurred with prior consent of the insurer are covered. All claims have to be made in writing against the insured during the policy period. The said liability is subject to limits of indemnity and other terms and conditions of the policy. It is not permissible to issue a public liability policy with unlimited liability. The ratio of limits of indemnity per accident to any one year would be 1:1, 1:2,1:3,1:4.

Pollution Risks

The standard policy wording does not include to cover for pollution liability. It has to be specifically included by prescribed endorsement under market agreement and premium there of is collected therefrom. The cover of risk is subject to the following conditions:

(1) Submission of additional information as per questionnaire appended to the proposal form and

(2) Submission of certificate or consent letter from Pollution Control Board granting permission to the insured to carry on their activities

(3) A single policy can be issued to cover various premises of the insured whether manufacturing process is carried on or not or as otherwise specified in the proposal form. In case, more than one unit is covered the rate has to be appropriately loaded

(4) It is not permissible to issue policy for more than 12 months:

Transportation Risk

This is an exclusion, However, in case the insured desires extension for the coverage of transportation risk, separate limits of indemnity per any one accident to any one year has to be selected. However, these limits will form part of the overall limits of indemnity so stipulated in the policy. The additional premium would be based on (1) indemnity limits for transportation cover (2) turnover in transit loading shall apply, if opted.

Exclusions

The following are the exclusions of any liability.

1. Arising out of any agreement by the insured, which would not attach in the absence of such agreement.
2. Arising out of convulsions of nature, atmospheric disturbances.
3. Arising out of wilful non-compliance of any statutory provisions.
4. Financial loss or loss of goodwill
5. Arising out of personal injury on infringement of plans, designs, etc.,
6. Arising out of fines, penalties or for any other damages, resulting from multiplication of compensatory damages.

II. Industrial All Risks Insurance

Salient Features

The following are the salient features of Industrial All Risks Insurance:

1. Applicable to risks having sum insured of Rs.100 and above (other than petrochemicals)
2. Multiple situation risks cumulative sum insured has to be above Rs.100 crore
3. Comprehensive package policy of All Risk Nature
4. Not named peril insurance
5. Specific exclusion whose significance to be carefully studied and communicated.
6. Insurance on reinstatement value basis except stock under insurance up to 15% waived.
7. No depreciation deducted from machinery breakdown total loss or partial loss.
8. Theift, Burglary, Accidental Damage included
9. Machinery Breakdown Lop option
10. Business interruption covers can be extended to include suppliers, customer premises.
11. Transit inside compound of industrial risks covered.
12. No declaration facility can given on stock
13. Single Document policy
14. Considerable premium saving on account of different discounts for good features, claim experience, package policy and voluntarily deductible able.

Procedures

The following procedural formalities to be adopted for all industrial risk insurance:

(a) Application form to be completed and signed by insured and insurer.

(b) Has a schedule with block wise description of risk, class of construction and sum insured. The schedule has to be completed.

(c) Requires details of the sum insured, premium paid with claims dates for the past 15 years.

(d) Inspection of risk by Company's Engineer.

(e) Authority for fixing provision rates – Head Office.

(f) Authority for fixing final rates – Head Office.

Non-Industrial Risks Insurance

Market agreement is introduced with effect from 1.1.1991 for non-industrial risk such as Hotels, Club Houses, Restaurants, Boarding and Lodging Houses, Cinema Halls, Auditorium, Theatres, Residential, Office premises, Medical Establishment, Airport premises, warehouses, Godown, shops, Tank Exhibition, and similar such non-industrial risks. Proposal would be required to fill up in standard proposal form at inception as well as subsequent renewals together with duly signed declaration that all statutory requirements relating to business activities are complied with.

Scope of Cover

This covers legal liability to third party on account of accidental bodily injury or death or disease or loss or damage to their property arising out of claim made for any incidence occurred during the policy period. This includes legal costs payable provided agreed by the company. Maximum liability being limits of indemnity under the policy. No policy can be issued with unlimited liability. The ratio of indemnity limits with regard to anyone accident to anyone year shall not exceed exceed 1:4 and shall be either 1:1,1:2, 1:3 and 1:4.

Pollution Risk and Premium

Unless specifically included, this policy does not cover pollution risks and additional premium thereof is paid as defined in the agreement. The proposer will be required to furnish consent certificate letter from the Pollution Control Board granting permission to carry on the activities. Rate of premium for various categories of risks is defined in the agreement. The agreement also provides for short period scale of premium for policies issued for less than 12 months. In no case can the policy be issued for more than 12 months.

Rating for Non-Industrial Risks

The following are the basis of rating which is related to rating for non-industrial risk:

1. Types of constructions
2. Ratio of Indemnity limits as per AOA; AOY
3. Communication unless 15 metres away from main construction structure.
4. Occupancy or storage
5. Highest exceeding 22 metres-loading 10% of premium
6. Risk group and Turnover.

Questions

1. What do you understand by Public Liability Insurance?
2. Explain the type of Public Liability Insurance Risks.
3. Write short notes on:
   (a) Industrial Risks Insurance
   (b) Industrial All Risks Insurance
   (c) Non-Industrial Risks Insurance
4. Explain the salient features of Industrial All Risks Insurance.
5. Public Liability Insurance Discuss its scope and utility.
6. What are the risks covered under public liability insurance? Explain its significance.

Chapter 35

Insurance Regulatory and Development Authority (IRDA)

Introduction

The Insurance Act 1938 provides that the Government should appoint a Controller of insurance to ensure that insurance companies registered under the Act, comply with the various provisions of the Act. His duties include approval of the terms and conditions of various plans being offered by the companies, including the adequacy on the basis of premium. Scrutiny of the various returns on investments, annual accounts, periodicals, actuarial valuations etc. required to be submitted by the companies. The controller also has powers to order special investigations and also to take over the management of the companies.

After the nationalisation of the insurance industry, the responsibilities of supervision had reduced considerably. But with the proposal to open up the industry, following the policy of liberalisation and globalisation, and the likelihood of private companies being permitted to transact insurance business in India, it became necessary to establish an authority to regulate insurance corporations.

The government of India in April 1993 appointed the Committee of Reforms in insurance sector with Shri R.N. Malhotra, a former governer of the Reserve Bank of India as its chairman. The committee submitted its report to the Government of India in Jan. 1994. As per the committee's recommendations, the government set up a regulatory body known as the ***"Insurance Regulatory Development Authority".*** The insurance bill was passed in both houses of parliament, after the subject matter was discussed and debated and subsequently government enacted the Act, *viz.*, Insurance Regulatory and Development Authority (IRDA) Act. 1999. The Insurance Regulatory and Development Authority Act, 1999 seeks to open up the insurance sector for private companies with a foreign equity of 26 per cent. It is also aimed at ending the monopoly of the Life Insurance Corporation and General Insurance Corporation in the insurance sector of the country.

Constitution of the IRDA

The IRDA shall consist of not more than nine members, not more than five members of whom, including the chairperson to be full time. The whole time members shall hold office for 5 years or until the age of 62 (65 in the case of chairperson) whichever is earlier, part time members will hold office not more than 5 years. The above said members to be appointed by the Central Government from among persons of ability and standing who have knowledge or experience in life insurance, general insurance, actuarial science, finance, economics, law, accountancy, administration or any other discipline which would, in the opinion of the Central Government, be useful to the Authority.

Objectives of IRDA

The main objectives of the Insurance Regulatory and Development Authority are:

(1) To take care of the policy holders' interest.

(2) To open the insurance sector for private sector.

(3) To ensure continued financial soundness and solvency.

(4) To regulate insurance and reinsurance companies.

(5) To eliminate dishonesty and unhealthy competition.

(6) To supervise the activities of intermediaries.

(7) To amend the Insurance Act, 1938, the Life Insurance Corporation Act, 1956 and the General Business Nationalisation Act, 1972.

Duties and Powers of IRDA

For smooth running of insurance business, the regulatory authority has been vested with adequate power and duties.

The duties and powers of the IRDA are:

(1) To regulate, promote and ensure orderly growth of the insurance business.

(2) To exercise all powers and functions of the controller of insurance.

(3) To protect the interest of the policy holders in settlement of claims and terms and conditions of policies.

(4) To promote and regulate professional organisations connected with insurance business.

(5) To call for information from, undertake inspection and conduct investigations including audit of the insurer, intermediaries and other connected organisations and persons.

(6) To control and regulate the rates and terms and conditions that may be offered by the insurers in respect of general insurance matters, not so controlled by the Traiff Advisory Committee under Section 64 (U) of the Insurance Act.

(7) To prescribe the manner and form in which accounts will be maintained and submitted by insurers and intermediaries.

(8) To regulate investment of funds.

(9) To regulate margins if solvency.

(10) To adjudicate disputes between insurers and intermediaries.

Role of IRDA in Appointment of Agents

The conditions of appointment of agents are regulated by LIC of India (Agents) Regulations, 1972. The procedure for appointment and renewal of licenses of agents as stipulated in IRDA Insurance Agents Regulations, 2000 will have to be strictly adhered to from the date of notification. Accordingly,

(1) A person (natural person, Registered Society, Panchayat, Co-operative Society or Firm or Company registered under Companies Act, 1956) can be appointed as insurance agent, in any place within India for soliciting or procuring insurance business, by the insurer or a designated person provided he holds a valid certificate of license issued by IRDA at the time of appointment.

(2) The certificate of license will be issued by IRDA as per the procedure prescribed in the Insurance Agents Regulations 2000. The designated person (appointed by the insurer having authority to appoint agents, and notified to the authority) will receive and forward the application for issue or renewal of license, with requisite fees prescribed by IRDA, to IRDA in the manner prescribed in the Insurance Agents Regulations, 2000.

Excerpts from Insurance Regulatory and Development Authority (Appointed Actuary) Regulations, 2000

Procedure for appointment of an Appointed Actuary:

(1) An insurer registered to carry on insurance business in India shall, subject to sub-regulation.

(2) Appoint an actuary, who shall be known as the 'Appointed Actuary' for the purposes of the Act.

(3) A person shall be eligible to be appointed as an appointed actuary for an insurer, if he or she shall be —

(i) ordinarily resident in India;

(ii) a Fellow Member of the Actuarial Society of India;

(iii) an employee of the life insurer, in case of life insurance business;

(iv) an employee of the insurer or a consulting actuary, in case of general insurance business;

(v) a person against whom no disciplinary action by the Actuarial Society of India or any other actuarial professional body is pending;

(vi) not an appointed actuary of another insurer;

(vii) a person who possesses a Certificate of Practice issued by the Actuarial Society of India; and

(viii) not over the ago of seventy years.

Powers of Appointed Actuary

(1) An appointed actuary shall have access to all information or documents in possession, or under control, of the insurer if such access is necessary for the proper and effective performance of the functions and duties of the appointed actuary.

(2) The appointed actuary may seek any information for the purpose of sub-regulation. (1) of this regulation from any officer or employee of the insurer.

(3) The appointed actuary shall be entitled —

(a) to attend all meetings of the management including the directors of the insurer;

(b) to speak and discuss on any matter, at such meeting —

(i) that relates to the actuarial advice given to the directors;

(ii) that may affect the solvency of the insurer;

(iii) that may affect the ability of the insurer to meet the reasonable expectations of policyholders; or

(iv) on which actuarial advice is necessary;

(c) to attend —

(i) any meeting of the shareholders or the policyholders of the insurer; or

(ii) any other meeting of members of the insurer at which the insurer's annual accounts or financial statements are to be considered or at which any matter in connection with the appointed actuary's duties is discussed.

Duties and Obligations

In particular and without prejudice to the generality of the for going matters, and in the interests of the insurance industry and the policyholders, the duties and obligations of an appointed actuary of an insurer shall include:

(a) Rendering actuarial advice to the management of the insurer, in particular in the areas of product design and pricing, insurance contract wording, investments and reinsurance;

(b) Ensuring the solvency of the insurer at all times;

(c) Complying with the provisions of the section 64V if the Act in regard to certification of the assets and liabilities that have been valued in the manner required under the said section;

(d) Complying with the provisions of the section 64VA of the Act in regard to maintenance of required solvency margin in the manner required under the said section;

(e) Drawing the attention of management of the insurer, to any matter on which he or she thinks that action is required to be taken by the insurer to avoid—

(i) any contravention of the Act; or

(ii) prejudice to the interest of policyholders;

(f) Complying with the Authority's directions from time to time;

(g) In the case of the insurer carrying on life insurance business—

(i) to certify the actuarial report and abstract and other returns as required under section 13 of the Act;

(ii) to comply with the provisions of section 21 of the Act in regard of further information required by the Authority;

(iii) to comply with the provisions of section 40-B of the Act in regard to the bases of premium;

(iv) to comply with provisions of the section 112 of the Act in regard to recommendation of interim bonus or bonuses payable by life insurer to policyholders whose policies mature for payment by reason of death or otherwise during the inter-valuation period;

(v) to ensure that all the requisite records have been made available to him or her for the purpose of conducting actuarial valuation of liabilities and assets of the insurer;

(vi) to ensure that the premium rates of the insurance products are fair;

(vii) to certify that the mathematical reserves have been determined taking into account the guidance notes issued by the Actuarial Society of India and any directions given by the Authority;

(viii) to ensure that the policyholders' reasonable expectations have been considered in the matter of valuation of liabilities and distribution of surplus to the participating policyholders who are entitled for a share of surplus;

(ix) to submit the actuarial advice in the interests of the insurance industry and the policyholders;

(h) In the case of the insurer carrying on general insurance business to ensure —

(i) that the rates are fair in respect of those contracts that are governed by the insurer's in-house tariff;

(ii) that the actuarial principles, in the determination of liabilities, have been used in the calculation of reserves for incurred but not reported claims (IBNR) and other reserves where actuarial advice is sought by the Authority;

(i) Informing the Authority in writing of his or her opinion, within a reasonable time, whether —

(i) the insurer has contravened the Act or any other Acts;

(ii) the contravention is of such a nature that it may affect significantly the interests of the owners or beneficiaries of policies issued by the insurer;

(iii) the directors of the insurer have failed to take such action as is reasonably necessary to enable him to exercise his or her duties and obligations under this regulation; or

(iv) an officer or employee of the insurer has engaged in conduct calculated to prevent him or her exercising his or her duties and obligations under this regulation.

Absolute Privilege of Appointed Actuary

(1) An appointed actuary shall enjoy absolute privilege to make any statement, oral or written, for the purpose of the performance of his functions as appointed actuary. This is in addition to any other privilege conferred upon an appointed actuary under any other Regulations.

(2) Any provision of the letter of appointment of the appointed actuary, which restricts or prevents his duties, obligations and privileges under these regulations, shall be of no effect.

Applicability to Reinsurance Business

These regulations shall apply to reinsures carrying on reinsurance business in India.

II Excerpts From Insurance Regulatory and Development Authority (Actuarial Report and Abstract) Regulations, 2000

(1) The Abstract and Statements must be so arranged the number and letters of the paragraphs correspond with Regulation 4.

(2) The Abstracts and Statements shall be furnished to the Authority, within nine months from the end of the period to which they refer to, in accordance with sub-section (1) of section 15 of the Act.

(3) Four copies of the Abstract and Statements shall be furnished to the Authority in accordance with sub-section (1) of section 15 of the Act, and one of the four copies so furnished shall be signed by the persons as mentioned in sub-section (2) section 15 of the Act.

(4) There shall be appended to every such Abstract and Statement.

(a) a certificate signed by the principal officer that full and accurate particulars of every policy under which there is a liability, either actual or contingent, has been furnished to the appointed actuary for the investigation; and

(b) a certificate signed by the appointed actuary with his remarks, if any, to the effect that:-

(i) the data furnished by the principal officer has been included in conducting the valuation of liabilities for the purpose of investigation;

(ii) reasonable steps have been taken to ensure the accuracy and completeness of the data;

(iii) he has complied with provisions of the Act;

(iv) he has complied with guidance notes issued by the Actuarial Society of India with the concurrence of the Authority; and

(v) in his opinion, the mathematical reserves are adequate to meet the insurer's future commitments under the contracts, ar d the policyholders' reasonable expectations.

Requirements Applicable to Abstract and Statements

(1) Abstracts and statements shall be prepared separately in respect of—

(a) Linked Business;

(b) Non-Linked Business; and

(c) Health Insurance Business

(2) An insurance shall prepare the following statements which shall be annexed to the abstract prepared in accordance with these regulations, namely:—

(a) in respect of Linked Business —

(i) From LB-1;

(ii) From LB-2;

(iii) From LB-3;

(iv) Form LB-4;

(v) Form IA;

(b) in respect of Non- Linked Business —

(i) Form NLB-1;

(ii) Form NLB-2;

(iii) Form DD;

(iv) Form DDD;

(v) Form DDDD;

(vi) Form IA;

(c) in respect of Health Insurance Business —

(i) From LB-1;

(ii) From LB-2;

(iii) From LB-3;

(iv) From NLB-1;

(v) From IA.

(d) Summary statements —

(i) Form K;

(ii) Form IDRA- AA as specified under Regulation 4 of Insurance Regulatory and Development Authority (Assets, Liabilities, and Solvency Margin of Insurers) Regulation 2000;

(iii) From H;

(iv) Form I;

(v) Statement of Composition and Distribution of surplus in respect of policyholders' fund as specified under Regulation 8;

(3) Each Abstracts shall show—

(a) The Valuation Date — The date on which valuation (investigation) is done;

(b) New Products—A brief description of new products introduced during the inter-valuation period giving salient features ;

(c) Foreign Operations — A brief description of the foreign operations of the insurer, during the inter-valuation period;

(d) Valuation Method — A brief description of—

(i) the methods adopted in the determination of mathematical reserves in respect of insurance products;

(ii) the method by which age at entry, premium term maturity date, valuation date to the maturity date, have been treated for the purpose of valuation;

(iii) the method of allowing for —

(I) incidence of premium income; and

(II) premiums payable otherwise than annually.

(e) Valuation Bases

(i) Valuation parameters used in the valuation shall be furnished in the manner as specified in the table hereunder:—

Description	Mortality basis used	Morbidity basis	Inflation rate	Interest rate	Exp-penses	Future bonuses	Others Please specify	Remarks
(1)	(2)	(3)	(4)	(5)	(6)	(7)	(8)	(9)
(a) Insurance Product:								
(i) Regular Premium								
(ii) Single Pemium and Fully paid up								
(iii) Reduced Paid up								
(b) Insurance Product								
(i) Regular Premium								
(ii) Single Premium and Fully paid up								
(iii) Reduced Paid up								

(ii) Expenses related to premiums, sum assured, annuity, etc., and per policy shall be specified separately under Column (5) of the table;

(iii) Items such as terminal bonus, in case of with profit contracts, management charges, etc., in respect of linked business, shall be specified under Column (8) of the table;

(f) Other Adjustments (Provisions):

The methods by which provision, if any, has been made for the following matters, including a statement of bases wherever necessary

(i) Policies in respect of which extra premiums have been charged on account of underwriting of under-average lives that are subject to extra risks such as occupation hazard, over weight, under-weight, smoking history, health, climatic or geographical conditions;

(ii) Lapsed policies not included in the valuation but under which a liability exists or may arise;

(iii) Options available under individual and group insurance policies;

(iv) Guarantees available to individual and group insurance policies;

(v) The rate of exchange at which benefits in respect of policies issued in foreign currencies have been converted into India Rupees and what provision has been made for possible increase of mathematical reserves arising from future variations in rates of exchanges;

(g) Further Information

The following information shall be appended:

Group Code

(a) Category Code I — Linked Business — Consisting of Insurance Products—

(1) In respect of Division Code I — Individual Business, and under each Sub-Class Code —

(i) with guarantees – with participation in profits : A;

(ii) with no guarantees – with participation in profits : B;

(iii) with guarantees – without participation in profits : C;

(iv) with no guarantees – without participation in profits : D;

(2) in respect of Division Code 2–Group Business, and under each Sub-Class Code —

(i) with guarantees – with participation in profits : A;

(ii) with no guarantees – with participation in profits : B;

(iii) with guarantees – without participation in profits : C;

(iv) with no guarantees – without participation in profits : D;

(b) Category Code 2 – Non-Linked Busines—consisting of Insurance Products—

(I) in respect of Division code I - Individual Business ¾

(1) Sub-Class Code 1- Sub-Class — Life Business, —

(i) with participation in profits :A;

(ii) with deferred participation in profits : B;

(iii) under discounted Bonus system : C;

(iv) without participation in profits : D;

(II) Sub-Class Codes 2,3 — Sub-Class—General Annuity/Pension, as the case may be —

(i) Immediate Annuities with participation in profits : A;

(ii) Immediate Annuities without participation in profits : B;

(iii) Deferred Annuities with participation in profits : C;

(iv) Deferred Annuities without participation in profits : D;

(2) In respect of Division Code 2 - Group Business —

(I) Sub-Class Code I - Sub-Class-Life Business, where ¾

(i) Premiums are guaranteed for not more than one year:—

(a) with participation in profits : A;

(b) without participation in profits : B;

(ii) Premiums are guaranteed for more than one year:-

(a) with participation in profits : C;

(b) without participation in profits : D;

(II) Sub-Class Codes 2,3 — Sub-Class—General Annuity/Pension as the case may be —

(i) Immediate Annuities with participation in profits : A;

(ii) Immediate Annuities without participation in profits : B;

(iii) Deferred Annuities with participation in profits : C;

(iv) Deferred Annuities without participation in profits: : D;

(f) Amount of surplus, from policyholders' funds, brought forward preceding valuation:

(g) Total Surplus (total of the items (a) to (f):

Distribution of Surplus

Policyholder's Fund:

(a) To Interim Bonuses Paid;

(b) To Terminal Bonuses

(c) To Loyalty Additions or any other forms of bonuses, if any;

(d) Among policyholders with immediate participation giving the number of policies which participated and the sums assured thereunder (excluding bonuses);

(e) Among policyholders with deferred participation, giving the number of policies which participated and the sums assured thereunder (excluding bonuses);

(f) Among policyholders in the discounted bonus class giving the number of policies which participated an the sums assured thereunder (excluding bonues);

(g) To every reserve fund or other fund or account (any such sums passed through the accounts during the inter valuation period to be separately stated);

(h) As carried forward un-appropriated.

Shareholders' Fund

(i) To the shareholders; funds (any such sums passed through the accounts during the inter valuation period to be separately stated);

Totals :

(1) Total Surplus allocated: (total of the items (a) to (i)

(2) Specimen of Bonuses allotted to policies for one thousand rupees together with the amounts apportioned under the various manners in which the bonus is receivable, for each type of participating product, shall be furnished.

Negative Reserves and Guaranteed Surrender Value Deficiency Reserves — A brief description of treatment adopted for negative, reserves and guaranteed surrender value deficiency reserves shall be furnished.

(3) There shall be two Classifications, namely, Business within India, and Total Business (consisting of Business within India and Business outside India), with Classification Codes 1 and 2 respectively.

(4) There shall be three Categories, namely, Linked Business, Non-linked Business and Health Insurance Business, with Category Codes 1, 2 and 3 respectively, under each Classification;

(5) There shall be two Divisions, namely, Individual Business and Group Business, with Divisions Codes I and 2 respectively under Category Codes 1, 2 and 3;

(6) There shall be three Sub–Classes, Namely, Life Business, General Annuity, and Pension, with Sub–Class Codes 1, 2 and 3 respectively, under Category Codes 1 and 2, and two Sub–Classes, namely, Linked Business, Non-Linked Business, with Sub–Class Codes 1, and 2 respectively, under Category Code 3.

(7) There shall be four Groups under each Sub-Class, with Group Codes as specified under sub-regulation (7).

(8) The details of Group Codes under each Category shall be as follows:

  (i) Returns on Assets as specified under Regulation 5;

  (ii) Distribution of surplus as specified under Regulation 6;

  (iii) Principles adopted in distribution of surplus as specified under Regulation 7;

  (iv) Negative Reserves and Guaranteed Surrender Value Deficiency Reserves as specified under Regulation 8;

  (v) Miscellaneous, if any.

Returns on Assets

(1) The average gross rates of interest yielded by the assets may be determined expressing the investment income as percentage of the mean fund. [I = 2 x I / (A + B–I) ; where is the gross yield; I = Investment Income; A = the assets at the beginning of the financial year, and B = the assets at the end of the financial year; Investment Income (shown in the Revenue Account) should include the amount of the unrealized gain taken into revenue account, A and B have to be adjusted value of assets shown in the Balance Sheet].

(2) The average gross rates of interest, referred to under sub-regulation (1) shall be furnished for each fund maintained by an insurer.

Distribution of Surplus

The basis adopted in the distribution of surplus as between the shareholders and the policyholders, and whether such distribution was determined by the instruments constituting the company, or by its regulations or by-laws or how otherwise shall be mentioned.

Principles adopted in distribution of profits

The general principles adopted in distribution of profits among policyholders, including statements on following points, shall be furnished.

(i) Whether the principles were determined by instruments constituting the insurer, or by its regulations or by-laws or how otherwise;

(ii) The number of year's premium to be paid, period to elapse and other conditions to be fulfilled before a bonus is allotted;

(iii) Whether the bonus is allocated in respect of each year's premium paid, or in respect of each calendar year or year of assurance or how otherwise; and

(iv) Whether the bonus vests immediately on allocation, or, if not conditions of vesting.

Statement of composition of surplus and distribution of surplus in respect of policyholders' funds

(1) A statement, showing total amount of surplus arising during the inter-valuation period, and the allocation of such surplus, shall be furnished separately for participating business and for non-participating business, with the particulars as mentioned below:

Composition of Surplus

(a) Surplus shown under Form I;

(b) Interim Bonuses paid during the inter-valuation period;

(c) Terminal Bonuses paid during the inter-valuation period;

(d) Loyalty Additions or other forms of bonuses, if any, paid during the inter-valuation period;

(e) Sum transferred from shareholders funds during the inter-valuation period;

(f) Category Code 3 — Health Insurance Business — consisting of Insurance Products:

(1) in respect of Division Code 1 —Individual Business:-

(I) Sub-Class 1 ¾ Linked Business;

(i) with guarantees — with participation in profits : A; —

(ii) with no guarantees—with participation in profits : B; —

(iii) with guarantees — without participation in profits : C; —

(iv) with no guarantees — without participation in profits : D; —

(II) Sub-Class Code 2—Non Linked Business:—

(i) with participation in profits : A;

(ii) with deferred participation in profits : B;

(iii) under discounted Bonus system : C;

(iv) without participation in profits : D;

(2) in respect of Division code 2—Group Business:-

(I) Sub-Class Code 3 — Linked Business;

(i) with guarantees-with participation in profits : A; —

(ii) with no guarantees-with participation in profits : B; —

(iii) with guarantees-without participation in profits : C; —

(iv) with no guarantees-without participation in profits : D; —

(II) Sub-Class Code 4 Non-Linked Business:—

(i) Premiums are guaranteed for not more than one year:

(a) with participation in profits : A;

(b) without participation in profits : B;

(ii) Premiums are guaranteed for more than one year:

(a) with participation in profits : C;

(b) without participation in profits : D;

(8) "Nil" Statements shall be furnished for those Forms where the insurer has no transactions.

(9) Information relating to insurance products shall be given in Forms in the following order of insurance products, wherever required.

Whole Life Assurances,

Endowment Assurances,

Anticipated Endowment Plan (Money Back Plans),

Pure Endowments,

Double Endowments,

Term Insurance Contract, and

Others (specifying each)

(10) All figures shall be furnished in thousands and all amounts shall be furnished in Indian rupees.

(11) In respect of Group Business, 'the number of policies' in Forms, wherever applicable, shall be read as 'number of schemes'.

(12) Rider Benefits shall be furnished in Forms, wherever required, in the order of (a) Accident Covers – double, triple, (b) Disability Covers, (c) Dread Disease Covers, and (d) Others (specifying each).

(13) Other Adjustments, shall be furnished in Forms, wherever necessary, for instance, Provision for Deaths due to AIDS.

III Excerpts from Insurance Regulatory and Development Authority (Assets, Liabilities, and Solvency Margin of Insurers) Regulations, 2000

Every insurer shall prepare a statement of the value of assets in Form IRDA. Assets AA in accordance with Schedule I.

Determination of Amount of Liabilities

Every insurer shall prepare a statement of the amount of liabilities in accordance with Schedule II-A, in respect of life insurance business, and in Form HG in accordance with Schedule II-B, in respect of general insurance business, as the case may be.

Determination of Solvency Margin

Every insurer shall prepare a statement of solvency margin in accordance with Schedule III-A, respect of life insurance business, and in Form KG in accordance with Schedule III-B, in respect of general insurance business, as the case may be.

Health Insurance Business

Where the insurer transacts health insurance business, providing health covers, the amount of liabilities shall be determined in accordance with the principles specified under these Regulations.

Business outside India

Where the insurer transacts insurance business in a country outside India, and submits statements or returns or any such particulars to a public authority of that country, he shall enclose the same along with the Forms specified in accordance with these Regulations and the Insurance Regulatory and Development Authority (Actuarial Report and Abstract) Regulations, 2000.

Provided that if the appointed actuary is of the opinion that it is necessary to set additional reserves over and above that reserves shown in the statements or returns or any such particulars submitted to the public authority of a country outside India, he may set such additional reserves.

Furnishing of Forms

The forms, namely, Form IRDA-Assets-AA, Form HG. and Form KG. shall be furnished separately for Business within India and Total Business Transacted by the Insurer.

Personal visit of appointed actuary to the Authority

The Authority may, if considered necessary and expedient, ask the appointed actuary to make a personal visit to the office of the Authority to elicit from him any further information.

Valuation of Assets

(1) **Interpretation:** In this Schedule, unless the context otherwise requires, 'non-mandated investments' means neither those investments that are neither approved securities nor approved investments.

(2) **Values of Assets:** (1) The following assets should be placed with value zero —

(a) Agent's balances and outstanding premiums in India, to the extent they are not realised within a period of thirty days;

(b) Agents' balances and outstanding premiums outside India, to the extent they are not realisable;

(c) Sundry debts, to the extent they are not realizable;

(d) Advances of an unrealisable character;

(e) Deferred expenses;

(f) Profit and loss appropriation account balance and any fictitious assets other than pre-paid expenses;

(g) Reinsurer's balances outstanding for more than three months;

(h) Preliminary expenses in the formation of the company;

(2) The value of computer equipment including software shall be computed as under —

(i) seventy five per cent of its cost in the year of purchase;

(ii) fifty per cent of its cost in the second year;

(iii) twenty-five per cent of its cost in the third year; and

(iv) zero per cent thereafter.

(3) All other assets of an insurer have to be value in accordance with the Insurance Regulatory and Development Authority (Preparation of Financial Statements and Auditor's Report of Insurance Companies) Regulations, 2000.

3. Statement of Assets

Every insurer shall prepare a statement of assets in Form IRDA Assets- AA.

Valuation of Liabilities—Life Insurance

I. Interpretation – In this Schedule —

(a) "valuation date", in relation to an actuarial investigation means the date to which the investigation relates.

(b) "universal life contracts" means those contracts that are presented in an unbundled form. The contracts where policyholders have an option to invest; in units of insurer's segregated fund(s) shall be treated as "linked business"; and others shall be treated as "non-linked business".

(c) "segregated funds" means funds earmarked in respect of linked business.

2. Method of Determination of Mathematical Reserves

(1) Mathematical Reserves shall be determined separately for each contract by a prospective method of valuation in accordance with sub-paras (2) to (4).

(2) The valuation method shall take into account all prospective contingencies under which any premiums (by the policyholder) or benefits (to the policy holder/beneficiary) may be payable under the policy, as determined by the policy conditions. The level of benefits shall take into account the reasonable expectations of policyholders (with regard to bonuses, including terminal bonuses, if any) and any established practices of an insurer for payment of benefits.

(3) The valuation method shall take into account the cost of any options that may be available to the policyholder under the terms of the contract.

(4) The determination of the amount of liability under each policy shall be based on prudent assumptions of all relevant parameters. The value of each such parameter shall be based on the insurer's expected experience and shall include an appropriate margin for adverse deviations (hereinafter referred to as MAD) that may result in an increase in the amount of mathematical reserves.

(5) (i) The amount of mathematical reserve in respect of a policy, determined in accordance with sub-para (4), may be negative (called "negative reserves") or less than the guaranteed surrender value available (called "guaranteed surrender value deficiency reserves") at the valuation date.

(ii) The appointed actuary shall, for the purpose of section 35 of the Act, use the amount of such mathematical reserves without any modification;

(iii) The appointed actuary shall, for the purpose of sections 13, 49, 64V and 64VA of the Act, set the amount of such mathematical reserve to zero, in case of such negative reserve, or to the guaranteed surrender value, in case of such guaranteed surrender value deficiency reserves, as the case may be.

(6) The valuation method shall be called "Gross Premium Method".

(7) If in the opinion of the appointed actuary, a method of valuation other than the Gross Premium Method of valuation is to be adopted, then, other approximations (e.g. retrospective method) may be use.

Provided that the amount of calculated reserve is expected to be atleast equal to the amount that shall be produced by the application of Gross Premium Method.

(8) The method of calculation of the amount of liabilities and the assumptions for the valuation parameters shall not be subject to arbitrary discontinuities from one year to the next.

(9) The determination of the amount of mathematical reserves shall take into account the nature and term of the assets representing those liabilities and the value placed upon them and shall include prudent provision against the effects of possible future changes in the value of assets on the ability of the insurer to meet its obligations arising under policies as they arise.

4. Policy Cash Flows

The gross premium method of valuation shall discount the following future policy cash flows at an appropriate rate of interest—

(a) premiums payable, if any, benefits payable, if any, on death; benefits payable, if any, on survival; benefits payable, if any, onvoluntary termination of contract, and the following, if any:—

(i) basic benefits,

(ii) rider benefits,

(iii) bonuses that have already been vested as at the valuation date,

(iv) bonuses as a result of the valuation at the valuation date, and

(v) future bonuses (one year after valuation date), including terminal bonuses (consistent with the valuation rate of interest).

(b) commission and remuneration payable, if any, in respect of a policy (This shall be based on the Current practice of the insurer).

No allowance shall be made for non-payment of commissions in respect of the orphaned policies;

(c) policy maintenance expenses, if any, in respect of a policy, as provided under sub-para (4) of para 5;

(d) allocation of profit to shareholders, if any, where there is a specified relationship between profits attributable to shareholders and the bonus rates declared for policyholders.

Provided that allowance must be made for tax, if any,

Policy Options

Where a policy provides built-in options, that may be exercised by the policyholder, such as conversion or addition of coverage at future date(s) without any evidence of good health, annuity rate guarantees at maturity of contract, etc., the costs of such options shall be estimated and treated as special cash flows in calculating the mathematical reserves.

Valuation Parameters

(1) The valuation parameters shall constitute the bases on which the future policy cash flows shall be computed and discounted. Each parameter shall have to be appropriate to the block of business to be valued. An appointed actuary shall take into consideration the following

(a) The value(s) of he parameter shall be based on the insurer's experience study, where available. If reliable experience study is not available, the value(s) can be based on the industry study, if available and appropriate. If neither is available, the values may be based on the bases used for pricing the product. In establishing the expected level of any parameter, any likely deterioration in the experience shall be taken into account;

(b) The expected level, as determined in clause (a) of this sub-para, shall be adjusted by an appropriate Margin for Adverse Deviations (MAD), the level of MAD in each parameter shall be based on the Guidance Notes issued by the Actuarial Society of India, with the concurrence of the Authority.

(c) The values used for the various valuation parameters should be consistent among themselves.

Mortality rates to be used shall be by reference to a published table, unless the insurer has constructed a separate table based on his own experience:

Provided that such published table shall be made available to the insurance industry by the Actuarial Society of India, with the concurrence of the Authority.

Provided further that such rates determined by reference to a published table shall not be less than hundred per cent of that published table.

Provided further that such rates determined by reference to a published table may be less than hundred per cent of that published table if the appointed actuary can justify a lower per cent.

Morbidity rates to be used shall be by reference to a published table, unless the insurer has constructed a separate table based on his own experience.

Provided that such published table shall be made available to the insurance industry by the Actuarial Society of India, with the concurrence of the Authority.

Provided further that such rates determined by reference to a published table may be less than hundred per cent of that published table if the appointed actuary can justify a lower per cent.

Policy maintenance expenses shall depend on the manner, in which they are analysed by the insurer, viz., fixed expenses and variable expenses. The variable expenses shall be related to sum assured or premiums or benefits. The fixed expenses may be related to sum assured or premiums or benefits or per policy expenses. All expenses shall be increased in future years for inflation, the rate of inflation assumed should be consistent with the valuation rate of interest. Valuation rates of interest, to be used by appointed actuary.

(e) Shall be not higher than the rates of interest, for the calculation of the present value of policy cash flows referred to in para 4, determined from prudent assessment of the yields from existing assets attributable to blocks of life insurance business, and the yields which the insurer is expected to obtain from the sums invested in the future, and such assessment shall take into account.

  (i) the composition of assets supporting the liabilities, expected cash flows from the investments on hand, the cash flows from the block of policies to be valued, the likely future investment and disinvestments strategy to be employed in dealing with the future net cash flows;

  (ii) the risks associated with investment in regard to receipt of income on such investment or repayment of principal;

  (iii) the expenses associated with the investment functions of the insurer;

(f) shall not be higher than, for the calculation of present value of policy cash flows in respect of a particular category of contracts, the yields on assets maintained for the purpose of such category of contacts;

(g) in respect of non-participating business, shall recognize the risk of decline in the future interest rates;

(h) in respect of participating business, shall be based on the assumption (with regard to future investment conditions), that the scale of future bonuses used in the valuation is consistent with the valuation rate of interest; and

(i) in respect of single premium business, shall take into account the effect of changes in the risk-free interest rates.

Other parameters, may be taken into account, depending on the type of policy. In establishing the values of such parameters, the considerations set out in this Schedule shall be taken into account.

Applicability to Reinsurance

(1) This Schedule shall also apply to the valuation of business in the books of reinsurers.

(2) As regards the business ceded by insurers, this Schedule shall be applicable to the net sums at risk retained by the insurer.

(3) Reinsurance arrangement with an element of borrowing in the form of deposit or credit of any kind from insurer's reinsurers with the prior approval of the Authority shall not be treated as credit for reinsurance for the purpose of determination of required solvency margin.

Additional Requirements for Linked Business

(1) Reserves in respect of linked business shall consist of two components, namely, unit reserves and general fund reserves.

(2) Unit reserves shall be calculated in respect of the units allocated to the policies in force at the valuation date using unit values at the valuation date.

(3) General fund reserves (non-unit reserves) shall be determined using a prospective valuation method set out in, this Schedule, which shall take into account of the following, namely:—

1. Premiums, if any, payable in future;
2. Death benefits, if any, provided by the general fund (over and above the value of units);
3. Management charges paid to the general fund;
4. Guarantees, if any, relating to surrender values or minimum death any maturity benefits;
5. Fund growth rates and management charges (the values of these parameters, along with others, shall be determined in accordance with para 5);

6. Negative reserves, if any, shall be dealt with in accordance with sub-para (5) of para 2.

Additional Requirements for Provisions

The appointed actuary shall make aggregate provisions in respect of the following, where it is not possible to calculate mathematical reserves for each policy, in the determination of mathematical reserves:

(a) Policies in respect of which extra premiums have been charged on account of underwriting of under-average lives that are subject to extra risks such as occupation hazard, over-weight, under-weight, smoking history, health, climatic or geographical conditions;

(b) Lapses policies not included in the valuation but under which a liability exists or may arise;

(c) Options available under individual and group insurance policies;

(d) Guarantees available to individual and group insurance policies;

(e) The rates of exchange at which benefits in respect of policies issued in foreign currencies have been converted into Indian Rupees and what provision has been made for possible increase of mathematical reserves arising from future variations in rates of exchange;

(f) Other, if any.

Statement of Liabilities

An insurer shall furnish a statement of liabilities in accordance with the Insurance Regulatory and Development Authority (Actuarial Report and Abstract) Regulations, 2000.

Development in the Insurance Sector

Nationalisation of the Life Insurance Corporation business in 1956 and the General Insurance Business on 1st January 1973.

It was on Jan. 19, 1956 that the management of 245 Indian and Foreign Insurance Companies and provident societies operating in the life insurance business was taken up by the Union Government and then nationalised on September 1956 when the Life Insurance Corporation (LIC) was formed with the capital contribution of Rs. 5 crores. As for the general insurance business, the government nationalised 107 different companies, 63 domestic and 44 foreign and formed the General Insurance Corporation of India (GIC) as a holding company with four subsidiaries which compete among themselves.

In the case of the LIC, business has increased from five million polices at the time of nationalisation to over 56 million at present. The GIC too has progressed similarly in the last 24 years with business volume of premium growing from Rs. 207 crores in 1973 to Rs. 6,000 crores in 1995-96.

According to Dr. Joy Cherian, a former Director of International Insurance Law of the American Council of Life Insurance in Washington, India has a fast growing middle class of 25-30 crore people who can afford to buy life insurance, health insurance, disability, insurance and pension plan products. LIC has covered only 23% of the Insurable population. Hence, 77% of the insurable population according to Dr. Cherian is uninsured. Foreign insurance companies are attracted by this vast insurance market in India.

Business Growth of GIC

On nationalisation, GIC formed with four subsidiaies, *viz.*,

(1) New India Assurance Co. LTD.

(2) United India Insurance Co. Ltd.

(3) Oriental Insurance Co. LtD. and

(4) National Insurance Co. Ltd. All business is transacted through these four subsidiaries. General Insurance Corporation is the controlling body. Expect crop insurance, aviation business of India Airlines and Air India, GIC does not involve itself directly in business. Each of the subsidiaries has about 1,000 divisional offices and 40,000 operating offices spread all over India. The total manpower employed by the industry is 86,000, The main income and expenditure of the insurance companies is as follows. Income from (a) claim (insured) (b) establishment and other expenses (c) commission to agents (d) dividends to shareholders.

In 1970, the total premium income of 108 insurance companies was Rs. 105 crores. Today, the four nationalized insurances company's premium income totals upto Rs. 10,000 crores. The GIC and its four subsidiaries gross premium and profit before tax from 1990-91 to 1998-99 are given below.

Statement of Gross Premium and Profit (1986-90 – 2000-01)

Year	Gross Premium Rs. In Crores	Profit (Before tax) Rs. In Crores
1989-90	2279	371
1990-91	2931	482
1991-92	3503	669
1992-93	4070	779
1993-94	4766	1082
1994-95	5271	503
1995-96	6377	8311
1996-97	7348	1084
1997-98	80666	1623
1998-99	9158	1467
1999-2000	9982	1153
2000-01	10772	729

Market share of the insurance business of GIC and its Four subsidiaries is given below:

Company	Market %
United	25
Oriental	22
Natioral	20
New India	32
GIC	1

[*Source*: K.N. Bhandari "*Agenda for Insurance*" Economic Times 31, Jan 1999.]

Despite this, India remains one of the least insured countries in the world. While India ranks tents in terms of corporate presence among the 78 industries national in the world, in terms of insurance covers it ranks 51st

The GIC not only does the mobilization of resources and redistribute the funds to those who suffered losses but also as per the government guidelines the funds are invested for industrial development, social oriental sectors such as housing sectors and State and Central Government Securities. In 1997, out of the total investment of Rs. 14.392 crores the GIC subsidiaries invested Rs. 2,648 crores in Industries, Rs. 856 crores in state and Central Government Securities and Rs. 1,073 crores in housing sector.

Presently, the insurance industries contributes only 0.55% to GDP against 4% to 5%^ in developed countries like the USA Canada and Japan etc. It is expected that current level of premium of 2 billion dollars in non-life sector, can easily be around 20 billion dollars in the next years. Market liberalization will also bring new challenges.

The opening of the insurance sector, therefore, would immensely help the Indian economy, particularly in mobilizing substantial amounts of resources which could then be channeled into infrastructure development. But it is also true that insurance companies would command huge funds at their disposal which make reforms critics to voice apprehensions for throwing open this sector to the private sector and foreigners, more so because these funds could be utilized to procure equity stake in Indian Companies as has been cone by the LIC and the GIC.

Role of Insurance in International Economy

Insurance plays an important role not only in the national economy but also in the international economy. Marine cargo Insurance, for example, provides risks coverage for shippers and importers and the banks which finance international trade. This role becomes all the more important in the context of an active government policy to encourage export.

Indian Insurance operate in more than 30 counters through agencies, branches and subsidiary/associate companies. These operations earn foreign exchange and represent invisible exports. The U.K. insurance, for example earn more premium overseas than from their domestic operations.

The Indian insurance have also an international presence through an active reinsurance exchange program with insurers with in over 100 countries. Another dimension of international insurance found in regional co-operations is reinsurance. Asian Reinsurance Corporation (of which Indian is a members) with head quarters in Bangkok, Thailand's is one example. Large industrial and infrastructural project set up in India through joint venture or otherwise with overseas fiancé need tailor made specialized insurance covers.

Questions

1. Explain the special features Insurance Regulatory and Developoment Authority.
2. Write a brief note on Insurance Regulatory and Development and Development Authority.
3. What are the important duties and power of IRDA?

Annexure

SECTION-A

Choose the correct answer:

(1) A certain percentage of the sum assured is paid periodically according to the terms of policy

(a) Term policy (b) Endowment Life policy

(C) Money-back policy (d) Group Insurance policy

(2) The principle of indemnity does not apply to

(a) Burglary Insurance (b) Fire Insura

(c) Marine Insurance (d) Life and personal accident Insurance

(3) Transfer of rights and remedies of the insured to the insurer after indemnity has been effected is called

(a) Insurable Interest (b) Subrogation

(c) Proximate cause (d) Money back policy

(4) Guarantees for employer for the loss out of employee's dishonest is

(a) Burglary Insurance (b) Fidelity Insurance

(c) Third Party Insurance (d) Medical Insurance

(5) Motor Insurance has its beginning in the

(a) U.S.A (b) U.S.S.R

(c) U.K (d) U.A.E

(6) Fidelity Guarantee Insurance does not gurantee

(a) The death of the employer

(b) The death of the employee

(c) The employee's honesty

(d) The employer's honesty

(7) Insurance is based on the principle of

(a) Co-operation (b) Democracy

(c) Equality (d) Welfare

(8) This policy covers all risks to the ship and its cargo while the ship is at a particular port

(a) Voyage policy (b) Floating policy

(c) Time policy (d) Port risk policy

(9) Fire Insurance can be taken in respect of

(a) Movable properties only

(b) Immovable properties only

(c) Both movable and Immovable properties

(d) Persons Only

(10) The principle of indemnity is applicable to ________________ only

(a) Life Insurance (b) Personal Accident Insurance

(c) Proximate cause (d) Property Insurance

(11) Except life assurance the maximum term of other insurance is ________________

(a) 12 months (b) 24 months

(c) 6 months (d) 36 months

(12) The person whose risk is insured is called the________________

(a) Insured (b) Assured

(c) Indemnity (d) Both a and b

(13) The person who agrees to compensate the loss arising from the risk is called the ____________

(a) insurer (b) assurer

(c) underwriter (d) all the above

(14) ______________ Policy matures on the assured death or on his attainment of a particular age whichever occurs earlier

(a) Endowment policy (b) Money back policy

(c) Joint life policy (d) Single premium policy.

(15) In marine insurance, insurable interest is enough at the time of ___________

(a) Claim (b) loss

(c) maturity (d) Insurance

(16) In fire insurance, insurable interest is enough at the time of _________

(a) Effecting the policy (b) Loss

(c) maturity (d) both a and b

(17) ____________ is an agreement where by the insurer agrees to indemnity the insured against marine losses

(a) Life insurance (b) Fire Insurance

(c) Marine Insurance (d) Public Liability Insurance

(18) _____________ are those terms, which are implied in every contract of marine insurance unless they are expressly excluded

(a) Guarantee (b) Express warranties

(c) Implied warranties (d) Waiver Clause

(19) _____________ are those terms, which are written on the policy.

(a) Express warranties (b) Implied warranties

(c) Memorandum clause (d) Valuation clause

(20) Notice of abandonment is necessary in the case of _____________

(a) Actual total loss (b) Constructive total loss

(c) Partial total loss (d) None of the above

(21) When the subject matter insured is destroyed wholly refers to ____________

(a) Partial total loss (b) Actual total loss

(c) Constructive total loss (d) None of the above

(22) ___________ Policy issued on the basis of the number of persons assured

(a) Annuity policy (b) Multiple life policy

(c) Single life policy (d) Level premium policy

(23) Assignment of life policy means ____________

(a) Transferring rights to the assignee

(b) Policy holder is entitled to the paid up value

(c) Paid up value is always higher than surrender value

(d) Value payable on Assurd's death or maturity

(24) _________ means a wilful and intentional act on part of the self destroyer

(a) Death (b) Suicide

(c) Murder (d) Accident

(25) The central office of Life Insurance Corporation of India is located at _________

(a) New Delhi (b) Kolkata

(c) Mumbai (d) Chennai

(26) A person employed to do any act for another or to represent another in dealing with a third person refers to ____________

(a) Principal (b) Employee

(c) Agent (d) Development Officer

(27) The person for whom such act is done or who is so represented is called _________

(a) Principal (b) Worker

(c) Agent (d) Development Officer

(28) Martine perils is also called as ______________

(a) Perils of the sea (b) Moral Hazards

(c) Morale Hazards (d) None of the above

(29) _____________ Policy in which the limits of the risks are determined by place of particular voyage.

(a) Valued (b) Time

(c) Voyage (d) Unvalued

(30) ______________ Policy in which covers the risk during

(a) Floating (b) Wagering

(c) Valued (d) Mixed

(31) The term 'run off' or 'fully declared' refers to

(a) Floating Policy (b) Wagering Policy

(c) Builders Risk Policy (d) Open Cover Policy

(32) Wagering Policy is otherwise termed as

(a) Policy Proof of Interest

(b) Open Policy

(c) Builders Risk Policy

(d) Port Risk Policies

(33) Risk insured against death is a contract of ____________

(a) Assurance (b) Agreement

(c) Indemnity (d) All the above

(34) Which of the following contract is not legally enforceable?

(a) Contract of Insurance

(b) Wagering contract

(c) Contract of sale of goods

(d) Contract of business

(35) Insurance contract is sort of contract which is approved by

(a) The Indian Contract Act (b) Indian Factory Act

(c) Indian Companies Act (d) The Indian Finance Act

(36) ____________ is a document which provides evidence of the contract of insurance

(a) Proposal Form (b) Policy Form

(c) Cover Note (d) Certificate of Insurance

(37) ____________ provides evidence of insurance to the police and Registration Authorities under Motor Vehicle Act.

(a) Cover Note

(b) Endorsements

(c) Certificate of Insurance

(d) Policy Form

(38) General Insurance Corporation was established during the year ____________

(a) 1956 (b) 1972

(c) 1955 (d) 1971

(39) General Insurance Business was nationalized under

(a) General Insurance Business Nationalisation Act 1971

(b) General Insurance Business Nationalisation Act 1972

(c) General Insurance Business Nationalisation Act 1973

(d) General Insurance Business Nationalisation Act 1974

(40) The Head office of New India Assurance & Co. Ltd., is

(a) New Delhi (b) Kolkata

(c) Chennai (d) Mumbai

(41) New Delhi is the head office of ______________

(a) New India Assurance & Co. Ltd.

(b) United India Assurance & Co. Ltd.

(c) Oriental Insurance Co. Ltd.

(d) National Insurance Co. Ltd.

(42) The subscribed capital of GIC contributed by the Central Government is ______________

(a) Rs. 5 Crore (b) Rs. 10 Crore

(c) Rs. 15 Crore (d) Rs. 20 Crore

(43) The Head Office of National Insurance Co. Ltd. is at ______________

(a) Mumbai (b) Kolkata

(c) Bangalore (d) Hyderabad

(44) The Head Office of United India Insurance Co. Ltd., is ______________

(a) Chennai (b) Bengaluru

(c) New Delhi (d) Mumbai

(45) Life Insurance in its present form came to India from

(a) The United Kingdom (b) The USA

(c) Canada (d) Germany

(46) Life Insurance Company was setup in ______________

(a) 1824 (b) 1823

(c) 1822 (d) 1821

(47) Life Insurance Corporation was nationalised in ______________

(a) 1951 (b) 1952

(c) 1954 (d) 1956

(48) Life Insurance Corporation was formed with a capital contribution of ______________

(a) Rs. 10 Crore (b) Rs. 15 Crore

(c) Rs. 5 Crore (d) Rs. 20 Crore

(49) The term 'Assurance' refers to ____________

(a) Life Insurance business

(b) Marine Insurance Business

(c) Fire Insurance Business

(d) Motor Vehicle Insurance Business

(50) The Oriental Life Insurance Company came to India during ____________

(a) 1919 (b) 1818

(c) 1899 (d) 1888

(51) The policies where the premium is payable thoughout the life of the assured is called ____________

(a) Whole Life Policies

(b) Renewable Term Policies

(c) Sinking Fund Policies

(d) Annuity Policy

(52) With Profit Policy is also termed as ____________

(a) Multiple Life Policy (b) Participating Policy

(b) Level Premium Policy (d) Lump sum Policy

(53) The Insurer who grants a guarantee from the direct insurer is called as ____________

(a) Direct Insurer (b) Ceding Insurer

(b) Re-Insurer (d) None of the above

(54) The proportion of the risk which the direct insurer holds on his own account refers to ____________

(a) Line (b) Retention

(c) Retrocession (b) Ceding Insurer

(55) A reinsurance of reinsurance refers to ____________

(a) Line (b) Retention

(b) Retrocession (d) Cession

(56) Reinsurance also termed as ____________

(a) Insurance of Insurance (b) Reinsurance of Reinsurance

(c) Double Insurance (d) Over Insurance

(57) When the same risk and subject matter is insured with more than one insurer is called as ____________

(a) Double Insurance

(b) Over Insurance

(c) Reinsurance

(d) Non-Proportional Reinsurance

(58) When the amount for which a subject matter is insured is more than its actual value it is called ____________

(a) Double Insurance (b) Reinsurance

(c) Over Insurance (d) External Insurance

(59) IRDA refers to

(a) Insurance Regulatory Development Authority

(b) Indian Regulatory Development Authority

(c) Institute of Regulatory Development Authority

(d) Insurance Regulatory Development Association

(60) Committee of Reforms in insurance sectors during 1993 headed by ______________

(a) R.N. Malhotra (b) S. Narashiman

(c) Manmohan Singh (d) P. Chidamabaram

(61) The danger of loss from the unforeseen circumstances in future refers to

(a) Risk (b) Perils

(c) hazard (d) Damage

(62) ______________ involves those losses that occur even if there were no changes in the economic environment.

(a) Dynamic Risks (b) Static Risks

(c) Fundamental Risk (d) Particular Risk

(63) Risks are not suited to treatment by. Insurance refers to

(a) Static Risk (b) Property Risk

(c) Dynamic Risk (d) Liability Risk

(64) Fundamental Risk is also termed as ______________

(a) Particular Risk (b) Speculative Risk

(c) Group Risk (d) Pure Risk

(65) Unemployment, war, inflation, earthquake etc are the examples of ______________

(a) Pure Risk (b) Particular Risk

(c) Personal Risk (d) Fundamental Risk

(66) Any risk involved a situation where there is a possibility of gain refers to ____________

(a) Liability Risk (b) Personal Risk

(c) Pure Risk (d) Speculative Risk

(67) Direct or Consequential losses refer to

(a) Dynamic Risk (b) Particular risk

(b) Property risk (d) Pure risk

(68) Spreading of risk otherwise termed as ______________

(a) Shifting of Risk (b) Acceptance of Risk

(b) Reduction of Risk (d) Spreading of Risk

(69) The principle of prevention is better than cure refers to

(a) Avoiding of Risk (b) Reduction of Risk

(b) Transferring of Risk (d) Shifting of Risk

(70) When the subject is partially lost by a peril insured against, it is called ____________

(a) General Average loss (b) Constructive Total Loss

(c) Actual Total Loss (d) Particular Average Loss

(71) An international code of York Antwerp Rules applied to

(a) Marine Losses (b) Losses of Fire

(c) Losses of Crop (d) Losses of human life.

(72) Cargo Ship caught by fire is an example of ______________

(a) Particular Average Loss

(b) Actual Total Loss

(c) Constructive Total Loss

(d) Actual Total Loss

(73) ____________ Policy is granted only in respect of stock of inventories of the insured under Fire insurance business.

(a) Floating (b) Declarations

(c) Replacement (d) Valued

(74) Under Fire Insurance, Loss of profit policy is also called as ____________

(a) Average policy (b) Consequential Loss policy

(c) Specific policy (d) Adjustable policy.

(75) Rashtriya Krishi Yojama of Crop Insurance Scheme Came to India during ______________

(a) 1999 (b) 1888

(c) 1988 (d) 1977

(76) Corpus fund is created with contributions from the Central Government and

State Government on _____________

(a) 75:25 basis (b) 50:50 basis

(c) 60:40 basis (d) 70:30 basis

(77) Motor Vehicle Insurance is compulsory under the Motor Vehicles Act, which was enacted in _____________

(a) 1988 (b) 1998

(c) 1939 (d) 1978

(78) Motor Vehicle Insurance had its beginning in

(a) The U.K (b) The U.S.A

(c) India (d) Canada

(79) The organisation structure of LIC refers to

(a) Two Tier structure (b) Three Tier Structure

(c) Four Tier structure (d) Five Tier structure

(80) The constitution of the Insurance Regulatory Development Authority consists of not more than ___________________ members.

(a) 10 members (b) 7 members

(c) 9 members (d) 8 members

Answers:

1. C – Money - back policy
2. D – Life and Personal Accident Insurance
3. B – Subrogation
4. B – Fidelity Insurance
5. C – U.K
6. C – the employee's honesty
7. A – Co-operation
8. D – Port Risk policy
9. C – Both Movable and Immovable properties
10. D – Property Insurance
11. A – 12 Months
12. D – Both a and b
13. D – All the above
14. A – Endowment Policy

15. B – Loss
16. D – Both a and b
17. C – Marine Insurance
18. C – Implied Warranties
19. A – Express Warranties
20. B – Constructive Total Loss
21. B – Actual Total Loss
22. B – Multiple Life Policy
23. A – Transferring rights to the assignee
24. B – Suicide
25. C – Mumbai
26. C – Agent
27. D – Development Officer
28. A – Perils of the Sea
29. C – Voyage
30. D – Mixed
31. A – Floating Policy
32. A – Policy Proof of Interest
33. A – Assurance
34. B – Wagering Contract
35. A – Indian Contract Act
36. B – Policy Form
37. C – Certificate of Insurance
38. A – 1956
39. B –General Insurance Business Nationalisation Act 1972
40. D – Mumbai
41. C – Oriental Insurance Co. Ltd.,
42. A – Rs. 5 Crore
43. B – Kolkata
44. A – Chennai
45. A – United Kingdom
46. B – 1823
47. D – 1956
48. C – Rs. 5 Crore
49. A – Life Insurance Business
50. B – 1818
51. A – Whole Life Policies
52. B – Participating Policy
53. C – Re-insurer
54. B – Retention
55. C – Retrocession
56. A – Insurance of Insurance
57. A – Double Insurance
58. B – Over Insurance
59. A – Insurance Regulatory Development Authority
60. A – R.N.Malhotra
61. A – Risk
62. B – Static Risk
63. C – Dynamic Risk
64. C – Group Risk
65. D – Fundamental Risk
66. D – Speculative Risk
67. C – Property Risk
68. D – Spreading of Risk
69. A – Avoiding of Risk
70. D – Particular Average Loss
71. A – Marine Loss
72. B – General Average Loss
73. B – Declaration
74. B – Consequential Loss Policy
75. A – 1999
76. B – 50:50 basis
77. C – 1939
78. A – U.K.
79. C – Four-Tier Structure
80. C – 9 Members.